PR
2820
.R5   Richard II
1984

| DATE | | | |
|---|---|---|---|
| | | | |
| | | | |
| | | | |
| | | | |
| | | | |
| | | | |
| | | | |
| | | | |
| | | | |
| | | | |
| | | | |
| | | | |
| | | | |

8901 8731

**WITHDRAWN**

**DAVID GLENN HUNT**
**MEMORIAL LIBRARY**
**GALVESTON COLLEGE**

© THE BAKER & TAYLOR CO.

# RICHARD II

Shakespearean Criticism
(Advisory Editor: Joseph G. Price)
Vol. 2

The dead body of Richard II (Paul Scofield) in the court of Henry IV (Eric Porter); Tennent Productions Ltd., Lyric Theatre, Hammersmith, London, December 24, 1952; directed by John Gielgud.

# RICHARD II
*Critical Essays*

Jeanne T. Newlin

GARLAND PUBLISHING, INC. • NEW YORK & LONDON
1984

© 1984 Jeanne T. Newlin
All rights reserved

**Library of Congress Cataloging in Publication Data**
Main entry under title:

Richard II: Critical essays.
(Shakespearean criticism ; vol. 2)

    1. Shakespeare, William, 1564–1616. King Richard II
—Addresses, essays, lectures. 2. Richard II, King of
England, 1367–1400, in fiction, drama, poetry, etc.—
Addresses, essays, lectures. I. Newlin, Jeanne T.
II. Series.
PR2820.R5   1984     822.3'3     82-48290
ISBN 0-8240-9238-4

Printed on acid-free, 250-year-life paper
Manufactured in the United States of America

# Acknowledgments

"Symphonic Imagery in *Richard II*" is reprinted with the permission of Richard D. Altick and The Modern Language Association of America. Excerpts from the books of John Russell Brown and Robert Ornstein are reprinted with the permission of the authors. The Folio Society has granted permission to reprint from John Gielgud's *Stage Directions*. The chapter from Ernst H. Kantorowicz's *The King's Two Bodies* is reprinted with the permission of Princeton University Press. *The Shakespeare Quarterly* has given permission to reprint Brents Stirling's "Bolingbroke's Decision." The chapter from E. M. W. Tillyard's *Shakespeare's History Plays* is reprinted with the permission of Chatto & Windus. Stanley Wells' critique, "John Barton's *Richard II*," is reprinted with the permission of the author and *Furman Studies*. Cambridge University Press has granted permission to reprint material from John Dover Wilson's edition of *Richard II*. The section from *Shakespeare's Histories at Stratford, 1951* is reprinted with permission of Max Reinhardt at The Bodley Head. The essay by William Butler Yeats is reprinted with the permission of Michael Yeats, Anne Yeats and Macmillan, London, Ltd.

I am indebted to Laurence P. Senelick for his translation of the Alessandro Manzoni letter in *Opere Complete*, 1843.

# Contents

| | |
|---|---|
| Editor's Preface | ix |
| Introduction | xi |
| Bibliography | xix |
| Part I. *Richard II*: The Historical and Political Dynamics | 1 |
| Queen Elizabeth I, "Remarks to William Lambarde" (1601) | 3 |
| John Dover Wilson, "Introduction to *Richard II*" (1939) | 5 |
| E.M.W. Tillyard, *Shakespeare's History Plays* (1944) | 23 |
| Robert Ornstein, *A Kingdom for a Stage* (1972) | 45 |
| E.H. Kantorowicz, *The King's Two Bodies* (1957) | 73 |
| Irving Ribner, "Bolingbroke, a True Machiavellian" (1948) | 95 |
| Part II. *Richard II*: The Theatre | 105 |
| C.E. Montague, "F.R. Benson's Richard II" (1899) | 107 |
| William Butler Yeats, "At Stratford-on-Avon" (1901) | 115 |
| T.C. Worsley, *Shakespeare's Histories at Stratford, 1951* (1952) | 127 |
| H. Granville-Barker, "Letter to John Gielgud" (1937) | 135 |
| John Gielgud, *Stage Directions* (1963) | 139 |
| John Russell Brown, *Shakespeare's Plays in Performance* (1966) | 145 |
| Stanley Wells, "John Barton's *Richard II*" (1976) | 163 |

Part III. *Richard II*: The Psychology of its Characters   185

Samuel Taylor Coleridge, "Lectures on Shakespeare
    and Milton" (1812)   187

Walter Pater, *Shakespeare's English Kings* (1889)   193

E.K. Chambers, *The Tragedy of King Richard the
    Second* (1891)   207

Brents Stirling, "Bolingbroke's 'Decision'" (1951)   217

Part IV. *Richard II*: Poetry and Rhetoric   231

Alessandro Manzoni, "Letter to Mr. Chauvet concerning
    the unities of time and place in Tragedy" (1820)   233

Algernon Charles Swinburne, "King Richard II" (1909)   239

Richard D. Altick, "Symphonic Imagery in *Richard II*"
    (1947)   249

# GENERAL EDITOR'S PREFACE

The Garland series is designed to bring together the best that has been written about Shakespeare's plays, both as dramatic literature and theatrical performance. With the exception of some early plays which are treated in related combinations, each volume is devoted to a single play to include the most influential historical criticism, the significant modern interpretations, and reviews of the most illuminating productions. The collections are intended as resource companions to the texts. The scholar, the student, the reader, the director, the actor, the audience, will find here the full range of critical opinion, scholarly debate, and popular taste. Much of the material reproduced has been extremely difficult for the casual reader to locate. Original volumes have long since been out of print; definitive articles have been buried in journals and editions now obscure; theatrical reviews are discarded with each day's newspaper.

"The best that has been written" about each play is the criterion for selection, and the volumes represent the collective wisdom of foremost Shakespearean scholars throughout the world. Each editor has had the freedom and responsibility to make accessible the most insightful criticism to date for his or her play. I express my gratitude to the team of international scholars who have accepted this challenge. One would like to say with Keats "that is all/Ye know on earth, and all ye need to know," but the universality of Shakespeare will stimulate new responses, yield fresh meanings, and lead new generations to richer understandings of human nature.

Generally the essays have been reproduced as they appeared originally. Some concessions in punctuation, spelling, and documentation have been made for the sake of conformity. In the case of excerpts, notes have been renumbered to clarify the references. A principle of the series, however, is to reproduce the full text, rather than excerpts, except for digressive material having no bearing on the subject.

Joseph Price

# Introduction

*Richard II* is very much a play of the twentieth century. Critics of earlier times would be astonished at the fourfold division of essays in this volume which signifies the politico-historical interest, the excitement for the psychological, the praise for the poetry, and the stage triumphs generated by the play in recent decades. Generations of critics from Dr. Johnson to Swinburne have disparaged these precise areas. Shakespeare, it was said, had failed to give dramatic movement and unity to the reign of Richard; in fact, neither audience nor reader could grasp the historical events and issues of Act I. Further, there was not enough subsequent action as Richard merely crumbled before Bolingbroke's threat. The historical sources provided battles, flights, and ambushes which Shakespeare ignored. And the protagonist? For the critics of the eighteenth and nineteenth centuries, little wonder that no actor could succeed in such a static and unsympathetic role. Audiences will delight in a hero or a villain, but they were not inclined toward the characterization of such a weak, vapid personality as Shakespeare's king seemed. To them, Richard wallowed in sentimental verse and turgid rhetoric. The play was rarely performed.[1] I have included Swinburne's essay in the volume not for its own merit but as the last great clap of thunder before the clouds dispersed over the sun-king. When set against traditional opinions such as Swinburne's, the arguments of modern critics gain clarity and emphasis.

It is poetic, or rather dramatic, justice that the impetus for reappraisal about the turn of the century came from the theatre. If Queen Elizabeth, upset by the theme of deposition, could complain that "this tragedy was played 40tie times in open streets and houses," we can rejoice that key performances over the last eighty years have propelled the play into the ranks of Shakespeare's masterpieces. The entire canon has profited from twentieth-century productions, and less popular plays such as *Two Gentlemen of Verona, Titus Andronicus, All's Well That Ends Well, Troilus and Cressida, Coriolanus, Pericles, Timon of Athens,* and *Cymbeline* have been restored to something like the initial enthusiasm with which Elizabethan and Jacobean audiences greeted them. Perhaps only *Troilus,* however, can rival the radical change which the reputation of *Richard II* has undergone. *Richard* leads the way into the new-found appreciation for the full Shakespearean canon. This appreciation distinguishes twentieth-century audiences, readers, and critics from earlier generations.

The rags-to-riches story began in 1889 with Walter Pater's *Shakespeare's English Kings.* Recalling Charles Kean's revival, Pater praised Richard as "the most sweet-tongued" of all Shakespeare's kings, the deposition scene as a Handelian anthem, and the play as a musical composition, possessing "a certain concentration of all its parts, a simple continuity, and evenness in execution, which are rare in the great dramatist." This image of Richard as poet was realized on stage in the 1899 Stratford-upon-Avon production of F.R. Benson and, in a rare instance of theatrical reviewing, C.E. Montague wrote an extensive and insightful critique of both play and performance. His review prodded scholars and audiences to reconsider the merits of the play. One theatre-goer needed no prodding. In 1901, William Butler Yeats wrote a charming essay on his experiences at Stratford and, among the plays which he had seen, singled out Shakespeare's weak king for his special approval. The interpretation of Richard as a sensitive poet who loved to "monarchize" remote from the realities of monarchy was now set, no doubt influenced by Freud's exploration of the subconscious. Its fulfillment in the theatre materialized in Sir John Gielgud's first portrayal of the role in 1937. In the interim, one of the most successful Richards was the young Harley Granville-Barker. His experience as actor, director, critic prompted his critique of Gielgud's performance in an invaluable letter to Gielgud dated October 15, 1937. Since that production, which drew out all the emotional potential of

Introduction                                                                 xiii

the play, the role of Richard has competed with Hamlet in attracting and challenging major actors. As Gielgud wrote in 1962, "Richard is one of those rare parts in which the actor may indulge himself, luxuriating in the language he has to speak, and attitudinizing in consciously graceful poses." That conscious sense of self is in the characterizations of both Richard and Hamlet, and it is interesting that in the recent BBC televised productions Derek Jacobi played both roles. In 1951, the spotlight on the protagonist widened to cast new light on other aspects of the play. Produced at Stratford-upon-Avon as the first play in the cycle which included the two parts of *Henry IV* and *Henry V*, *Richard II* drew attention to its theme and to Henry Bolingbroke whose character gained complexity through the continuity of three plays. Productions of the last two decades have elaborated the full text, giving full play to the ambiguities which Shakespeare has woven into the design. Essays by John Russell Brown and Stanley Wells demonstrate the richness of both text and performance.

Among the ambiguities, of course, is the central question of the right to the throne. Is the legitimate heir to keep the throne though he is weak, irresponsible, and perhaps ruinous to the country? Should the crown be usurped by a strong, competent executive? It is the great debate among the characters of the play, and it became the great debate of historically-oriented critics in the first half of this century. This kind of scholarship illuminated all of Shakespeare's history plays as critics set them in their Elizabethan context. They were explicated with reference to Britain's epic wars, first with France, then within itself. Political doctrines such as the Tudor Divine Right theory, Machiavellianism, and Lancastrian-Yorkist attitudes to succession were brought to bear in interpreting the plays. New meanings were attached through the cosmology implied in the later phrase "Great Chain of Being" and a theology which stressed divine retribution. The search for contemporary significance found allusions particularly in *Richard II*, and the findings and conjectures were reinforced by the play's revival at the time of the Essex rebellion. All of these Tudor concerns and their relationship to Shakespeare's play are set forth with exceptional clarity by John Dover Wilson in his introduction to the New

Cambridge edition. Somewhat later, E.M.W. Tillyard, in assimilating this material, fashioned a coherent design for Shakespeare's two tetralogies. Tillyard considered these eight plays to be an epic drama, intended by its author to demonstrate the consequences of usurpation and the destructiveness of a country divided. *Richard II* is the prelude, the seed which blossomed during the Hundred Years' War and into the War of the Roses. For both Wilson and Tillyard, Richard is the royal martyr; for some later critics, the Christ-figure, the sacrificial lamb. As for Richard's crimes, they would cite Gaunt:

> God's is the quarrel, for God's substitute,
> His deputy anointed in His sight,
> Hath caus'd his death, the which if wrongfully,
> Let heaven revenge, for I may never lift
> An angry arm against His ministers.
>
> (I.ii.37–41)

The devil may quote scripture, and critics supportive of Bolingbroke find justification in Gaunt's dying words:

> O had thy grandsire with a prophet's eye
> Seen how his son's son should destroy his sons,
> From forth thy reach he would have laid thy shame
> Deposing thee before thou wert possess'd,
> Which art possess'd now to depose thyself.
>
> (II.i.104–108)

The ambivalence within Gaunt is characteristic of the political ambivalence throughout the play, perhaps deemed necessary by Shakespeare when confronted with the dilemma of Tudor Divine Right theory condemning all usurpation on the one hand and Elizabeth's lineage traced back through the Lancastrians to Henry IV on the other. To make either Richard or Henry hero or villain had its risks. Shakespeare seems to have chosen to strap the political question to the shoulders of Gaunt and York as chorus characters, representatives of England who finally adopt a pragmatic stance ("Nor friends, nor foes, to me welcome you are:/Things past redress are now with me past care.") as indeed England itself did in 1399. York's position is as pragmatic as that of the gardeners who know that superfluous branches must be lopped away "that bearing boughs may live." The tension and strain which Shakespeare mounts between political ideals and political realities is analyzed most perceptively by Robert Ornstein in his chapter on *Richard II* in *A Kingdom for a Stage*.

The political ambiguities within the characters of Richard and Bolingbroke are put into historical perspective in significant work by E.H. Kantorowicz and Irving Ribner. The sensitive, self-pitying poet who insists on his divine right to rule is related by Kantorowicz to the legal notion of the king's public, corporate role and his private, personal morality. Irving Ribner's systematic correlation of *The Prince* with the progressive steps of Bolingbroke illustrates for the modern reader what Shakespeare might have considered the "true Machiavellian."

The great interest in the play, however, remains with the psychological ambivalence of the protagonist and, to a lesser degree, with his antagonist. Scholarly journals over the last thirty years abound in what might be called loosely psychoanalytic studies of Richard. Yet perhaps no one in itself is as rich as the three earlier essays I have included in Part III. In fact, taken together they comprise a psychological portrait of Richard which anticipates later perspectives. Coleridge may not have known the term manic-depressive as applied to Richard in criticism of the 1970s, but consider his symptomatic analysis:

> He scatters himself into a multitude of images, and in conclusion endeavours to shelter himself from that which is around him by a cloud of his own thoughts. Throughout his whole career may be noticed the most rapid transitions —from the highest insolence to the lowest humility—from hope to despair, from the extravagance of love to the agonies of resentment, and from pretended resignation to the bitterest reproaches.

Pater's description of the "most sweet-tongued" of Shakespeare's kings is unsurpassed; one curious measure of its influence is how many subsequent analyses assume a "fatal" physical beauty in Richard, an elaboration of Pater's, not of the text. The psychology of all the *dramatis personae* and, in particular, the contrasting character traits of Richard and Henry are treated compellingly by E.K. Chambers. Writing only two years after Pater, he expresses a similar admiration for this neglected play: "And after all, in this play, it is the effect on the emotions that is the great thing; there is hardly another that moves us, that overwhelms us, like this."

Among modern studies of characterization in *Richard II*, most impressive is Brents Stirling's "Bolingbroke's 'Decision.'" Its achievement lies in the integration of character and structure in resolving the crucial question of the play: at what point does Henry decide to take the crown?

European criticism of the play is neither as innovative nor as distinguished as with other Shakespearean plays. *Richard II* suffered the same slights on the Continent as it did at home, although there is a body of nineteenth-century German criticism.[2] In the twentieth century, there is a distinguished discussion of the play's imagery by Wolfgang Clemen in his book *The Development of Shakespeare's Imagery*. Objections to *Richard II* in France and Italy were based on the general charge against Shakespeare that he violated the classical principle of the unities. The great Italian novelist and playwright Alessandro Manzoni used *Richard II* to counter this charge. In one of the earliest Romantic rebuttals to classical rules, Manzoni elevated the demands of poetry above those of critical principles. I have excerpted this little-known, charming letter not only for its historical value but also for his appreciation of the play's "most exalted poetry."

At least from Pater on, each critic who has written about *Richard II* directly or indirectly pays tribute to its poetry. Indeed, any study of Shakespeare's language, poetry, rhetoric, or imagery will contain rewarding analyses of the great speeches in the play. In addition to Clemen, M.C. Bradbrook, Caroline Spurgeon, and Derek Traversi are especially helpful.[3] Richard Altick, in the outstanding essay on the subject, synthesizes Shakespeare's poetic techniques. The essay is reproduced in Part IV.

The great quality of this lyrical play sings out passionately to us in the most poignant, and perhaps finest, passage:

> No matter where—of comfort no man speak:
> Let's talk of graves, of worms, and epitaphs,
> Make dust our paper, and with rainy eyes
> Write sorrow on the bosom of the earth.
> Let's choose executors and talk of wills;

# Introduction

> And yet not so, for what can we bequeath
> Save our deposed bodies to the ground?
> Our lands, our lives, and all are Bullingbrook's,
> And nothing can we call our own but death,
> And that small model of the barren earth
> Which serves as paste and cover to our bones.
> For God's sake let us sit upon the ground
> And tell sad stories of the death of kings:
> How some have been depos'd, some slain in war,
> Some haunted by the ghosts they have deposed,
> Some poisoned by their wives, some sleeping kill'd,
> All murthered—for within the hollow crown
> That rounds the mortal temples of a king
> Keeps Death his court, and there the antic sits,
> Scoffing his state and grinning at his pomp,
> Allowing him a breath, a little scene,
> To monarchize, be fear'd, and kill with looks,
> Infusing him with self and vain conceit,
> As if this flesh which walls about our life
> Were brass impregnable; and humor'd thus,
> Comes at the last and with a little pin
> Bores thorough his castle wall, and farewell king!
> Cover your heads, and mock not flesh and blood
> With solemn reverence, throw away respect,
> Tradition, form, and ceremonious duty,
> For you have but mistook me all this while.
> I live with bread like you, feel want,
> Taste grief, need friends: subjected thus,
> How can you say to me I am a king?
>
> (III.ii.144-76)

Swinburne, who disparages so much of the play, writes of the "magnificent poetry" in this scene. It "might almost have been uttered by the divine and unknown and unimaginable poet who gave to eternity the Book of Job."

### NOTES

1. For a concise review of the stage history, see Arthur Colby Sprague, *Shakespeare's Histories: Plays for the Stage* (London, 1964).
2. Christian Eidam, "Über die Einleitung in Shakespeares *Richard II*," *Die Neueren Sprachen*, XIX (1911-12), 277-95.

3. W.H. Clemen, *The Development of Shakespeare's Imagery* (London, 1951); Muriel Bradbrook, *Shakespeare and Elizabethan Poetry* (London, 1951); Caroline Spurgeon, *Shakespeare's Imagery and What It Tells Us* (London, 1935); Derek Traversi, *An Approach to Shakespeare*, 3rd ed., 2 vols. (London, 1968-69).

# Bibliography

Altick, Richard D. "Symphonic Imagery in *Richard II.*" *PMLA*, 62 (1947), 339-65.
Brown, John Russell. *Shakespeare's Plays in Performance*. London: Edward Arnold, Ltd., 1966, pp. 115-30.
Chambers, E.K., ed. *The Tragedy of King Richard the Second*. London and New York: Longmans, Green and Co., 1891, pp. vii-xxvii.
Coleridge, Samuel T. "Lectures on Shakespeare and Milton." *Coleridge's Shakespearean Criticism*. Ed. Thomas Middleton Raysor. Cambridge, Mass.: Harvard University Press, 1930, Vol. II, pp. 186-92.
Elizabeth I. "Remarks to William Lambarde," Aug. 4, 1601, *Memorandum*, pr. Nichols, *Eliz.* iii,552, from Lambard family MS. Quoted in E.K. Chambers. *William Shakespeare*. Oxford: University Press, 1951 (first ed., Clarendon Press, 1930), Vol. II, p. 326.
Gielgud, John. "King Richard the Second." *Stage Directions*. New York: Random House, 1963, pp. 28-35.
Kantorowicz, Ernst H. *The King's Two Bodies: A Study in Medieval Political Theology*. Princeton: Princeton University Press, 1957, pp. 24-41.
Manzoni, Alessandro. "Lettre à M. Chauvet sur l'unité de temps et de lieu dans la tragédie." *Opere Complete*. Paris, 1843, pp. 257-60. Unpublished translation by Laurence P. Senelick, 1982.
Montague, C.E. "F.R. Benson's *Richard II.*" Manchester *Guardian*, Dec. 4, 1899.
Ornstein, Robert. *A Kingdom for a Stage: The Achievement of Shakespeare's History Plays*. Cambridge, Mass.: Harvard University Press, 1972, pp. 102-24.
Pater, Walter. *Appreciations with an Essay on Style*. London: Macmillan & Co., 1911, pp. 185-204.
Purdom, C.B. *Harley Granville-Barker: Man of the Theatre, Dramatist and Scholar*. Cambridge, Mass.: Harvard University Press, 1956, pp. 251-55.

Ribner, Irving. "Bolingbroke, a True Machiavellian." *MLQ*, 9 (June, 1948), 177-84.
Stirling, Brents. "Bolingbroke's Decision." *SQ*, 2 (Jan., 1951), 27-34.
Swinburne, Algernon Charles. "King Richard II." *Three Plays of Shakespeare*. London and New York: Harper and Brothers, 1909, pp. 59-85.
Tillyard, E.M.W. *Shakespeare's History Plays*. London: Chatto & Windus, 1948, pp. 244-63.
Wells, Stanley. "John Barton's *Richard II*." *Furman Studies*, N.S., 23 (June, 1976), 64-81.
Wilson, John Dover, ed. *King Richard II*. New Cambridge Edition. Cambridge: Cambridge University Press, 1939, pp. xvi-xxxviii.
Wilson, John Dover, and Worsley, T.C. *Shakespeare's Histories at Stratford, 1951*. London: Max Reinhardt, 1952, pp. 34-43.
Yeats, William Butler. *Ideas of Good and Evil*. London: A.H. Bullen, 1903, pp. 142-67.

# PART I
## *RICHARD II*
## The Historical and Political Dynamics

# Queen Elizabeth I

# Remarks to William Lambarde (1601)

I am Richard II, know ye not that?

. . . . . . . .

He that will forget God, will also forget his benefactors; this tragedy was played 40^tie times in open streets and houses.

*John Dover Wilson*

# Introduction to Richard II (1939)

"The significance of Richard's fall to the contemporaries of Shakespeare"

To the contemporaries of Shakespeare Richard was no ordinary man; and it is by failing to realize this that modern criticism, despite all its penetrating, and for the most part just, analysis of his human qualities, leaves every thoughtful reader and spectator of the drama baffled and dissatisfied. Richard was a king, and a good deal more. First of all he stood in the eyes of the later middle ages as the type and exemplar of royal martyrdom; of a king not slain in battle, not defeated and killed by a foreign adversary, not even deposed owing to weakness or tyranny in favor of his heir, but thrust from the throne in his may of youth by a mere usurper, under color of a process at law utterly illegal, and then foully murdered. One may catch something of this aspect of his tragedy by turning to the "form of prayer with fasting," for "the day of the martyrdom of the Blessed King Charles I," which was printed in the Book of Common Prayer until half-way through the nineteenth century,[1] or by remembering the passionate devotion which the memory of Mary Queen of Scots inspired until an even later date. Richard combined the personal attractiveness of Mary with the wrongs of Charles, and moreover belonged to a period when men were far more swayed by the glamor of kingship and the tendency to canonize those they admired than they have been during the last three centuries. Not that the admiration was universal; there were, as ever in such cases, two parties, the idolaters and the defamers. As long as the house of Lancaster, which triumphed in Richard's fall, ruled the country, it was of course treasonable for Englishmen to take his side. But from the first on the Continent, where thought was free, the reading public, already rejoicing in Boccaccio's most popular book, *De Casibus Illustrium Virorum* (1360-74), which Shakespeare's Richard seems to be describing in the well-known lines:

> For God's sake let us sit upon the ground,
> And tell sad stories of the death of kings—
> How some have been deposed, some slain in war,
> Some haunted by the ghosts they have deposed,
> Some poisoned by their wives, some sleeping killed;
> All murdered, . . .

had found in Richard's own "casus" a peculiar appeal; so much so indeed that no fewer than three different contemporary accounts of it, favorable to Richard, have come down to us in the French tongue, while yet a fourth of similar sympathies, though in Latin not French, reposes in the library of Gray's Inn.[2] One of the French chronicles exists in some twenty or more MS. copies to be found in various continental libraries.

This widespread interest may, it is suggested, have been due in part to anti-English feeling among French patriots during the latter half of the Hundred Years' War.[3] But that the "sad story" was also valued for its own sake is proved by the persistence of its popularity, which, when the accession of the Tudors healed the dynastic breach, found voice in England itself, so that the tragedy of Richard appears, not it is true very sympathetically told, in *The Mirror for Magistrates*, 1559-63.[4] This well-known book, an immense corpus of such "casus," was a continuation and enlargement of Lydgate's *Falls of Princes*, which in turn was itself an adaptation of Boccaccio's original collection. Moreover, the most remarkable fact about the four original pro-Richard chronicles is that they already, as we shall see later, give utterance to that mystical conception of the martyred king which we find in Shakespeare, and compare his betrayal with that of Christ and his enemies with Pilate and Judas, much as the play itself does. Nor is it certain that they are not in this nearer the truth than the orthodox modern historian who has on the whole accepted the Lancastrian version of the revolution of 1399. The official story, embodied in the Parliament Roll, was being denounced by a scholar in 1824 as "a gross fabrication of Henry IV for purposes of state";[5] and a recent study of the evidence by Professor Galbraith and Miss Clarke comes to very much the same conclusion.[6]

Yet the fall of Richard fascinated the late medieval and Elizabethan world as much by its magnitude and its unaccountableness as by its pathos and the sacrilege that brought it to pass.

> Down, down I come, like glist'ring Phaethon:
> Wanting the manage of unruly jades,

are words which Shakespeare places in his mouth, and some critics have taken them as the keynote of the play. But though in their sun-imagery they express the splendor of the catastrophe, like that of Lucifer from the empyrean, they do not touch its mystery, of which all at that period who studied the young king's career were conscious, and which is one of the main impressions that Shakespeare's play still leaves upon our minds. This mystery was closely associated with the supposed workings of Fortune, a Roman deity which continued to exercise under Providence a potent influence over men's thought during the middle ages, and was conceived of by Elizabethan England far more concretely than by the England of our own day, despite its daily race-meetings, its football pools and its almost universal habit of gambling. The symbol and attribute of Fortune was, of course, her wheel, which is hardly ever absent from any of the countless pictures and references to her in medieval art and literature. Shakespeare makes no mention of the wheel in *Richard II*, though he employs the less familiar figure of Fortune's buckets in the deposition scene.[7]

His reticence, however, is part of his subtlety. For the wheel is constantly in his mind throughout the play. Indeed, it determines the play's shape and structure, which gives us a complete inversion.[8] The first act begins immediately after the death of the Duke of Gloucester, when, as Froissart notes, Richard was "hygh uppon the whele,"[9] and exhibiting all the hybris and tyranny expected of persons in that position, while, at the same time, his opponent, Bolingbroke, is shown at the lowest point of his fortune, at the bottom. But from the beginning of Act II the wheel begins to turn mysteriously of itself, or rather by the action of Fortune. The will of the King seems paralyzed; he becomes an almost passive agent. Bolingbroke acts, and acts forcibly; yet he too appears to be borne upward by a power beyond his volition.

This last is an important point, since it rules out those indications of deep design which some subtle critics, following Coleridge, think they discover in the character of the usurper from the very beginning, but which I feel sure were not intended by Shakespeare. Circumstance drives Bolingbroke on from point to point: he takes what Fortune and Richard throw in his path. The attitude of the nobles toward him in II.iii shows that they regard him as a claimant to the throne, and by that time the larger horizon has begun to open out before him. But this is quite a different thing from entertaining deep designs. Bolingbroke is an opportunist, not a schemer.[10] And when, the hand of Death upon him, he looks back over the events that had led to his accession, and solemnly declares:

> Though then, God knows, I had no such intent,
> But that necessity so bowed the state
> That I and greatness were compelled to kiss,[11]

the deep note of contrition proves the sincerity of the words. In fact Shakespeare followed Daniel, who himself accepted the judgment of the historians of his time upon this matter. As we shall see, Daniel considered that Bolingbroke

> Was with occasion thrust into the crime,

for which Fortune was more responsible than the criminal, while the relations between the two cousins throughout the play are already defined, as a recent scholar has noted, in the following passage from Holinshed, which is itself borrowed from Hall:[12]

> This suerlie is a verie notable example, and not vnwoorthie of all princes to be well weied, and diligentlie marked, that this Henrie duke of Lancaster should be thus called to the kingdome, and haue the helpe and assistance (almost) of all the whole realme, which perchance neuer

thereof thought or yet dreamed; and that king Richard should thus be left desolate, void, and in despaire of all hope and comfort, in whom if there were anie offense, it ought rather to be imputed to the frailtie of wanton youth, than to the malice of his hart: but such is the deceiuable judgement of man, which not regarding things present with due consideration, thinketh euer that things to come shall haue good successe, with a pleasant & delitefull end. But in this deiecting of the one, & aduancing of the other, the prouidence of God is to be respected, & his secret will to be woondered at.[13]

The second great attraction, then, of the story of Richard of Bordeaux and Henry, Duke of Lancaster, for the men of the fifteenth and sixteenth centuries was that it afforded, in its spectacle of the "dejecting of the one and advancing of the other," a perfect example of the mysterious action of Fortune, working of course under the inscrutable "providence of God," according to the quasi-mechanical symbolism under which they conceived that action. And this in turn constituted one of the main appeals of *Richard II* for the spectators who first witnessed it. For, though the operations of Fortune were most evident and potent in the lives of the great, everything human was subject to them. It is a point which did not escape Pater, who has seen so much in this play. "His grief," he writes of Richard, "becomes nothing less than a central expression of all that in the revolutions of Fortune's wheel goes *down* in the world."[14] Shakespeare's play was a mirror, not only for magistrates, but for every son of woman; and when on Shakespeare's stage the "dejected" king gazed into the glass—incomparable symbol for that age!—what he saw there was the brittleness both of his own glory and of all earthly happiness.

In the third place, the reign of Richard II possessed a peculiar significance in the history of England, as the Elizabethans understood that history. In itself, and for the two protagonists who brought it to an end, a striking example of a turn of Fortune's wheel, it marked the beginning of a much greater revolution in the story of the nation's fortunes. Shakespeare and his contemporaries, rejoicing in the Tudor peace and looking back with horror to the period of civil strife, known as the Wars of the

Roses, which preceded the accession of Henry VII, were haunted by fears of a return of such anarchy, and found its origin in the events of the last few years of Richard II's reign. And rightly so; for the deposition and murder of Richard not only shocked the conscience of Christendom, they struck at the legal basis of the monarchical, that is to say the whole constitutional, system of England. As Professor Galbraith puts it, "The procedure of deposition as well as the act itself was a cause of the 'disorder, horror, fear, and mutiny' of the fifteenth century."[15]

In *King John* Shakespeare had dealt, for the one and only time, with the question of the relations between this country and the Papacy, which was one of the two main problems of Tudor England. In *Richard II*, which I think followed immediately after, he now handles the other and, in Tudor eyes, still more important problem, the problem of government, or rather of the Governor or Prince. Writing on "the nature of Tudor despotism," Neville Figgis, our chief authority on the history of the idea of kingship in England, remarks:

> The exaltation of the royal authority was due to the need of a strong government. The crime of the Lancastrian dynasty had been, not that it was capricious or self-seeking or oppressive, but that it was weak, that law and order were not maintained and private war was once again becoming prevalent. It is as "saviours of society" that the Yorkists and afterwards the Tudors win their position. In the statutes of liveries and in the Star Chamber is to be found the *raison d'être* of Tudor despotism. Government must be effective, private oppression must be punished, great offenders must be forced to submit to the authority of the Crown. That is the general sentiment. In a word, obedience must be enforced. The very causes, which drove men to support the Tudors at all, drove them also to insist on the paramount importance of obedience, and to proclaim the iniquity of rebellion.[16]

In that age men could not think of government except as embodied in a single person. Indeed, only a very small proportion of the human race is capable of thinking otherwise today. Dangers for government and order might therefore arise from three causes: from weakness of character on the part of the monarch, from the accession of a monarch with a weak claim to the throne, and from the turbulence and ambition of the great nobles surrounding him, who might take advantage of either of the two weaknesses just mentioned or of some other occasion. Except for the abortive insurrection of Essex at the end of her reign, Elizabeth had little trouble from her nobles, who were for the most part "new men" and close adherents of her dynasty from motives of self-interest. But the other two dangers made a special appeal to the fears of her subjects. Not only was her own title, as also her legitimacy, open to question, but being unmarried she had no heir, so that the succession was left at hazard. Writing on *The State of England, Anno Dom. 1600*,[17] a contemporary lawyer, Sir Thomas Wilson, enumerates no fewer than twelve different "competitors that gape for the death of that good old Princess the now Queen." Moreover, though history in retrospect depicts her as a strong character and a great statesman, to her contemporaries, who judged her conduct from day to day and could neither see her reign as a whole nor appreciate to the full the difficulties that faced her, she probably appeared a weak and vacillating woman. In any event, as we shall see, there is plenty of evidence that her courtiers spoke of her not infrequently as "Richard II" and that she herself was conscious of their doing so.

All this being so, the Elizabethans felt much the same interest in the Lancastrian and Yorkist period, culminating in "the glorious union of Henry VII," as Englishmen of the eighteenth and the nineteenth centuries felt in the Civil Wars and the "Glorious Revolution of 1688." And just as the reign of Charles I marked the beginning of the one struggle, so that of Richard II marked the beginning of the other. The period 1398–1485 was, moreover, a self-contained one, was sufficiently remote to be safe to write about, and possessed something of an epical quality, inasmuch as it embraced the martyrdom of a king, the efforts of a usurper to establish his rule, the brilliant episode of Henry V's victories over the foreign foe, the downfall of government and the reign of chaos during the quarrels of the rival dynasties, and finally the restoration of order at the hands of a new dynasty, heir to the claims of both houses. It is not surprising, therefore, that no fewer than three elaborate accounts of this critical period have come down from the sixteenth century. The first is that earliest of Tudor histories, Hall's *Chronicle* (1548), which set the tone for all the histories that followed;[18] the second is the poem already spoken of, a poem in eight books, entitled *The Civil Wars between the two houses of Lancaster and York* (1595-1609) by Samuel Daniel; and the third is the dramatic cycle of Shakespeare's English Histories, composed during the years 1590-99.

What Englishmen, in the age of the Tudor peace, thought about the Wars of the Roses, and the usurpation of Henry Bolingbroke in connection with them, finds eloquent, if quaint, expression on the very title-page of Hall's book, which runs:

> *The union of the two noble and illustre famelies of Lancastre & Yorke, beyng long in continuall discension for the croune of this noble realme, with all the actes done in both the tymes of the Princes, both of the one linage & of the other, beginnyng at the tyme of kyng Henry the fowerth, the first aucthor of this deuision, and so successively proceding to the reigne of the High and Prudent Prince Kyng Henry the Eight, the indubitate flower and very heire of both the saied linages.*

And I do not know of any better text to set in the forefront of this, the first (though not the first written) of Shakespeare's series of historical plays upon the same theme, than Hall's title and the following words with which his book opens, and which, as we shall find, were themselves inspired by a passage in Froissart:

> What mischiefe hath insurged in realmes by intestine deuision, what depopulacion hath ensued in countries by ciuill discenciō, what detestable murder hath been cōmitted in citees by seperate faccions, and what calamitee hath ensued in famous regiōs by domestical discord & vnnaturall controuersy: Rome hath felt, Italy can testifie, Fraunce can bere witnes, Beame[19] can tell, Scotlande maie write, Denmarke can shewe, and especially this noble realme of Englande can apparantly declare and make demonstracion. For who abhorreth not to expresse the heynous factes comitted in Rome, by the ciuill war betwene Julius Cesar

and hardy Pōpey by whose discorde the bright glory of the triūphant Rome was eclipsed & shadowed? Who can reherce what mischefes and what plages the pleasant countree of Italy hath tasted and suffered by the sedicious faccions of the Guelphes and Gebelynes? Who can report the misery that daiely hath ensued in Faunce, by the discorde of the houses of Burgoyne and Orliens: Or in Scotland betwene the brother and brother, the vncle and the nephew? Who can curiously endite the manifolde battailles that were fought in the realme of Beame, betwene the catholikes and the pestiferous sectes of the Adamites and others? What damage discencion hath dooen in Germany and Denmarke, all christians at this daie can well declare. And the Turke can bere good testimony, whiche by the discord of christen princes hath amplified greatly his seigniory and dominion. But what miserie, what murder, and what execrable plagues this famous region hath suffered by the deuision and discencion of the renoumed houses of Lancastre and Yorke, my witte cannot comprehende nor my toung declare nether yet my penne fully set furthe.

For what noble man liueth at this daie, or what gentleman of any aunciient stocke or progeny is clere, whose linage hath not ben infested and plaged with this vnnaturall deuision. All the other discordes, sectes and faccions almoste liuely florishe and continue at this presente tyme, to the greate displesure and preiudice of all the christian publike welth. But the olde deuided controuersie betwene the fornamed families of Lācastre and Yorke, by the vnion of Matrimony celebrate and consummate betwene the high and mighty Prince Kyng Henry the seuenth and the lady Elizabeth his moste worthy Quene, the one beeyng indubitate heire of the hous of Lancastre, and the other of Yorke was suspended and appalled in the person of their most noble, puissāt and mighty heire kyng Henry the eight, and by hym clerely buried and perpetually extinct. So that all men (more clerer than the sonne) maie apparantly perceiue, that as by discord greate thynges decaie and fall to ruine, so the same by concord be reuiued and erected. In likewise also all regions whiche by deuisiō and discencion be vexed, molested and troubled, bee by vnion and agrement releued pacified and enriched. . . .

## Richard II and Queen Elizabeth

But while Elizabeth lived, the older anxieties governed men's thoughts and in their fears that her reign might be the prelude to yet another period of anarchy, they naturally bent eagerly enquiring eyes upon the events of the reign of Richard II which had led up to the earlier period of trouble and particularly upon the actions of the usurper Henry IV, who was, as Hall taught them, "the first aucthor of this deuision."

> There are [writes Sir Edmund Chambers] many indications of an analogy present to the Elizabethan political imagination between the reign of Richard II and that of Elizabeth herself. A letter of Sir Francis Knollys on 9 January 1578 excuses himself for giving unwelcome counsel to the queen. He will not "play the partes of King Richard the Second's men"; will not be a courtly and unstatesmanlike flatterer. Clearly the phrase was familiar. Henry Lord Hunsdon similarly wrote at some date before 1588, "I never was one of Richard II's men." More cryptic is a letter from Raleigh to Robert Cecil on 6 July 1597, "I acquaynted my L: generall [Essex] with your letter to mee & your kynd acceptance of your enterteynemente, hee was also wonderfull merry att ye consait of Richard the 2. I hope it shall never alter, & whereof I shalbe most gladd of as the trew way to all our good, quiett & advancement, and most of all for her sake whose affaires shall therby fynd better progression." All these allusions are of course in perfect loyalty, the utterances of devoted, if critical, officials.[20]

Others, however, might employ the analogy for different ends. *Thomas of Woodstock*, the only other extant Elizabethan play on the subject,[21] is patently unsympathetic to Richard, its theme being the glorification of his uncle the Duke of Gloucester, whose murder was the first link in the chain of events that led to the King's downfall. And that this play was not unconnected with contemporary politics may be surmized from the fact that the Earl of Essex traced his descent from the same duke, which remote alliance with the blood royal constituted his sole claim to the crown. Moreover, after the summer of 1597 (when for a brief space Essex, Raleigh and Cecil were in accord), as the Earl

## The Historical and Political Dynamics

fell by degrees into disfavor and began to entertain seditious thoughts toward his royal mistress, he seems to have identified himself more and more in imagination with Bolingbroke, and to have contemplated with increasing equanimity the possibility of Elizabeth's deposition in his favor. In January, 1599, one John Hayward was foolish enough to publish a prose history entitled *The First Part of the Life and Raigne of King Henrie IIII* with an epistle dedicatory to Essex in which the Earl is described as "magnus et presenti iudicio et futuri temporis expectatione"; words that suggest an heir to the throne at the least. Apart from this the book seems innocent enough to the modern eye; but it was considered seditious by the authorities, and suppressed.

The most remarkable of all occurrences, however, connecting the fortunes of Elizabeth and Essex with those of Richard and his rival was the performance at the Globe theatre, by the express wish of the Earl's supporters, who added an honorarium to their other persuasions, of a play, *Richard II*, generally assumed to be Shakespeare's, on the eve of the attempted rebellion, which took place on 8 February 1601, and came, as all men know, utterly to grief. The transaction at the Globe was discussed at length in the trial that followed; but Shakespeare was not among the Globe players brought to book, and there is no evidence that he and his company suffered in any way for their part therein. On the contrary, they are found playing at Court before the Queen on the day preceding Essex's execution. Anyone who knew the play, as Cecil did, would have been able to acquit its author of treasonable intent. Nevertheless, the Queen herself appears to have nourished a grudge against it. At least that seems the natural deduction from the famous story told by William Lambarde, keeper of the Tower records. While he was visiting her at Greenwich on 4 August 1601, and presenting her

> with his Pandecta of all her rolls, bundells, membranes, and parcells that be reposed in her Majestie's Tower at London . . . her Majestie fell upon the reign of King Richard II, saying, "I am Richard II, know ye not that?"
> 
> W.L. Such a wicked imagination was determined and attempted by a most unkind Gent. the most adorned creature that ever your Majestie made.

*Her Majestie*. He that will forget God, will also forget his benefactors; this tragedy was played 40$^{tie}$ times in open streets and houses.²²

Unhappily no theatrical records of Shakespeare's company have come down to us; but from Henslowe's *Diary* it appears that the longest run for a play belonging to their rivals, the Admiral's Servants, was thirty-one performances spread over two and a half years.²³ Queen Elizabeth, therefore, in mentioning the forty performances of *Richard II*, was emphasizing something quite out of the common. She refers, we must suppose, not to the revival of 1601, which was for one occasion only (and when, as the players averred to those who urged them to act it, the drama was so "stale" that "they should get nothing by playing" it²⁴), but to the original performances in 1595-96, at which time, it was asserted in official notes concerning Essex drawn up in 1600, "the Erle himself" was "often present at the playing thereof, . . . with great applause giving countenance and lyking to the same."²⁵

It is to be presumed also that the deposition scene, which was not printed until after Elizabeth's death, had been acted on all these occasions. As Sir Edmund Chambers remarks, it "was evidently given at the 1601 performance"; and I agree with him that "it was probably given in 1595 also."²⁶ Certainly it is unlikely that Sir Edward Hoby would have offered a maimed and deformed play when he desired "K. Richard" to "present himselfe to" the view of Sir Robert Cecil. Furthermore, had the scene been forbidden by the Censor, the players could hardly have acted it with impunity, as they appear to have done, in 1601. Clearly, the whole play, as we now have it, received the Censor's endorsement in 1595—as why should it not, at a time before suspicions had begun to attach themselves to the Earl of Essex and while he yet stood high in the Queen's favor?—and was acted from the original "allowed book" at the revival six years later. Not that the deposition scene contained anything in the least seditious; on the contrary, its whole tenor might seem to appeal for the sympathy of the audience on behalf of the distressed King. And I believe this obvious fact may have stood the Chamberlain's Servants in good stead during the trial of Essex. Yet, what in normal times would seem quite innocuous might take on a dangerous complexion when treason was abroad. That Shakespeare's *Richard II* exhibited the spectacle of a monarch being actually dethroned, and that monarch popularly regarded as the prototype of the Queen, was enough to render it "good propaganda," as the modern political jargon goes, in the eyes of the hotheads of Essex's party, who would remember perhaps the private comments by their leader upon it after seeing it in 1595. And that the same spectacle had been cut out by the Censor of books, who was a different functionary from the Censor of plays, when the drama came to be printed in the autumn of 1597, is, perhaps, an indication that by that date the authorities were beginning to grow nervous about the intentions of the headstrong Earl, and more conscious of the analogy between Richard and Elizabeth.[27] Or may it have been decided that what was safe enough to perform in loyal and Protestant London might prove too exciting for heady wits to read at the universities or in the Catholic north?

The foregoing paragraphs are offered as an explanation of a situation which has hitherto baffled enquirers by presenting a series of apparently irreconcilable contradictions. How came a play which is patently loyalist in tone, if critical of Richard's actions, to be used for seditious ends? Why was a scene, allowed by one censor, considered dangerous by another? How was it that the Chamberlain's men, having enacted a play at the request of conspirators and for seditious purposes, escaped scot-free from the vengeance of the authorities? The probability that *Richard II* was well known to these authorities, and particularly to Cecil, in 1595, and known to have had nothing whatever to do with the disaffection of Essex, taken together with the progressive deterioration of the relations between Essex and Elizabeth during the years 1597–1601, is sufficient, I think, to account for all the circumstances.

## Richard and Bolingbroke

Whatever, then, Shakespeare's personal attitude toward Essex may have been, the association of his *Richard II* with the Earl's schemes was an accidental one, and has no relevance either to the purpose of the dramatist or to our understanding of the play. The play is, nevertheless, steeped in Elizabethan political notions, and unless we grasp them we are likely to miss much that the author intended us to perceive. Not that he was attempting anything in the nature of a political argument. On the contrary, the political situation he dealt with was merely the material for drama. He takes sides neither with Richard nor with Bolingbroke; he exhibits without concealment the weakness of the King's character, but he spares no pains to evoke our whole-hearted pity for him in his fall. Indeed, it is partly because it succeeds in holding the balance so even that *Richard II* is a favorite play with historians. It develops the political issue in all its complexity, and leaves judgment upon it to the spectator. Shakespeare's only prejudices are a patriotic assertion of the paramount interests of England above those of king or subject, an assertion which, following a hint in Froissart, he places upon the lips of the dying John of Gaunt, and a quasi-religious belief in the sanctity of an anointed monarch; and it is part of his dramatic setting that these two prejudices or ideals are irreconcilable under the historical circumstances with which the play deals.

Another reason why the modern historian tends to delight in *Richard II* is that, unlike most of Shakespeare's other chronicle-plays, the events it relates are with minor exceptions regarded as historically correct. Thus we have our greatest imagination at work, in the disinterested spirit of true art, upon a series of facts, admirably adapted for dramatic treatment, which are still for the most part attested by modern history. And how closely Shakespeare's diagnosis of Richard's character tallies with that of a typical historian of our time may be seen from the following extract from Sir Charles Oman's *Political History of England, 1377-1485*:

> Richard's temper on any given occasion was incalculable. Energy and apathy, over-confidence and abject depression came to him at the inappropriate moments. . . . He was a creature of moods, and his moods always visited him at the wrong time. If he had not been thoughtless, arrogant, and overbearing in 1398, he might have reigned for many a

year. If he had shown common resolution in 1399, he might have made a fair fight for his crown: it was by deserting his army at Milford that he ruined himself. Later events showed that he possessed many friends, and that they would have defended him if he had given them the chance. It was not the deaths of Gloucester and Arundel that doomed him to destruction, but his vain boasting, his petty interferences with the liberties of his subjects, his fits of passion, his senseless acts of injustice to men of minor importance. . . . Yet few tyrants have shed so little blood—if few have made so many foolish boasts concerning their prerogative. Richard cannot be called cruel, nor was he a notorious evil liver, nor a thriftless weakling. Nevertheless he fooled away the crown which kings intellectually, as well as morally, his inferiors preserved to their death-day. . . . No sovereign was ever more entirely the author of his own destruction.[28]

There, except for his poetry—a large exception—and for other slighter variations and small differences of emphasis, stands Shakespeare's Richard as Coleridge saw him.

And yet, if we follow Coleridge and most modern critics in isolating the figure of Richard from the dramatic composition of which it is only a part, and ignoring the political prepossessions of the audience for whom the play was written, we miss much, perhaps most, that Shakespeare intended. For his Richard, as often happens with his characters for one reason or another, is to be viewed on a double plane of vision: at once realistically as a man, and symbolically as the royal martyr whose blood, spilt by the usurper, cries out for the vengeance which tears England asunder for two generations. Looked at merely from within the framework of the play of which he is the central figure, he seems the rather contemptible person that Coleridge has depicted; seen in the secular perspective of the whole cycle, his personal failings, the $\alpha\mu\alpha\rho\tau\iota\alpha$ of his peculiar tragedy, become the occasion of something much larger than himself, the deposition and death of the Lord's anointed. For that break in the lineal succession of God's deputies-elect meant the beginning of political chaos.

> Take but degree away, untune that string,
> And hark what discord follows!

is the moral of Shakespeare's series of English chronicles as of everything else he wrote that touches political issues.

And what is true of Richard is true also of the lesser characters in the play. The prophetic voice of Gaunt, for example, pronounces judgment not only upon the spendthrift King, whose deposition it foretells,[29] but also by implication upon Bolingbroke, the son who lifts

> An angry arm against God's minister,[30]

and becomes the sacrilegious instrument of his deposition. As I have said above, Bolingbroke is not rightly understood until he is regarded as in part at least the puppet of Fortune. And, successful as he is in *Richard II*, we feel even here that he has been caught up into the tragic net by usurpation, so that it is with no surprise we find him at the beginning of the sequel not only renewing his vow to go on a crusade in expiation of his guilt, but pronouncing himself "shaken" and "wan with care." Indeed, the whole play is as full of foreboding as it is of patriotic sentiment. Civil war is already implicit in the strife between Bolingbroke and Mowbray, with which it opens, and in the wrangling of the nobles before Richard's deposition, while it is explicit in the prophecy of the Bishop of Carlisle (IV.i.129-49) and in the scarcely less significant words of Richard to Northumberland at V.i.55-68. Thus when Richard's tragedy is ended, we are left with the feeling that England's has only just begun.

Yet the foreboding has almost entirely evaporated in the Histories that immediately follow. When Shakespeare came to give us the *Henry IV* we know, his mood had changed. In 1595 he had evidently no inkling that Sir John Falstaff was waiting for him round the corner.

NOTES

*Note*: Original footnotes have been renumbered.

1. Our latter-day "royalist," Mr. T.S. Eliot, is still found referring to the execution of Charles I as "the Martyrdom" sans phrase, in a

recent publication; see *Seventeenth Century Studies in Honour of Sir Herbert Grierson*, p. 242. On the other hand a Catholic historian like Mr. Hilaire Belloc, who speaks of Richard II as the "sacramental man," and of his dethroning as "sacrilege," shows that the medieval conception of Richard is not yet extinct (see *History of England*, III.90-91).
2. Reprinted with a valuable introduction by M.V. Clarke and V.H. Galbraith as "The Deposition of Richard II" (*Rylands Library Bulletin*, vol. XIV, Jan. 1930).
3. P. viii of Preface to *Chronicque de la Traïson et Mort de Richard Deux roy Dengleterre* (ed. B. Williams, 1846); see below.
4. "I would (quoth one of the company)," runs the prose preface, "gladly say sumwhat for King Richard. But his personage is so sore intangled as I thinke fewe benefices be at this day" (p. 110, ed. L.B. Campbell, 1938).
5. See *Archaeologia*, XX.138.
6. See note 2.
7. Cf. IV.i.184-89.
8. Cf. *The Goddess Fortuna in Medieval Literature*, by H.R. Patch, 1927, and *The Medieval Heritage of Elizabethan Tragedy*, by W. Farnham, 1936, pp. 415-18.
9. Berners' *Froissart*, VI.307 (Tudor Translations).
10. The passage depicting Bolingbroke as a deep politician occurs in Coleridge's 1818 notes. In the lectures of 1811-12 he took a different view. "In Bolingbroke," he then declared, "we find a man who in the outset has been sorely injured: then, we see him encouraged by the grievances of his country, and by the strange mismanagement of the government, yet at the same time scarcely daring to look at his own views, or to acknowledge them as designs. He comes home under the pretence of claiming his dukedom, and he professes that to be his object almost to the last; but, at the last, he avows his purpose to its full extent, of which he was himself unconscious in the earlier stages" (T.M. Raysor, *Coleridge's Shakespearean Criticism*, II.188-89).
11. *2 Henry IV*, III.i.72-74.
12. Farnham, *op. cit.*
13. Holinshed, *Chronicles*, ed. 1587, vol. III, p. 499/2/50.
14. *Appreciations*, p. 199.
15. Clarke and Galbraith, *op. cit.*, p. 33.
16. *Divine Right of Kings* (2nd ed.), p. 88.
17. Edited from the manuscripts among the State Papers in the Public Record Office by F.J. Fisher (*Camden Miscellany*, vol. XVI, p. 2).

18. Cf. C.L. Kingsford, *Prejudice & Promise in XVth Century England*, p. 3: "Hall's presentment of past history appealed naturally to those who came after him, and was embedded firmly in the opinion of the time."
19. I.e., Bohemia.
20. *William Shakespeare*, I.353.
21. *Jack Straw* (1593) deals with the Peasants' Revolt, 1381, and has nothing to do with the Deposition. The entry in Simon Forman's *Booke* concerning a *Richard II*, seen in 1611, does not describe this play. For the authenticity of the *Booke* see *RES*, July 1947.
22. Chambers, *William Shakespeare*, II.326-27.
23. Chambers, *Elizabethan Stage*, II.148.
24. *William Shakespeare*, II.326.
25. *Ibid.*, I.354, II.323.
26. *Ibid.*, I.355.
27. See above, p. 11.
28. *Political History of England, 1377-1485*, pp. 150-51.
29. II.i.108.
30. I.ii.40-41.

# E.M.W. Tillyard

## Shakespeare's History Plays (1944)

*Richard II* is imperfectly executed, and yet, that imperfection granted, perfectly planned as part of a great structure. It is sharply contrasted, in its extreme formality of shape and style, with the subtler and more fluid nature of *Henry IV*; but it is a necessary and deliberate contrast; resembling a stiff recitative composed to introduce a varied and flexible *aria*. Coming after *King John* the play would appear the strangest relapse into the official self which Shakespeare had been shedding; taken with *Henry IV* it shows that Shakespeare, while retaining and using this official self, could develop with brilliant success the new qualities of character and style manifested in the Bastard. *Richard II* therefore betokens no relapse but is an organic part of one of Shakespeare's major achievements.

But the imperfections are undoubted and must be faced. As a separate play *Richard II* lacks the sustained vitality of *Richard III*, being less interesting and less exacting in structure and containing a good deal of verse which by the best Shakespearean standards can only be called indifferent. Not that there is anything wrong with the structure, which is that of *2 Henry VI*, the rise of one great man at the expense of another; but it is simple, as befits an exordium, and does not serve through the excitement of its complications to make the utmost demand on the powers of the author. For illustrating the indifferent verse I need not go beyond the frequent stretches of couplet-writing and the occasional quatrains that make such a contrast to the verse of *Henry IV*. It is not that these have not got their function, which will be dealt with later, but that as poetry they are indifferent stuff. They are as necessary as the stiff lines in

*3 Henry VI* spoken by the Father who has killed his Son, and the Son who has killed his Father; but they are little better poetically. For present purposes it does not matter in the least whether they are relics of an old play, by Shakespeare or by someone else, or whether Shakespeare wrote them with the rest. They occur throughout the play and with the exception of perhaps two couplets are not conspicuously worse in the fifth act than anywhere else. There is no need for a theory that in this act, to save time, Shakespeare hurriedly began copying chunks from an old play. Until there is decisive proof of this, it is simplest to think that Shakespeare wrote his couplets along with the rest, intending a deliberate contrast. He had done the same thing with the Talbots' death in *1 Henry VI*, while, to account for the indifferent quality, one may remember that he was never very good at the couplet. The best couplets in *A Midsummer Night's Dream* are weak compared with the best blank verse in that play, while few of the final couplets of the sonnets are more than a competent close to far higher verse.

I turn now to a larger quality of the play, of which the couplets are one of several indications.

Of all Shakespeare's plays *Richard II* is the most formal and ceremonial. It is not only that Richard himself is a true king in appearance, in his command of the trappings of royalty, while being deficient in the solid virtues of the ruler; that is a commonplace: the ceremonial character of the play extends much wider than Richard's own nature or the exquisite patterns of his poetic speech.

First, the very actions tend to be symbolic rather than real. There is all the pomp of a tournament without the physical meeting of the two armed knights. There is a great army of Welshmen assembled to support Richard, but they never fight. Bolingbroke before Flint Castle speaks of the terrible clash there should be when he and Richard meet:

> Methinks King Richard and myself should meet
> With no less terror than the elements
> Of fire and water, when their thundering shock
> At meeting tears the cloudy cheeks of heaven.

## The Historical and Political Dynamics 25

But instead of a clash there is a highly ceremonious encounter leading to the effortless submission of Richard. There are violent challenges before Henry in Westminster Hall, but the issue is postponed. The climax of the play is the ceremony of Richard's deposition. And finally Richard, imprisoned at Pomfret, erects his own lonely state and his own griefs into a gigantic ceremony. He arranges his own thoughts into classes corresponding with men's estates in real life; king and beggar, divine, soldier, and middle man. His own sighs keep a ceremonial order like a clock:

> Now, sir, the sound that tells what hour it is
> Are clamorous groans, which strike upon my heart,
> Which is the bell: so sighs and tears and groans
> Show minutes, times, and hours.

Second, in places where emotion rises, where there is strong mental action, Shakespeare evades direct or naturalistic presentation and resorts to convention and conceit. He had done the same when Arthur pleaded with Hubert for his eyes in *King John*, but that was exceptional to a play which contained the agonies of Constance and the Bastard's perplexities over Arthur's body. Emotionally Richard's parting from his queen could have been a great thing in the play: actually it is an exchange of frigidly ingenious couplets.

> *Rich.* Go, count thy ways with sighs; I mine with groans.
> *Qu.* So longest way shall have the longest moans.
> *Rich.* Twice for one step I'll groan, the way being short,
>   And piece the way out with a heavy heart.

This is indeed the language of ceremony not of passion. Exactly the same happens when the Duchess of York pleads with Henry against her husband for her son Aumerle's life. Before the climax, when York gives the news of his son's treachery, there had been a show of feeling; but with the entry of the Duchess, when emotion should culminate, all is changed to prettiness and formal antiphony. This is how the Duchess compares her own quality of pleading with her husband's:

> Pleads he in earnest? look upon his face;
> His eyes do drop no tears, his prayers are jest;

> His words come from his mouth, ours from our breast:
> He prays but faintly and would be denied;
> We pray with heart and soul and all beside:
> His weary joints would gladly rise, I know;
> Our knees shall kneel till to the ground they grow:
> His prayers are full of false hypocrisy;
> Ours of true zeal and deep integrity.

And to "frame" the scene, to make it unmistakably a piece of deliberate ceremonial, Bolingbroke falls into the normal language of drama when, having forgiven Aumerle, he vows to punish the other conspirators:

> But for our trusty brother-in-law and the abbot,
> And all the rest of that consorted crew,
> Destruction straight shall dog them at the heels.

The case of Gaunt is different but more complicated. When he has the state of England in mind and reproves Richard, though he can be rhetorical and play on words, he speaks the language of passion:

> Now He that made me knows I see thee ill.
> Thy death-bed is no lesser than thy land
> Wherein thou liest in reputation sick.
> And thou, too careless patient as thou art,
> Commit'st thy anointed body to the cure
> Of those physicians that first wounded thee.
> A thousand flatterers sit within thy crown,
> Whose compass is no bigger than thy head.

But in the scene of private feeling, when he parts from his banished son, both speakers, ceasing to be specifically themselves, exchange the most exquisitely formal commonplaces traditionally deemed appropriate to such a situation.

> Go, say I sent thee for to purchase honour
> And not the king exil'd thee; or suppose
> Devouring pestilence hangs in our air
> And thou art flying to a fresher clime.
> Look, what thy soul holds dear, imagine it
> To lie that way thou go'st, not whence thou com'st.

> Suppose the singing birds musicians,
> The grass whereon thou tread'st the presence strew'd,
> The flowers fair ladies, and thy steps no more
> Than a delightful measure or a dance;
> For gnarling sorrow hath less power to bite
> The man that mocks at it and sets it light.

Superficially this may be maturer verse than the couplets quoted, but it is just as formal, just as mindful of propriety and as unmindful of nature as Richard and his queen taking leave. Richard's sudden start into action when attacked by his murderers is exceptional, serving to set off by contrast the lack of action that has prevailed and to link the play with the next of the series. His groom, who appears in the same scene, is a realistic character alien to the rest of the play and serves the same function as Richard in action.

Thirdly, there is an elaboration and a formality in the cosmic references, scarcely to be matched in Shakespeare. These are usually brief and incidental, showing indeed how intimate a part they were of the things accepted and familiar in Shakespeare's mind. But in *Richard II* they are positively paraded. The great speech of Richard in Pomfret Castle is a tissue of them: first the peopling of his prison room with his thoughts, making its microcosm correspond with the orders of the body politic; then the doctrine of the universe as a musical harmony; then the fantasy of his own griefs arranged in a pattern like the working of a clock, symbol of regularity opposed to discord; and finally madness as the counterpart in man's mental kingdom of discord or chaos. Throughout the play the great commonplace of the king on earth duplicating the sun in heaven is exploited with a persistence unmatched anywhere else in Shakespeare. Finally (for I omit minor references to cosmic lore) there is the scene (III.iv) of the gardeners, with the elaborate comparison of the state to the botanical microcosm of the garden. But this is a scene so typical of the whole trend of the play that I will speak of it generally and not merely as another illustration of the traditional correspondences.

The scene begins with a few exquisitely musical lines of dialogue between the queen and two ladies. She refines her grief in a vein of high ceremony and sophistication. She begins by asking what sport they can devise in this garden to drive away care. But to every sport proposed there is a witty objection.

> *Lady.* Madam, we'll tell tales.
> *Queen.* Of sorrow or of joy?
> *Lady.* Of either, madam.
> *Queen.* Of neither, girl:
>   For if of joy, being altogether wanting,
>   It doth remember me the more of sorrow;
>   Or if of grief, being altogether had,
>   It adds more sorrow to my want of joy.
>   For what I have I need not to repeat,
>   And what I want it boots not to complain.

Shakespeare uses language here like a very accomplished musician doing exercises over the whole compass of the violin. Then there enter a gardener and two servants: clearly to balance the queen and her ladies and through that balance to suggest that the gardener within the walls of his little plot of land is a king. Nothing could illustrate better the different expectations of a modern and of an Elizabethan audience than the way they would take the gardener's opening words:

> Go, bind thou up yon dangling apricocks,
> Which, like unruly children, make their sire
> Stoop with oppression of their prodigal weight.

The first thought of a modern audience is: what a ridiculous way for a gardener to talk. The first thought of an Elizabethan would have been: what is the symbolic meaning of those words, spoken by this king of the garden, and how does it bear on the play? And it would very quickly conclude that the apricots have grown inflated and overweening in the sun of the royal favor; that oppression was used with a political as well as a physical meaning; and that the apricots threatened, unless restrained, to upset the proper relation between parent and offspring, to offend against the great principle of order. And the rest of the gardener's speech would bear out this interpretation.

> Go thou, and like an executioner
> Cut off the heads of too fast growing sprays,
> That look too lofty in our commonwealth.

> All must be even in our government.
> You thus employ'd, I will go root away
> The noisome weeds, which without profit suck
> The soil's fertility from wholesome flowers.

In fact the scene turns out to be an elaborate political allegory, with the Earl of Wiltshire, Bushy, and Green standing for the noxious weeds which Richard, the bad gardener, allowed to flourish and which Henry, the new gardener, has rooted up. It ends with the queen coming forward and joining in the talk. She confirms the gardener's regal and moral function by calling him "old Adam's likeness," but curses him for his ill news about Richard and Bolingbroke. The intensively symbolic character of the scene is confirmed when the gardener at the end proposes to plant a bank with rue where the queen let fall her tears, as a memorial:

> Rue, even for ruth, here shortly shall be seen
> In the remembrance of a weeping queen.

In passing, for it is not my immediate concern, let me add that the gardener gives both the pattern and the moral of the play. The pattern is the weighing of the fortunes of Richard and Bolingbroke:

> Their fortunes both are weigh'd.
> In your lord's scale is nothing but himself
> And some few vanities that make him light;
> But in the balance of great Bolingbroke
> Besides himself are all the English peers,
> And with that odds he weighs King Richard down.

For the moral, though he deplores Richard's inefficiency, the gardener calls the news of his fall "black tidings" and he sympathizes with the queen's sorrow. And he is himself, in his microcosmic garden, what neither Richard nor Bolingbroke separately is, the authentic gardener-king, no usurper, and the just represser of vices, the man who makes "all even in our government."

The one close Shakespearean analogy with this gardener is Iden, the unambitious squire in his Kentish garden, who stands for "degree" in *2 Henry VI*. But he comes in as an obvious foil to the realistic disorder just exhibited in Cade's rebellion. Why was it that in *Richard II*, when he was so much more mature, when his brilliant realism in *King John* showed him capable of making his gardeners as human and as amusing as the gravediggers in *Hamlet*, Shakespeare chose to present them with a degree of formality unequalled in any play he wrote? It is, in a different form, the same question as that which was implied by my discussion of the other formal or ceremonial features of the play: namely, why did Shakespeare in *Richard II* make the ceremonial or ritual form of writing, found in differing quantities in the *Henry VI* plays and in *Richard III*, not merely one of the principal means of expression but the very essence of the play?

These are the first questions we must answer if we are to understand the true nature of *Richard II*. And here let me repeat that though Richard himself is a very important part of the play's ceremonial content, that content is larger and more important than Richard. With that caution, I will try to explain how the ritual or ceremonial element in *Richard II* differs from that in the earlier History Plays, and through such an explanation to conjecture a new interpretation of the play. There is no finer instance of ceremonial writing than the scene of the ghosts at the end of *Richard III*. But it is subservient to a piece of action, to the Battle of Bosworth with the overthrow of a tyrant and the triumph of a righteous prince. Its duty is to make that action a matter of high, mysterious, religious import. We are not invited to dwell on the ritual happenings as on a resting-place, to deduce from them the ideas into which the mind settles when the action of the play is over. But in *Richard II*, with all the emphasis and the point taken out of the action, we are invited, again and again, to dwell on the sheer ceremony of the various situations. The main point of the tournament between Bolingbroke and Mowbray is the way it is conducted; the point of Gaunt's parting with Bolingbroke is the sheer propriety of the sentiments they utter; the portents, put so fittingly into the mouth of a Welshman, are more exciting because they are appropriate than because they precipitate an event; Richard is ever more concerned with how he behaves, with the fitness of his conduct to the occasion, than with what he actually does; the gardener may foretell the deposition of Richard yet he is far

## The Historical and Political Dynamics 31

more interesting as representing a static principle of order; when Richard is deposed, it is the precise manner that comes before all—

> With mine own tears I wash away my balm,
> With mine own hands I give away my crown,
> With mine own tongue deny my sacred state,
> With mine own breath release all duty's rites.

We are in fact in a world where means matter more than ends, where it is more important to keep strictly the rules of an elaborate game than either to win or to lose it.

Now though compared with ourselves the Elizabethans put a high value on means as against ends they did not go to the extreme. It was in the Middle Ages that means were so elaborated, that the rules of the game of life were so lavishly and so minutely set forth. *Richard II* is Shakespeare's picture of that life.

Of course it would be absurd to suggest that Shakespeare pictured the age of Richard II after the fashion of a modern historian. But there are signs elsewhere in Shakespeare of at least a feeling after historical verity; and there are special reasons why the age of Richard II should have struck the imaginations of the Elizabethans.

I noted elsewhere that at the end of *2 Henry VI* Clifford and York, though enemies, do utter some of the chivalric sentiments proper to medieval warfare. Such sentiments do not recur in *3 Henry VI*, where we have instead the full barbarities of Wakefield and Towton. Shakespeare is probably recording the historical fact that the decencies of the knightly code went down under the stress of civil carnage. But the really convincing analogy with *Richard II* is the play of *Julius Caesar*. There, however slender Shakespeare's equipment as historian and however much of his own time he slips in, he does succeed in giving his picture of antique Rome, of the dignity of its government and of the stoic creed of its great men. T.S. Eliot has rightly noted how much essential history Shakespeare extracted from Plutarch. And if from Plutarch, why not from Froissart likewise?

Till recently Shakespeare's debt to Berners's translation of Froissart's Chronicle has been almost passed over, but now it is rightly agreed that it was considerable. To recognize the debt helps one to understand the play. For instance, one of the minor puzzles of the play is plain if we grant Shakespeare's acquaintance with Froissart. When York, horrified at Richard's confiscating Gaunt's property the moment he died, goes on to enumerate all Richard's crimes, he mentions "the prevention of poor Bolingbroke about his marriage." There is nothing more about this in the play, but there is a great deal about it in Froissart—Richard had brought charges against the exile Bolingbroke which induced the French king to break off Bolingbroke's engagement with the daughter of the Duke of Berry, the king's cousin. If Shakespeare had been full of Froissart when writing *Richard II* he could easily have slipped in this isolated reference. But quite apart from any tangible signs of imitation it is scarcely conceivable that Shakespeare should not have read so famous a book as Berners's Froissart, or that having read it he should not have been impressed by the bright pictures of chivalric life in those pages. Now among Shakespeare's History Plays *Richard II* is the only one that falls within the period of time covered by Froissart. All the more reason why on this unique occasion he should heed this great original. Now though Froissart is greatly interested in motives, he also writes with an eye unmatched among chroniclers for its eager observation of external things and with a mind similarly unmatched for the high value it placed on the proper disposition of those things. In fact he showed a lively belief in ceremony and in the proprieties of heraldry akin to Elizabethan belief yet altogether more firmly attached to the general scheme of ideas that prevailed at the time. Shakespeare's brilliant wit must have grasped this; and *Richard II* may be his intuitive rendering of Froissart's medievalism.

But there were other reasons why the reign of Richard II should be notable. A.B. Steel, his most recent historian, begins his study by noting that Richard was the last king of the old medieval order:

> the last king ruling by hereditary right, directed and undisputed, from the Conqueror. The kings of the next hundred and ten years . . . were essentially kings *de facto* not *de jure*, successful usurpers recognised after the event, upon conditions, by their fellow-magnates or by parliament.

## The Historical and Political Dynamics

Shakespeare, deeply interested in titles as he had showed himself to be in his early History Plays, must have known this very well; and Gaunt's famous speech on England cannot be fully understood without this knowledge. He calls England

> This nurse, this teeming womb of royal kings,
> Fear'd by their breed and famous by their birth,
> Renowned for their deeds as far from home,
> For Christian service and true chivalry,
> As is the sepulchre in stubborn Jewry
> Of the world's ransom, blessed Mary's son.

Richard was no crusader, but he was authentic heir of the crusading Plantagenets. Henry was different, a usurper; and it is with reference to this passage that we must read the lines in *Richard II* and *Henry IV* which recount his desire and his failure to go to Palestine. That honor was reserved for the authentic Plantagenet kings. Richard then had the full sanctity of medieval kingship and the strong pathos of being the last king to possess it. Shakespeare probably realized that however powerful the Tudors were and however undisputed their hold over their country's church, they had not the same sanctity as the medieval kings. He was therefore ready to draw from certain French treatises, anti-Lancastrian in tone, that made Richard a martyr and compared him to Christ and his accusers to so many Pilates giving him over to the wishes of the London mob. Shakespeare's Richard says at his deposition:

> Though some of you with Pilate wash your hands,
> Showing an outward pity; yet you Pilates
> Have here deliver'd me to my sour cross,
> And water cannot wash away your sin.

Holy and virtuous as the Earl of Richmond is in *Richard III*, he does not pretend to the same kingly sanctity as Richard II. Such sanctity belongs to a more antique, more exotically ritual world; and Shakespeare composed his play accordingly.

Not only did Richard in himself hold a position unique among English kings, he maintained a court of excessive splendor. Froissart writes as follows in the last pages of his chronicle:

> This King Richard reigned king of England twenty-two year in great prosperity, holding great estate and signory. There was never before any king of England that spent so much in his house as he did by a hundred thousand florins every year. For I, Sir John Froissart, canon and treasurer of Chinay, knew it well, for I was in his court more than a quarter of a year together and he made me good cheer. . . . And when I departed from him it was at Windsor; and at my departing the king sent me by a knight of his, Sir John Golofer, a goblet of silver and gilt weighing two mark of silver and within it a hundred nobles, by the which I am as yet the better and shall be as long as I live; wherefore I am bound to pray to God for his soul and with much sorrow I write of his death.

But Shakespeare need not have gone to Froissart for such information. In an age that was both passionately admiring of royal magnificence and far more retentive of tradition than our own, the glories of Richard's court must have persisted as a legend. Anyhow, that Shakespeare was aware of them is plain from Richard's address to his own likeness in the mirror:

> Was this face the face
> That every day under his household roof
> Did keep ten thousand men?

The legend must have persisted of this court's continental elegance, of the curiosities of its dress, of such a thing as Anne of Bohemia introducing the custom of riding side-saddle, of Richard's invention of the handkerchief for nasal use. Then there were the poets. Shakespeare must have associated the beginnings of English poetry with Chaucer and Gower; and they wrote mainly in Richard's reign. There must have been much medieval art, far more than now survives, visible in the great houses of Elizabeth's day, illuminated books and tapestry; and it would be generally associated with the most brilliant reign of the Middle Ages. Finally in Richard's reign there was the glamor of a still intact nobility: a very powerful glamor in an age still devoted to heraldry and yet possessing an aristocracy who, compared with the great men of Richard's day, were upstarts.

## The Historical and Political Dynamics

All these facts would have a strong, if unconscious, effect on Shakespeare's mind and induce him to present the age of Richard in a brilliant yet remote and unrealistic manner. He was already master of a certain antique lore and of a certain kind of ceremonial writing: it was natural that he should use them, but with a different turn, to do this particular work. Thus he makes more solemn and elaborates the inherited notions of cosmic correspondences and chivalric procedure and he makes his ritual style a central and not peripheral concern. Hence the portentous solemnity of the moralizing gardeners, the powerful emphasis on the isolated symbol of the rue-tree, the elaborate circumstances of the tournament between Bolingbroke and Mowbray, and the unique artifice of Richard's great speeches: speeches which are the true center of the play but central with a far wider reference than to the mere character of Richard.

In speaking of medieval illuminated books and tapestry I do not wish to imply anything too literal: that Shakespeare had actual examples of such things in mind when he wrote *Richard II*. But it is true that many passages in this play call them up and that unconscious memory of them *might* have given Shakespeare help. Take a passage from one of Richard's best-known speeches.

> For God's sake, let us sit upon the ground
> And tell sad stories of the death of kings:
> How some have been depos'd, some slain in war,
> Some haunted by the ghosts they have depos'd;
> Some poison'd by their wives, some sleeping kill'd;
> All murder'd: for within the hollow crown
> That rounds the mortal temples of a king
> Keeps Death his court, and there the antic sits,
> Scoffing his state and grinning at his pomp,
> Allowing him a breath, a little scene,
> To monarchise, be fear'd, and kill with looks,
> Infusing him with self and vain conceit,
> As if this flesh which walls about our life
> Were brass impregnable, and, humour'd thus,
> Comes at the last and with a little pin
> Bores through his castle wall, and farewell king!

Critics have seen a reference here to the *Mirror for Magistrates*, but Chaucer's *Monk's Tale* would suit much better. Death, keeping his court, is a pure medieval motive. Still, these motives were inherited and need imply nothing unusual. But Death the skeleton watching and mocking the king in his trappings is a clear and concrete image that reminds one of the visual arts, and above all the exquisiteness, the very remoteness from what could have happened in an actual physical attempt, of someone boring through the castle wall with a little pin precisely recaptures the technique of medieval illumination. Before the tournament Bolingbroke prays God:

> And with thy blessings steel my lance's point
> That it may enter Mowbray's waxen coat.

That again is just like medieval illumination. When a wound is given in medieval art there is no fusion of thing striking with thing stricken; the blow simply rests in a pre-existing hole, while any blood that spouts out had pre-existed just as surely. This is the kind of picture called up by Mowbray's "waxen coat." Or take this comparison. If anywhere in *Henry IV* we might expect medievalism it is in the description of the Prince performing the most spectacular of chivalric actions: vaulting onto his horse in full armor.

> I saw young Harry, with his beaver on,
> His cuisses on his thighs, gallantly arm'd,
> Rise from the ground like feather'd Mercury,
> And vaulted with such ease into his seat,
> As if an angel dropp'd down from the clouds,
> To turn and wind a fiery Pegasus
> And witch the world with noble horsemanship.

There is nothing medieval here. It is a description recalling the art of the high Renaissance with fused colors and subtle transitions. Set beside it Gaunt's advice to Bolingbroke about to go into exile:

> Suppose the singing birds musicians,
> The grass whereon thou tread'st the presence strew'd,
> The flowers fair ladies, and thy steps no more
> Than a delightful measure or a dance.

Here each item is distinct, and the lines evoke the mincing figures of a medieval tapestry in a setting of birds and flowers.

## The Historical and Political Dynamics

The case for the essential medievalism of *Richard II* is even stronger when it is seen that the conspirators, working as such, do not share the ceremonial style used to represent Richard and his court. Once again the usual explanation of such a contrast is too narrow. It has been the habit to contrast the "poetry" of Richard with the practical common sense of Bolingbroke. But the "poetry" of Richard is all part of a world of gorgeous tournaments, conventionally mournful queens, and impossibly sententious gardeners, while Bolingbroke's common sense extends to his backers, in particular to that most important character, Northumberland. We have in fact the contrast not only of two characters but of two ways of life.

One example of the two different ways of life has occurred already: in the contrast noted between the mannered pleading of the Duchess of York for Aumerle's life and Henry's vigorous resolve immediately after to punish the conspirators. The Duchess and her family belong to the old order where the means, the style, the embroidery matter more than what they further or express. Henry belongs to a new order, where action is quick and leads somewhere. But other examples are needed to back up what to many readers will doubtless seem a dangerous and forced theory of the play's significance. First, a new kind of vigor, the vigor of strong and swift action, enters the verse of the play at II.i.224, when, after Richard has seized Gaunt's property and announced his coming journey to Ireland, Northumberland, Ross, and Willoughby remain behind and hatch their conspiracy. Northumberland's last speech especially has a different vigor from any vigorous writing that has gone before: from the vigor of the jousters' mutual defiance or York's moral indignation at the king's excesses. After enumerating Bolingbroke's supporters in Brittany, he goes on:

> All these well furnish'd by the Duke of Brittain
> With eight tall ships, three thousand men of war,
> And making hither with all due expedience
> And shortly mean to touch our northern shore:
> Perhaps they had ere this, but that they stay
> The first departing of the king for Ireland.
> If then we shall shake off our slavish yoke,
> Imp out our drooping country's broken wing,

> Redeem from broken pawn the blemish'd crown,
> Wipe off the dust that hides our sceptre's gift
> And make high majesty look like itself,
> Away with me in post to Ravenspurgh.

The four lines describing by different metaphors how the land is to be restored are not in a ritual manner but in Shakespeare's normal idiom of Elizabethan exuberance. It is not for nothing that the next scene shows the Queen exchanging elegant conceits about her sorrow for Richard's absence with Bushy and Green. But the largest contrast comes at the beginning of the third act. It begins with a very fine speech of Bolingbroke recounting to Bushy and Green all their crimes, before they are executed. It has the full accent of the world of action, where people want to get things and are roused to passion in their attempts:

> Bring forth these men.
> Bushy and Green, I will not vex your souls
> (Since presently your souls must part your bodies)
> With too much urging your pernicious lives,
> For 'twere no charity.

That is the beginning, and the speech goes on to things themselves not to the way they are done or are embroidered. And when at the end Bolingbroke recounts his own injuries it is with plain and understandable passion:

> Myself a prince by fortune of my birth,
> Near to the king in blood, and near in love
> Till you did make him misinterpret me,
> Have stoop'd my neck under your injuries
> And sigh'd my English breath in foreign clouds,
> Eating the bitter bread of banishment.

The scene is followed by Richard's landing in Wales, his pitiful inability to act, and his wonderful self-dramatization. As a display of externals, as an exaltation of means over ends (here carried to a frivolous excess), it is wonderful; yet it contains no lines that for the weight of unaffected passion come near Bolingbroke's single line,

> Eating the bitter bread of banishment.

The world for which Bolingbroke stands, though it is a usurping world, displays a greater sincerity of personal emotion.

Thus *Richard II*, although reputed so simple and homogeneous a play, is built on a contrast. The world of medieval refinement is indeed the main object of presentation but it is threatened and in the end superseded by the more familiar world of the present.

In carrying out his object Shakespeare shows the greatest skill in keeping the emphasis sufficiently on Richard, while hinting that in Bolingbroke's world there is the probability of development. In other words he makes the world of Bolingbroke not so much defective as embryonic. It is not allowed to compete with Richard's but it is ready to grow to its proper fullness in the next plays. This is especially true of the conspirators' characters. Hotspur, for instance, is faintly drawn, yet in one place he speaks with a hearty abruptness that shows his creator had conceived the whole character already. It is when Hotspur first meets Bolingbroke, near Berkeley Castle. Northumberland asks him if he has forgotten the Duke of Hereford, and Hotspur replies:

> No, my good lord, for that is not forgot
> Which ne'er I did remember: to my knowledge
> I never in my life did look on him.

At the beginning of the same scene Northumberland's elaborate compliments to Bolingbroke show his politic nature: it is the same man who at the beginning of *2 Henry IV* lies "crafty-sick." Bolingbroke too is consistent with his later self, though we are shown only certain elements in his character. What marks out the later Bolingbroke and makes him a rather pathetic figure is his bewilderment. For all his political acumen he does not know himself completely or his way about the world. And the reason is that he has relied in large part on fortune. Dover Wilson remarked truly of him in *Richard II* that though he acts forcibly he appears to be borne upward by a power beyond his volition. He is made the first mover of trouble in the matter of the tournament and he wants to do something about Woodstock's murder. But he has no steady policy and having once set events in motion is the servant of fortune. As such, he is not in control of events, though by his adroitness he may deal with the unpredictable as it occurs. Now a man who, lacking a steady policy, begins a course of action will be led into those "by-paths and indirect crook'd ways" of which Henry speaks to his son in *2 Henry IV*. Shakespeare says nothing of them in *Richard II*, but they are yet the inevitable result of Henry's character as shown in that play. It is worth anticipating and saying that Prince Hal differs from his father in having perfect knowledge of himself and of the world around him. Of all types of men he is the least subject to the sway of fortune.

Another quality shown only in embryo is humor. It is nearly absent but there is just a touch: sufficient to assure us that Shakespeare has it there all the time in readiness. It occurs in the scene where Aumerle describes to Richard his parting from Bolingbroke.

> *Rich.* And say, what store of parting tears were shed?
> *Aum.* Faith, none for me: except the north-east wind
>   Which then blew bitterly against our faces,
>   Awak'd the sleeping rheum, and so by chance
>   Did grace our hollow parting with a tear.

*Richard II* thus at once possesses a dominant theme and contains within itself the elements of those different things that are to be the theme of its successors.

It must not be thought, because Shakespeare treated history, as described above, in a way new to him that he has lost interest in his old themes. On the contrary he is interested as much as ever in the theme of civil war, in the kingly type, and in the general fortunes of England. And I will say a little on each of these before trying to sum up the play's meaning in the tetralogy to which it belongs.

*Richard II* does its work in proclaiming the great theme of the whole cycle of Shakespeare's History Plays: the beginning in prosperity, the distortion of prosperity by a crime, civil war, and ultimate renewal of prosperity. The last stage falls outside the play's scope, but the second scene with the Duchess of Gloucester's enumeration of Edward III's seven sons, her account of Gloucester's death, and her call for vengeance is a worthy exordium of the whole cycle. The speeches of the Bishop of Carlisle and of Richard to Northumberland, parts of which

## The Historical and Political Dynamics

were quoted near the beginning of this chapter, are worthy statements of the disorder that follows the deposition of the rightful king. In doctrine the play is entirely orthodox. Shakespeare knows that Richard's crimes never amounted to tyranny and hence that outright rebellion against him was a crime. He leaves uncertain the question of who murdered Woodstock and never says that Richard was personally responsible. The king's uncles hold perfectly correct opinions. Gaunt refuses the Duchess of Gloucester's request for vengeance, the matter being for God's decision alone. Even on his deathbed, when lamenting the state of the realm and calling Richard the landlord and not the king of England, he never preaches rebellion. And he mentions deposition only in the sense that Richard by his own conduct is deposing himself. York utters the most correct sentiments. Like the Bastard he is for supporting the existing government. And though he changes allegiance he is never for rebellion. As stated above, the gardener was against the deposition of Richard.

As well as being a study of medievalism, Richard takes his place among Shakespeare's many studies of the kingly nature. He is a king by unquestioned title and by his external graces alone. But others have written so well on Richard's character that I need say no more.

Lastly, for political motives, there is the old Morality theme of Respublica. One of Shakespeare's debts in *Richard II* is to *Woodstock*; and this play is constructed very plainly on the Morality pattern, with the king's three uncles led by Woodstock inducing him to virtue, and Tressilian Bushy and Green to vice. There are traces of this motive in Shakespeare's play, but with Woodstock dead before the action begins and Gaunt dying early in it the balance of good and evil influences is destroyed. Bushy, Green, and Bagot, however, remain very plainly Morality figures and were probably marked in some way by their dress as abstract vices. If Shakespeare really confused Bagot with the Earl of Wiltshire (according to a conjecture of Dover Wilson) he need not be following an old play heedlessly: he would in any case look on them all as a gang of bad characters, far more important as a gang than as individuals, hence not worth being careful over separately. Once again, as in the earlier tetralogy, England herself, and not the protagonist, is the main concern. Gaunt speaks her praises, the gardener in describing his own symbolic garden has her in mind. As part of the great cycle of English history covered by Hall's chronicle the events of the reign of Richard II take their proper place. But here something fresh has happened. The early tetralogy had as its concern the fortunes of England in that exciting and instructive stretch of her history. *Richard II* has this concern too, but it also deals with England herself, the nature and not merely the fortunes of England. In *Richard II* it is the old brilliant medieval England of the last Plantagenet in the authentic succession; in *Henry IV* it will be the England not of the Middle Ages but of Shakespeare himself. We can now see how the epic comes in and how *Richard II* contributes to an epic effect. Those works which we honor by the epic title always, among other things, express the feelings or the habits of a large group of men, often of a nation. However centrally human, however powerful, a work may be, we shall not give it the epic title for these qualities alone. It is not the parting of Hector and Andromache or the ransoming of Hector's body that make the *Iliad* an epic; it is that the *Iliad* expresses a whole way of life. Shakespeare, it seems, as well as exploiting the most central human affairs, as he was to do in his tragedies, was also impelled to fulfill through the drama that peculiarly epic function which is usually fulfilled through the narrative. Inspired partly perhaps by the example of Daniel and certainly by his own genius, he combined with the grim didactic exposition of the fortunes of England during her terrible ordeal of civil war his epic version of what England was.

This new turn given to the History Play is a great stroke of Shakespeare's genius. Through it he goes beyond anything in Hall or Daniel or even Spenser. Hall and Daniel see English history in a solemn and moral light and they are impressive writers. Spenser is a great philosophical poet and epitomizes the ethos of the Elizabethan age. But none of these can truly picture England. Of the epic writers Sidney in *Arcadia* comes nearest to doing this. It is indeed only in patches that authentic England appears through mythical Arcadia, but that it can, this description of Kalander's house in the second chapter of the book is sufficient proof:

## The Historical and Political Dynamics

> The house itself was built of fair and strong stone, not affecting so much any extraordinary kind of fineness as an honourable representing of a firm stateliness: the lights, doors and stairs rather directed to the use of the guest than to the eye of the artificer, and yet, as the one chiefly heeded, so the other not neglected; each place handsome without curiosity and homely without loathsomeness; not so dainty as not to be trod on nor yet slubbered up with good fellowship; all more lasting than beautiful but that the consideration of the exceeding lastingness made the eye believe it was exceedingly beautiful.

This expresses the authentic genius of English domestic architecture.

Of this great new epic attempt *Richard II* is only the prelude. What of England it pictures is not only antique but partial: the confined world of a medieval courtly class. In his next plays Shakespeare was to picture (with much else) the whole land, as he knew it, in his own day, with its multifarious layers of society and manners of living.

Robert Ornstein

# A Kingdom for a Stage (1972)

The naturalness and spontaneity of the Bastard's speeches signal Shakespeare's complete mastery of his poetic medium. Thoroughly at ease now with his blank verse line and able to mimic with it the accent and cadence of daily speech, he could have turned his back forever on the formal rhetoric of the *Henry VI* plays and the declamatory style of *Richard III* and *King John*. Instead of moving forward to explore the new horizons of his poetic powers, he chose to fashion *Richard II* in a style so richly textured and conceited as to appear almost mannered, and so orotund and sententious that the dialogue often consists of choric pronouncements. If this choice of poetic style is retrograde, it is intentionally so, because even as the racy idiom of the Bastard's speeches aims at Elizabethan "contemporaneousness," the ceremonious formality of *Richard II* summons up remembrance of an antique past. Creating through poetic manner the medieval ambiance and setting of his play,[1] Shakespeare is less concerned to individualize the voices of his characters than to project in their sentences the collective consciousness of an age which treasured formality and order, and which found their analogical and symbolic expression everywhere in the universe. More than a dramatic protagonist, Richard is also the poetic voice of his era and the quintessential expression of its sensibility. When he falls, a way of life and a world seem to fall with him.

Whatever scorn Renaissance humanists professed for the monkish superstition of the middle ages, Shakespeare's contemporaries treasured and enjoyed its artistic legacy. The ancient ballads moved as severe a critic as Sir Philip Sidney, and the chivalric romances, which inspired the sage and serious

Spenser, had an enormous vogue with bourgeois as well as aristocratic readers. To be sure, the winds of change were blowing away the last vestiges of medieval feudalism in the sixteenth century. The manorial system was in decay; castles and abbeys were falling into ruin, and the old aristocracy was losing its preeminent place in the life of the nation. But the past lived on in the immemorial customs of town and country, in centuries-old observances and rituals, and in the pageantries and jousts staged by Tudor monarchs, who sought to recreate the magnificence of medieval courts. Because much of the enduring character of the nation was inscribed in its ancient traditions, Elizabethans hoped to find in the past recorded in the Chronicles and recreated by poets and dramatists a mirror for their own times. Where the "great debates" over the royal succession in the first tetralogy merely expose the ironies of political expediency, the speeches of Gaunt and York in *Richard II* defined for Shakespeare's audiences the aristocratic and conservative bias of their society. Here was incarnate the English reverence of tradition and the English conviction that time-honored right descends inviolate from generation to generation. Thus, while *Richard II* described for Elizabethans days that were no more, it also reaffirmed for them the continuity of past and present that made tradition so vital a force in English life.

There is an artistic pleasure in the evocation of a medieval ethos in *Richard II*, not a political nostalgia for an earlier time. There is no intimation that England under Richard was a prelapsarian paradise, a world of order and harmony that was to be destroyed by a primal sin of disobedience. The opening scenes introduce us to a world which already knows violent contention and mortal enmity, in which men have shed the blood of their nearest kin and fear their father's brother's son. Death in the form of political murder has blighted the garden of state, and serpents' tongues have hissed their temptation of vanity into the ears of the King, whose extravagance threatens to bankrupt the realm. But if Richard's court is "hollow," as Derek Traversi suggests,[2] it is not an *ancien régime* grown oversophisticated and decadent. Although not cast in the heroic mold of his ancestors, Richard is the son and grandson of warriors; his barons are proud, courageous men like Gaunt, York, Mowbray, and

Bolingbroke, for whom honor is a supreme value. Such men are the true representatives of the feudal aristocracy, on which upstarts like Bushy, Bagot, and Green are parasitic growths. Rather than the shuddering destruction of a political order grown effete and impotent, *Richard II* dramatizes the convulsion of a still vigorous political order which turns against the king who wantonly threatens its existence. Paradoxically, it is the would-be preservers of the status quo who become the agents of revolutionary change; it is the defenders of the old regime who become the leaders of the new. Thus, when the old order gives way to the new, there is no radical change in the moral temper of English politics. Northumberland's manner is blunter than Bushy's, but his words and gestures are not more sincere or admirable. The play acting does not end at Court when the rebels triumph, because they also know how to pretend, how to fawn, and how to stage-manage political shows.[3]

The opening scenes of *Richard II*, then, do not establish the harmony or stability of the medieval state. What they express is the importance of the idea of order to the medieval mind. More than an "elaborate game,"[4] the ceremonies of Richard's court project the decorums that order his kingdom. Courtesy is a supreme chivalric value, not simply a refinement of manner; and manner of speech counts because it bespeaks breeding, even as the forms of language count because the feudal oaths of allegiance are the foundation upon which all hierarchy rests. In such a world, height of name has a literal reality, because lowliness must hug the ground, kneeling in supplication to stated majesty. Mowbray flings himself at Richard's feet in the opening scene; Mowbray and Bolingbroke kneel together before Richard as their joust begins, and they must swear together an oath of allegiance before they depart to exile. Richard is amazed to see Northumberland erect before him at Flint Castle, but Bolingbroke is quick to kneel before York and to stoop before Richard, who raises his cousin up to the throne itself. On that throne, Henry later watches Aumerle, York, and his wife kneel to him in supplication. The climactic moments of the play are ceremonies of ascension and declension acted out on the heights and depths of the playhouse stage. It is from the gallery that Richard descends at Flint Castle to the "ground," the base court where kings grow base. It is from the ground that Bolingbroke ("in God's name") ascends the steps to platformed majesty.

Even as the ceremonies of *Richard II* dramatize hierarchical decorums, the poetry sounds a rhetoric of order in elaborate balances, symmetries, and alliterations, and the dialogue returns again and again to the fundamental sanctities of feudal life: blood, name, family, birth, possession, honor, pride, and courage. The thematic images of the first tetralogy refer to the things of this world, to sights and sounds of nature and human activity; they allude to the harvesting of fields, the hunting and slaughtering of animals, the fury of storms, the swarming of insects. The elaborate conceits of *Richard II* are more immediately "philosophical" in that they body forth the world as emblem and idea, as a metaphysical landscape composed of the Ptolemaic elements, earth, water, air, and fire, each theoretically in its proper place in the ascending hierarchical order. If one looks for Hooker's vision of cosmological order, one can find something like it in the speeches of *Richard II*. Yet one must wonder at a play which describes an ideal cosmological scheme in its poetry and mocks it in its dramatic action.[5] To find in the great speeches of *Richard II* an "Elizabethan World Picture" and in its plot a depiction of the brute realities of power politics is to distort Shakespeare's sense of the complex relationship between political ideals and political realities. As a matter of fact, the poetry of *Richard II* does not declare the universality of cosmic harmony; it speaks instead of the universality of contention and change. It suggests that if hierarchy is natural, sovereign place is neither fixed nor immutable. Stars fall and consume themselves; rivers overflow their banks; and clouds dim the radiance of the sun. The sea endlessly challenges the land, the falcon ventures into the eagle's space, and the elements themselves are protean in their qualities. The yielding water can be as forceful as the rage of blood and the swelling tide of oceans; it can drown land and quench fire. Such conceits do not project Shakespeare's belief in analogical order; they express in dramatic verse his awareness of man's will to discover pattern and stability in a universe of disorder and flux. There would be no need for metaphysical conceptions of hierarchy if every king, baron, and commoner were as he should be. It is precisely because the nature of kings is not always regal that the royal office must be made a religious mystery and the king an image of divine Authority. If enough men believe, as Gaunt does, that it is sacrilegious to lift an arm against anointed majesty, then, whatever gods may be, there is a divinity that hedges a king.

Medieval theologians used the idea of cosmological order to relate the imperfection of human existence to the perfect harmony and purposefulness of God's universe. In medieval feudalism the idea of order served as a restraining influence on political ambitions, because it made all authorities and privileges interrelated and interdependent. In the absence of institutions which could effectively maintain the status quo and equilibrium of power, it was essential that every member of a feudal society accept his place, acknowledge that of his superiors, and respect the rights of those beneath him. As York attempts to remind Richard, all feudal authorities are links of a single chain. All aristocratic privilege is supported by the same mystery of blood inheritance and guaranteed by the same rights of time. While the king's place is greater, his right is no different in kind from that of his lowliest peer. A king could be weak, extravagant, grasping, and capricious, as Richard was, and the feudal hierarchy still survive, but it could not survive if a king were allowed to disregard the rights of his subjects.

Coming to *Richard II* from *Richard III* and *King John*, we may think that its depiction of political conflict is somewhat attenuated or lacks immediacy and intensity. We have to keep in mind, however, that the earlier History Plays deal with extreme and melodramatically conceived political situations—with failures of order that loosed mere anarchy on the world in the rages and plots of Machiavellian conspirators. Because Richard is weak and irresponsible, his kingdom faces a political crisis in the opening scenes of the play, but because of the restraints of tradition, the power struggle is oblique, and the challenges masked by protocols. Capable now of artistic nuance and indirection, Shakespeare did not have to make history a study in blacks and whites, and he had available to him Daniel's poised and analytical account of the politics of Richard's fall in *The Civil Wars*. He found in Holinshed, moreover, a relatively sober chronicle of Richard's catastrophe, one that is untouched by the propagandistic distortions that made Margaret, Suffolk, and Richard III gloating villains. Although Holinshed roundly condemns Bolingbroke and his followers (and all his subjects, for that matter) for their disloyalty to Richard, he does not attempt to vilify them. He does not malign Bolingbroke's character or motives; and he passes no judgment on York, who failed to support Richard as the King's Lord Governor, or on Northumberland, who played a fairly treacherous role in bringing Richard into Bolingbroke's hands.

Of course, Shakespeare might have followed *Woodstock* in making Richard a criminal who brought down a just catastrophe upon himself, or followed the French Chronicles in making him a saintly martyr crucified by malicious traitors.[6] He was not tempted, however, toward these extreme, partisan perspectives, because he saw that there were neither heroes nor villains in the drama of Richard's fall, and neither simple rights nor simple wrongs on either side. Aware that Richard betrayed himself even as he was betrayed, Shakespeare sensed that there was a psychological mystery at the heart of his behavior, for though infatuated with his royalty, Richard surrendered it to Bolingbroke without a real struggle. He never fought against the rebels although there were men ready to bear arms to defend his right; he stole away from an army prepared to fight for him, and he bid his supporters flee. Captured without a struggle, he even consented to participate in the ceremony of his degradation. Daniel can think of very reasonable motives for Richard's acts.[7] Shakespeare more perceptively confronts the illogic of his behavior and the fascinating contradictions of his nature. Here was a king notorious for sensuality and extravagance, who lacked neither physical courage nor political acumen and tenacity. Engaged in bitter political struggles from his earliest days, he wrested control of his realm from powerful relatives, and while very young demonstrated extraordinary valor and coolness in dispersing the Jack Straw rebels, even as he proved his manliness at the last by slaying three of his murderers.[8] Not surprisingly, Shakespeare is unwilling to portray Richard as an effeminate Edward II or as the puppet of his sycophants as in *Woodstock*. Although York and others complain that the King is misled, the Richard we see is manipulated by no one. The one time he appears with his coterie, he clearly commands—he decides to farm out the realm, to allow blank charters, and to seize Gaunt's estates. York argues that too many vain tongues have buzzed in Richard's ears, but the Richard we see is too self-absorbed to listen to any words but his own and too shrewd to be easily corrupted. Neither indecisive nor ineffectual, he has lashed out at and murdered a powerful enemy. From the very first scene, however, it is apparent that he cannot meet the particular challenge which Bolingbroke represents, and his fear and hatred of Bolingbroke breeds in Richard something very like a will to disaster.

To see Richard only as a poet-*manqué* or a political fantasist is to see less than half of Shakespeare's portrait. With a poet's taste for language and an actor's hunger to hold the center of the stage, Richard looks forward as the play begins to the spectacle of Mowbray and Bolingbroke "frowning brow to brow." But he knows precisely what their quarrel is about, and he is not taken in by their high sentences and noble postures. He knows that, though they speak the same language of devotion, one of them merely flatters him. Because he is willful and arrogant like Lear, Richard is capable of stupendous folly and, like Lear, has much to learn about his nature and royal state. But he does not, like Lear, doom himself because in a moment of rash anger he forgets who loves him, or because he cannot recognize his enemies. Aware that Bolingbroke's ambition soars to a kingly pitch, he intuits also that Bolingbroke would be his kingdom's heir. His blindness comes, paradoxically, from too much light, from too lucid a recognition of the threat which he cannot admit to himself or to others.

Fully in command of his materials and fully engaged in his artistic task, Shakespeare triumphs in *Richard II* precisely where he failed in *King John*—in the subtle psychological revelation of his protagonist's nature. The portrayal of Richard is necessarily oblique in the opening scenes, because he strikes the conventional postures demanded by ceremonial occasions. We would more quickly grasp his character and more quickly fathom the political situation of the opening scene if, as Holinshed reports, Richard grew furious at Bolingbroke's mention of the murder of Gloucester.[9] The Richard whom Shakespeare conceives is incapable of meeting Bolingbroke's challenge in this direct fashion. Although he can turn with anger and scorn on those who represent Bolingbroke, he never dares pit either his rage or his authority against his cousin. He is vain and sophisticated enough, moreover, to enjoy the hidden drama of the encounter and the masking of motives; he takes pleasure in declarations of impartiality and gratitude which he edges with subtle and mocking irony. Perhaps Shakespeare demands too much from his audience in expecting them to follow the oblique exposition of the first scene, but a perceptive listener would not miss the curious fact that the King does not wish the issue of treason and murder to be pursued. He would note also that Richard's pretense of negligent indifference and impartiality is not very convincing. For, while Richard warns Bolingbroke that he is not prepared to think ill of Mowbray, he licenses Mowbray to say what he will about Richard's princely cousin, whom he carefully puts in his place as his "father's brother's son."[10] It is also revealing that Richard undertakes to calm Mowbray but calls on Gaunt to pacify Bolingbroke. Mowbray will not obey the King's command to throw down Bolingbroke's gage, but he turns toward Richard and flings himself at his feet in a gesture of submission, declaring: "My life thou shalt command, but not my shame." The obdurate Bolingbroke, in contrast, turns toward his father, unwilling to pick up his gage and unwilling also to make Mowbray's gesture of fealty. He refuses Richard's command because he would not seem crestfallen in his father's sight.

Because he is careless of his own reputation, Richard cannot fathom Mowbray's and Bolingbroke's rage, and he cannot quiet it. His clever jests accomplish nothing, his royal commands are disregarded; but he has immense skill in camouflaging his failure. Just as he artfully puts Gaunt between himself and Bolingbroke, he artfully avoids pressing the matter of his subjects' obedience to his commands:

> We were not born to sue, but to command;
> Which since we cannot do to make you friends,
> Be ready, as your lives shall answer it,
> At Coventry upon Saint Lambert's day.
>
> (I.i.196–99)

Every inch a king, he commands Mowbray and Bolingbroke to do that which only a moment before he forbade. With such sleights of hand, a weakling like Richard can maintain the semblance of authority. He cannot, however, settle issues by evading them. Because he has not met Bolingbroke's challenge, he has merely postponed the direct confrontation which must eventually come.

The first scene of *Richard II* intimates the King's shallowness and weakness; the second documents his unscrupulousness and sets forth the myth of royal authority that shores up his pretense of majesty. Urged by Gloucester's widow to revenge his murder, Gaunt confesses his obligation to act, but stronger than any familial tie is his conviction that Richard's office is sacrosanct. He cannot lift his arm in anger against "God's substitute / His deputy anointed in His sight." Yet even Gaunt's patience has its limits, especially when he is tricked by Richard in the third scene into becoming a partner to the banishing of his son. Precisely why Richard chooses to halt the joust between Bolingbroke and Mowbray at the very last moment we do not know, but we recognize the characteristic theatricality of the gesture: here is the weakling's pleasure in commanding (and humiliating) men stronger than himself. And, though we do not know what happens in the council that precedes the sentences of banishment, we recognize the triumph of Commodity in the inequitable terms: ten years of exile (quickly cut to six) for Bolingbroke; perpetual banishment for Mowbray—the first of the princely favorites to discover the meaning of courtly reward in the second tetralogy. Too politic to confess his obligation to Mowbray, Richard nevertheless hesitates to pronounce his sentence, and Mowbray, who expected better, is stunned by this betrayal of his "dearer merit." Shameful to the last, Richard callously dismisses his appeal—"It boots thee not to be compassionate"—and then seeks to appease Gaunt by cutting the term of Bolingbroke's exile. But he cannot, with sham solicitude, court Gaunt's favor any more than Gaunt can with platitudes teach Bolingbroke to think positively about his years of exile. As Daniel phrased it, Richard has "thought best to lose a friend to rid a foe";[11] he will soon learn that he needs friends, and that his clever words have won him only a security of words. He is safe from the threat of Bolingbroke only so long as Bolingbroke honors his oath of exile.

Where rhetoric had the power in *King John* to turn men and nations about, arguments and appeals seem impotent in *Richard II*. Gaunt's and York's counsel cannot save Richard, because he will not listen, and Richard's sentences cannot reconcile Bolingbroke and Mowbray or appease Gaunt or move Northumberland or affect the silent earls who witness his anguish in the deposition scene. On the other hand, words are of immense consequence in a feudal world, where so much depends on oaths, titles, and names, and where, for the sake of a name, men will take arms against a king, as Richard learns when he attempts to erase the name of Lancaster. He is not so foolish as to seize Bolingbroke's inheritance against all tradition and established right just to get money for his Irish wars. He strikes a coward's blow at his living fear, and the depth of that fear is momentarily revealed in the shrill fury with which he turns on the loyal Gaunt and in the bitterness of his response to York's defense of Hereford: "Right, you say true! As Hereford's love, so his [Gaunt's]; / As theirs, so mine; and all be as it is!" (II.i.145-46). Unable to outface Bolingbroke, Richard would destroy him in exile. He seeks, as Gaunt understands, to kill the name of Lancaster, but the name survives and becomes the rallying point of opposition to the King. It is the name of Lancaster which Bolingbroke says he comes to seek in England, and he must find that name on everyone's lips before he disbands his armies.

After the unpredictable twists and turns of plot in *King John*, the unfolding of the dramatic action in *Richard II* has a compelling simplicity and authority. Three great "public" scenes in Acts I and II are enough to chronicle Richard's infatuation with disaster. Spacing these "public" scenes are two brief "private" moments: first, when Gaunt speaks with Gloucester's widow, and, second, when Richard and his favorites joke about Bolingbroke's departure to exile. In the former, Gaunt recognizes the threat of Richard's irresponsibility but will not take arms against him; in the latter, Richard notes Bolingbroke's courting of the people but dismisses any fear of his rivalry. Self-indulgent and capricious, Richard seems to act on the spur of the moment, and yet the pattern of his behavior unfolds with an inexorable logic, because each of the public scenes in which he appears is a variation of the one before; each is another step toward, and a rehearsal for, his fateful encounter with Bolingbroke at Flint Castle. In the opening scene and in the tourney scene, Mowbray is Richard's surrogate. Then the dying Gaunt bears the brunt of Richard's hatred of Bolingbroke, while York struggles to remain neutral and Northumberland decides to take Bolingbroke's part.

The scene of Gaunt's death, too often regarded as simply an occasion for memorable sentences, is crucial to the political drama of *Richard II*, because here Richard commits the unpardonable sin against feudal right for which he must pay with his crown and his life. He comes prepared to patronize his uncle again, only to discover that the dying Gaunt cannot be cajoled and will no longer be still. Convinced that Richard will destroy England, Gaunt does not leave the quarrel to God; he is more concerned with saving England than with saving Richard, whom he considers already doomed. It is the "orthodox" Gaunt who speaks contemptuously of Richard's failings, who first declares him unfit to rule and suggests that if Richard's grandsire had known what crimes Richard would commit, he would have deposed Richard before Richard attained the throne. New inspired by his love of England, Gaunt speaks of it as a "blessed plot," another Eden, a "demi-paradise," but he does not imagine a divinity hedging a reckless king or an army of angels mustering to defend incompetent majesty. His advice to Richard is absolutely pragmatic: a king must use his head to save his head, because he cannot degrade the land without degrading himself. He cannot lose the affection and loyalty of his people without growing pale and sickly.

Where Gaunt is willing to risk Richard's ire by speaking bluntly, York would avoid conflict and risk. Knowing that Richard will not listen to good counsel, he urges Gaunt to be silent or at least circumspect. Silent himself while Richard heaps abuse on Gaunt, he then offers a timid plea on Gaunt's behalf and finds his tongue only when Richard seizes Gaunt's estates. Then his words sound a dangerous warning because they intimate the breaking point of loyalty: "How long shall I be patient? Ah, how long / Shall tender duty make me suffer wrong?" (II.i.163-64). York's patriotism, though as sincere as Gaunt's, is less ideal and less disinterested. He does not speak of the mystical entity of England; family, inheritance, and the rights of time are his themes. He sees Richard's lawlessness as a mortal danger to the aristocratic rights which guarantee his own place, for if Richard can take away Hereford's inheritance, no title or estate is safe. Where Gaunt places England above any other cause, York instinctively identifies the nation's well-being with his own, and he attacks Richard as one who, turning on his own blood, jeopardizes the very idea of right. Absolutely frank in expressing his disaffection, he warns Richard against seizing Hereford's lands:

> You pluck a thousand dangers on your head,
> You lose a thousand well-disposed hearts,
> And prick my tender patience to those thoughts
> Which honour and allegiance cannot think.
> (II.i.205–208)

Although York could not be blunter, Richard will not hear the threat in these words and foolishly appoints York to be his Lord Governor while he is in Ireland.

Just as York was too timid to speak out when Gaunt did, so the other barons say nothing while York protests Richard's act. Cautious and secretive, Northumberland will not open his discontented thoughts until the King has gone and only after he had heard Ross and Willoughby speak. Then his only concern is to protect his own possessions:

> The King is not himself, but basely led
> By flatterers; and what they will inform,
> Merely in hate, 'gainst any of us all,
> That will the King severely prosecute
> 'Gainst us, our lives, our children, and our heirs.
> (II.i.241–45)

These words carry us down from the heights of Gaunt's patriotism to the plains of self-interest. Unlike the outspoken Gaunt, Northumberland, Willoughby, and Ross offer no counsel to the King, and without any struggle of conscience take arms against him. First they blame the favorites, not Richard, but as they warm to their subject, they speak more freely of their "most degenerate king." Even here their plans for reforming the kingdom are ambiguous:

> . . . then we shall shake off our slavish yoke,
> Imp out our drooping country's broken wing,
> Redeem from broking pawn the blemish'd crown,
> Wipe off the dust that hides our sceptre's gilt,
> And make high majesty look like itself.
>
> (II.i.291-95)

Can high majesty look like itself so long as Richard is king? The question is so dangerous that the would-be reformers do not pause to consider it. They are content to speak in figures, though they act swiftly and directly enough. Yet they do not appear either unscrupulous or unconscionable; they rally to Hereford's cause because it is their own—in defending his right, they protect theirs.

So responsible seems Richard for the calamity that befalls him, and so inevitable seems his tragic fall, that one cannot believe Shakespeare wanted to persuade his audience that Richard should have been allowed to continue the rash blaze of riot which threatened to destroy England. According to Tillyard, the doctrine of *Richard II* is "entirely orthodox. Shakespeare knows that Richard's crimes never amounted to tyranny and hence that outright rebellion against him was a crime."[12] Yet in fact Richard was guilty of the lawlessness which medieval and Renaissance theorists defined as tyranny. Accused of tyranny by his contemporaries, he is called a "wanton Tirant" in *Woodstock*, whose author makes much of the corruption of the law by Richard's rapacious favorites.[13] Shakespeare grasps the more important issue of Richard's political lawlessness and leaves no doubt that at his worst he was, as *The Mirror for Magistrates* declares, a monarch who "ruled all by lust."[14]

When a king recklessly endangers the foundations of law and plunders his country, what is an honorable subject to do? He can remain loyal despite all; he can rebel; or he can like York try to avoid having to commit himself in either way. One can sympathize with York's hesitation because one can see as he does that Bolingbroke is wronged but not innocent. Where Hall relates that Bolingbroke came back to England only after the greatest men in the country sued for his return, Shakespeare has the report of Bolingbroke's return come at the very close of the scene in which Richard seizes Gaunt's estates. Perhaps Shakespeare telescopes time only to achieve a striking effect: no sooner does Richard overreach himself, than nemesis in the form of Bolingbroke appears. Yet this handling of events leaves open the possibility that Bolingbroke led an army to England and then discovered that Richard had given him a perfect excuse for rebellion.

Daniel more explicitly questions the motives of Bolingbroke, who swore on landing in England that he came back only to gain his ducal estates. Shunning the easy wisdom of hindsight, he refuses, however, to find Bolingbroke guilty of calculated ambition. Perhaps, he suggests, Fortune conspired with Pride and Time,

> To make so easie an ascent to wrong,
> That he who had no thought so hie to clime
> (With favouring comfort still allur'd along)
> Was with occasion thrust into the crime;
> Seeing others weakenes and his part so strong
> "And who is there, in such a case that will
> "Do good, and feare, that may live free with ill?[15]

Like Daniel, Shakespeare sees Bolingbroke as a "man of destiny," or, rather, as a man who gives himself to his destiny by refusing to think about the consequences of his acts. John Palmer describes him as "that most dangerous of all climbing politicians, the man who will go further than his rivals because he never allows himself to know where he is going."[16] Leading an army against the King, he declares himself obedient to the will of heaven; and heaven or fortune plays its part in events. Even as winds and tides delay Richard's return from Ireland, portents of disaster dismay those faithful to him. Had Bolingbroke met determined opposition, the height of his ambition would have been measured by his willingness to press on. Because there is no opposition, and commoners and nobles flock to him, his return from exile becomes a triumphant crusade. Declaring the hopelessness of resistance, the King's favorites scatter to save themselves. York, Richard's Lord Governor, is determined to do "somewhat," but not very much in Richard's behalf. Using his age as an excuse for hesitation, he contents himself with such feeble gestures as gathering carts of armor, and even before he meets Bolingbroke his decision to be "neuter" is made.

Meeting no obstacles, Bolingbroke does not have to decide consciously how far he will go. He can allow himself to be carried toward greatness on the tide of events. Even when he faces Richard at Flint Castle, he need not scale forbidden heights of power because Richard descends to his own abasement. Prey to hysteria as he lands again in England, Richard is incapable of dealing with the crisis of the rebellion. One moment he loses himself in fantasies about the earth which he has despoiled. The next moment he dreams that his dazzling radiance will dissolve the clouds of rebellion. This sense of omnipotence quickly fades, however, as reports of calamity, crowding one upon the other, drag his high thoughts down to the earth which is their resting place. It is not enough to say that Richard luxuriates in his sorrow or finds pleasure in the prospect of his degradation. When he substitutes the self-pity of imagined martyrdom for the fantasy of omnipotence, he surrenders to a destiny which has an unimpeachable authority because it has been so long dreaded—a destiny which seems unavoidable because his very attempts to prevent it have only brought it into being. He would like to imagine the self-affrighted Bolingbroke trembling at his sunlike radiance, but in fact it is he who trembles at the prospect of the meeting, and who is prepared beforetime to give all—his lands, his name, his life—to Bolingbroke. This abject surrender is an emotional relief as well as a torment because it ends Richard's need to pretend and to fear; it resolves the terrible contradiction between his imperious arrogance and his knowledge of his weakness.

Where Richard, despite the promptings of his followers, submits too readily to "destiny," his opponents avoid any mention of the future. Leading an army against sacred majesty, Bolingbroke and Northumberland discuss neither plans nor goals: they chat about the countryside and the pleasure or companionship during a journey. Despite the bland triviality of their conversation, however, they obviously understand each other. Out to rid the nation of sycophants, Northumberland fawns on Bolingbroke, deferring to him as if he were an heir apparent. Bolingbroke, in turn, as Hotspur will recall, is a very king of smiles and courtesy who graciously accepts proffers services even as he writes out verbal promissory notes that will fall due when his infant fortunes come of age. Quick to kneel before York and suave in his apologies for his actions, Bolingbroke, like his supporters, assumes the customary patriotic stance of rebels. What York knows to be "gross rebellion and detested treason," Bolingbroke, with some justification, describes as a challenging of law. Determined to rid the nation of its leeches, he does not hesitate to revenge himself on the hated sycophants, whom he accuses of misleading the King. Yet he is deferential of York's pose of neutrality and very cautious in moving against Richard. He swears devotion while he threatens devastation. He parades his army but does not hurl it against the defenseless king, because he knows that Richard is still armed with the mystery of the kingship. When in his fantasy Richard called on his name to arm, we smiled; yet twenty thousand men were ready to die for Richard, and if Bolingbroke proceeds too callously, or even too obviously, twice twenty thousand men may arm themselves again for Richard's sake. Before the magic potency of Richard's title, Bolingbroke and his followers must make the ancient gestures of fealty; they must insist to York and to Richard (and to themselves) that they come only for Bolingbroke's inheritance. Those who support Bolingbroke do not claim the right to put aside oaths of allegiance; on the contrary, they declare that they have taken solemn oaths to support his cause.

Although Bolingbroke is apprehensive about his meeting with Richard, the issue is never really in doubt. For, despite their protestations and their gestures of fealty, Bolingbroke's supporters no longer think of Richard as king. Northumberland, to be brief, omits Richard's title; the more loyal York is astonished that Richard "yet looks" like a king. The rebels' plans, moreover, reach beyond the meeting at Flint Castle; as Richard guesses, he must return with them to London whether he wishes to or not. Had Richard proved himself in this crisis to be as regal as the sun, Bolingbroke might possibly have been "the yielding water." Had he maintained his authority with unshakable confidence, Bolingbroke might have been trapped by his protestations of loyalty and forced to settle for his ducal estate. But, though Richard can outface the lackey Northumberland, his nerve fails at Bolingbroke's approach. Plunging toward calamity, he utters the thoughts that Bolingbroke cannot; he unkings himself even while his opponents speak of duty and devotion:

> What must the King do now? Must he submit?
> The King shall do it. Must he be depos'd?
> The King shall be contented. Must he lose
> The name of king? A God's name, let it go!
> I'll give my jewels for a set of beads,
> My gorgeous palace for a hermitage,
> My gay apparel for an almsman's gown,
> My figured goblets for a dish of wood,
> My sceptre for a palmer's walking staff,
> My subjects for a pair of carved saints,
> And my large kingdom for a little grave,
> A little little grave, an obscure grave.
> 
> (III.iii.143-54)

Advised by Aumerle to temporize, Richard, overwhelmed by a sense of impotence, seeks refuge in religious fantasies; when he must prove his kingliness, he proves unable to command his own nature: he wantons with his woes.

There is no indication in later scenes that Richard recovers from his failure at Flint Castle. He finds no fortitude in resignation and no strength to endure because his renunciation of the world is an aesthetic attitude self-pityingly struck. Yet he does begin to face the bitter truth about himself that he has so long known and denied. Too intelligent to delude himself, he realized as he landed in England that his tears were futile, his words idle, and his conjurations of earth and heaven senseless. A less intelligent man might have clung to the last tattered shreds of his royalty at Flint Castle, but Richard is no more deceived by the regal gestures he makes than by the kneelings and scrapings of his enemies. He flings away the pretense of rule because he is too humiliated by its feebleness; and although he would escape into fantasy, he also would confess the reality of his state to followers who have mistook him all the while. He is not the sun-king who can dissolve the clouds of rebellion; he is a glistering Phaethon, a mock-Phoebus who could not control the coursers of the sun. In earlier scenes Gaunt, York, and Northumberland served as choruses to the King's wantonness. Now that his princely education has begun, Richard can act as his own tragic chorus. Anatomizing his follies even while he exposes the shams of his enemies, he discovers too late what he is and needs, and he cherishes the tender feelings of York, who weeps for Richard but supports Bolingbroke.

As he falls from power, Richard rises in our sympathies, for calamity makes him wiser and more gracious, though less kingly and less capable of rule than before. His days of folly ended, he is in the mighty hold of the Bolingbroke he tried to beggar. Once he alone betrayed his responsibilities; now he is surrounded by men who have betrayed their oaths of allegiance but who continue their sham of obedience. Where Richard callously dismissed the loyal Mowbray, Bolingbroke facilely wipes the blood of Bushy and Green from his hands. Where Richard made a mockery of his princely obligations, his enemies throw away respect, form, and ceremonious duty. To preserve ancient right, they violate the sacred bond between subject and king, and would then judge the King guilty of all the disorder in the land.

At his deposition Richard will be asked to confess his political crimes. The Garden scene, which comes before, offers a more compassionate judgment in which the Gardener's indictment of Richard's failures is countered by the Queen's loving devotion.[17] Isabella speaks of Richard's degradation as a second fall of man. One scene later, Richard compares himself to Christ, and after the deposition, York speaks of Richard's entry into London as if it were a second journey to Calvary. How shall we interpret these religious allusions? We might say that Shakespeare "balances" the English view of Richard's lawlessness with the French view of his Christlike martyrdom, except that Richard's capriciousness and narcissism are nothing like Adam's innocence or Christ's selflessness. Like Christ, however, Richard stands for sacrifice. Like Christ's, his trial is a sham of justice that deposes a mockery king. He has a Judaslike Bagot to accuse him and for judges a host of "Pilates" who wash their hands of any complicity in the degradation of a king by listening to Richard's "willing" abdication.

York's announcement that Richard "with willing soul" adopts Bolingbroke as his heir is the cue for the ritual drama of the deposition to begin. Called forth to surrender his tired majesty in open view, Richard refuses, however, to play the role as it was cast, because though dazed and defeated, he will not, like the pliant Bagot, speak freely of his guilt. Outraged by the prospect of a public humiliation, he decides to expose the sham of his willing abdication and to change his part from defendant to prosecutor. Yet he cannot alter the script very much; nor can he escape the damning exposure of himself. We do not know what private reasons he had for agreeing to abdicate; all we know is that he consents to the mockery of his "willing" abdication, and that consent is damning, for a true king would have refused to collaborate in his degradation. Although it was probably not in Richard's power to save his crown, he alone could determine how he would lose it—what show of legitimacy he would lend to the proceedings against him. He appears at the deposition because he cannot resist the opportunity to be once more at the center of the political stage, and to make the emotional appeals which he knows will be futile.

Henry VI could lose a crown to find himself. Richard is too vain and self-absorbed to experience this kind of spiritual growth. Although he would wrap himself in the purple mantle of Christ, he knows the shamefulness of his conduct. Even as he calls his barons Judases, he admits that he is the greatest traitor of all, one who betrays his royalty by pretending, however badly, that he is willing to renounce it. Tormented by contradictory impulses, he would cast off the pretense of majesty, and he would also cling to it for a last few moments. He cannot sustain his part, however, before the tenacious Bolingbroke; intending to "expose" the fraudulence of the deposition, he ends by confessing his incompetence to rule and by acknowledging Bolingbroke's royalty.[18]

A purely impartial proceeding would have weighed Richard's crimes against those of his revolted followers. Here only the King is found guilty, and he must accept the verdict, for if he allows men to consider him a god on earth, he must be willing also to serve as their scapegoat. If in prosperous times the strength of twenty thousand loyal men flourishes in his cheeks, then he must accept as his own the guilt of the twenty thousand men who were driven to rebellion by his shameful conduct. If his carelessness must be their affliction, their disloyalty must be his princely "failure." The Mayor who acted as audience to Richard and Buckingham's posturing in rotten armor was a pliant hypocrite ready to believe anything he was told about Hastings' guilt. The earls who stand silent and shamefaced at Richard's deposition are another breed. They see what they want to believe: the orderly continuation of royal authority and the preservation of ancient ceremony, tradition, and form.

Among the silent witnesses is York, who later describes to his wife the shameful scene of Richard's return to London as Bolingbroke's prisoner:

> No man cried "God save him!"
> No joyful tongue gave him his welcome home.
> But dust was thrown upon his sacred head;
> Which with such gentle sorrow he shook off,
> His face still combating with tears and smiles
> (The badges of his grief and patience),
> That had not God for some strong purpose steel'd
> The hearts of men, they must perforce have melted
> And barbarism itself have pitied him.
> But heaven hath a hand in these events,
> To whose high will we bound our calm contents.
> To Bolingbroke are we sworn subjects now,
> Whose state and honour I for aye allow.
>
> (V.ii.28-40)

This is no hypocrite who sentimentalizes the man he betrayed. His heart grieves for the callous mistreatment of the King, but he is content to have Richard deposed and to attribute to God's will the course of events in which he played a significant role. Coming after the deposition scene, York's description of Richard's "Calvary" makes the rude jeering populace a larger audience to the preceding spectacle.[19] We know now that the ritual of deposition was not a politic fraud contrived to hoodwink a gullible commons. Thousands played their parts in the humiliation of the King, and though it was stage-managed by Bolingbroke, the ritual expressed the will of a nation.

The elegiac tone of York's speech makes events that have just occurred seem distant and "remembered." No longer the main actor in the drama of history, Richard faces a personal destiny that is more pathetic than tragic. Unable to win the crown of heaven, he also cannot accept his fate on earth, because without a crown he does not know what part to play or even who he is:

> I have no name, no title—
> No, not that name was given me at the font—
> But 'tis usurp'd. Alack the heavy day,
> That I have worn so many winters out
> And know not now what name to call myself!
> O that I were a mockery king of snow,
> Standing before the sun of Bolingbroke
> To melt myself away in water drops!
> (IV.i.255-62)

Like the dying Faustus, whose despairing speeches he echoes, Richard is tormented by a realization of loss and emptiness, for in giving up his kingship, he finds nothing except the nothingness of his existence, he sees only shadows and mocking images. Once he talked of the dazzling radiance of his majesty; now he knows that if men winked at him, it was only in contempt. No sun-god, not even a glistering Phaethon, he sees himself at the deposition as a mockery king of snow melting before the brightness of Henry's regality, and he can find no escape from this sense of his unreality. Lacking, as Isabella sees, the will to resist his fate, he is too shallow in his religious convictions and too accustomed to the presence of an audience to bear the solitude of imprisonment. His attempts at philosophy and theology are no more than facile, and though he tries to avoid the pain of self-realization by spinning out conceits, he cannot keep his thoughts from returning to the dead center of his nihilism:

> Sometimes am I king:
> Then treasons make me wish myself a beggar,
> And so I am. Then crushing penury
> Persuades me I was better when a king;

> Then am I king'd again; and by-and-by
> Think that I am unking'd by Bolingbroke,
> And straight am nothing. But whate'er I be,
> Nor I, nor any man that but man is,
> With nothing shall be pleas'd till he be eas'd
> With being nothing.
>
> (V.v.32-41)

One last moment of heroism and Richard is spared the mockery of his existence.

The crisis of Richard's incompetence ends with his deposition. The crisis of Henry's reign begins as soon as he is enthroned, because he can more easily seize the crown from Richard than possess it in peace and safety. Having made the crown stoop to armed might, he cannot quickly raise it again above the arena of political contention, for he has deposed a myth of authority in degrading Richard. If one king can be set aside, so can another; and if force can determine who wears the crown, there is no longer any limitation on the height of ambition. York may transfer to Henry the emotional loyalty he once felt for Richard, but other men will not acknowledge the new king, and Henry's authority cannot rest on his opportunistic alliance with the Percies—an alliance which Richard prophesies will not last. To strengthen his position Henry must, like Richard before him, manipulate the forms of judgment. Wringing all the political advantage he can out of Gloucester's murder, he stages a hearing before the deposition scene in which Bagot is called forth to speak of Richard's part in the murder of Gloucester. True to his kind, Bagot implicates Aumerle; other peers, eager for Bolingbroke's favor, add their accusations; and, as in the opening scene of the play, gages are flung down and charges of treason and murder hurled. The situation is tightly controlled, however, by Bolingbroke, who halts the show after Bagot has done his part in accusing Richard and the peers have tripped over one another in their desire to challenge Aumerle. Now the stage is set for the announcement of Richard's abdication, and when Carlisle tries to interfere, he is immediately arrested by the henchman Northumberland, who proves that it is as dangerous to speak honestly to the new King as to the old.

By the time the deposition scene has ended, there is no doubt of Henry's political qualities—he is strong, determined, shrewd, and ruthless, not particularly attractive but eminently capable. What he is like as a man is hidden until the fifth act, where something of his personal nature is revealed. We discover, almost with surprise, that this silent, skilled politician is a father disturbed by the waywardness of his son. We learn too that he has enough humor to appreciate the comedy of York's quarrel with his wife over the judgment of Aumerle. Tillyard would have us admire the conduct and the statements of York, who supposedly "utters the most correct sentiments."[20] At best, however, York is an odd specimen of Tudor orthodoxy—very slack in supporting the existing government when Richard was king and in defending Richard's right as his Lord Governor. Uttering the most correct sentiments, York warned Bolingbroke not to take too much and then helped him take the crown. Rather than a standard-bearer of Tudor royalism, York seems more accurately described by Palmer as a pragmatist,

> a sturdy, honest, well-meaning man, prompt with sensible advice but easily flustered, shrewd enough to see what's coming but not clever or resolute enough to prevent it. He stands for the average gentleman amateur in public life, as true to his friends and as firm in his principles as the times allow. Normally he makes the best of a bad business—which is usually not so bad after all, either for himself or for the nation. Such men are loyal to a government as long as it has legal or traditional status and the means to enforce it. With every appearance of probity and devotion—by no means wholly assumed—they contrive to find themselves in the long run sturdily swimming with the tide.[21]

True enough, and yet this sensible, adaptable creature is astonishingly adamant in condemning his only child. Unlike the callous Northumberland, who can pursue his advantage and advancement without qualm ("my sins on my head"), York would be true to the feudal values he cherishes. Having equivocated his loyalty to Richard, he is determined to prove a liegeman to Henry, if necessary by sacrificing an Isaac at the altar of loyalty.

Shakespeare did not enlarge the role and develop the character of York, who is a very minor and sketchy figure in the Chronicles, simply to make him a mouthpiece for pieties or to add him to the list of trimmers in the History Plays. Like More's Hythlodaye,[22] York lives under a political system which offers no satisfactory course for the subject of an arrogant, heedless king. He can offer counsel, which will be disregarded. He can flee the court and the problem of political action (which is York's first instinct), but if he is drawn back against his will into the toils of political crisis, he can only justify to himself the choice that he thinks right—or tell himself, as York does, that he really has no choice at all. Where characters like Blanch and France in *King John* debate their dilemmas, York lives his; and where the Bastard brushes aside his perplexity, York finds escape first in "inaction" and then in commitment. To recognize York's integrity, however, is not to agree with Bolingbroke that he is a "sheer, immaculate, and silver fountain" of truth, and Aumerle a muddy, defiled stream of treason. There can be no simple judgment of loyalties in a time of change when fidelity to the past becomes treason to the present. Although compared to the pragmatic and opportunistic alliances which support the new regime, Aumerle's devotion to Richard seems precious, it does not make the conspiracy to murder Henry any less vile. A futile attempt to call back yesterday, the plot dooms Richard and sacrifices the peace of England.

Instead of providing an ideological solution to the problem of political loyalty in *Richard II*, Shakespeare makes us aware of its enormous difficulty. We realize that men bow to circumstances in bowing to kings. Since there is no alternative to the rule of Henry, it is "right" for Aumerle to kneel before him; and if Henry is not the rightful heir to the throne, he is nevertheless the true king. Like Aumerle, Henry must bow to necessity. The barons rebelled to redeem the crown from "broking pawn," but the new king comes to power owing debts of gratitude that cannot be paid without cheapening his majesty. Because his claim to the throne is questionable, Henry must leave no doubt of his authority or his will to rule. Although he can forgive his not-very-dangerous cousin Aumerle, and be generous to Carlisle, whose courage he admires, he must hound the other conspirators and rebels to their destruction. And whether he wishes to or not, he must be rid of Richard, because Richard is his living fear, the excuse for if not the cause of murderous plots and bloody rebellion.

After the peaks of dramatic intensity reached in the fourth act, the plot of *Richard II* almost inevitably descends to an anticlimax in the fifth, in which Shakespeare's artistic interest or energy apparently wanes. The tone of the York-Henry-Aumerle episode is uncertain, and the rhyming couplets here and in the last scene are astonishingly pedestrian. In V.ii the unnamed Exton and his accomplices are thrust out on the stage, by the prompter's hand, it seems, not the playwright's. More awkward still—especially for the King—is Exton's intrusion on the royal council in the concluding scene, where he defies all rules of ceremony and decorum in his haste to exhibit the corpse of Richard. Nevertheless, the tableau of mourning that concludes *Richard II* has an artistic power and rightness lacking in the de casibus cliches that embroider the last scene of *King John*. Like Richard in the opening scene, Henry in the closing scene must pretend to judge a henchman for a crime in which he is complicit. At the same time that he makes Exton his scapegoat, he is honest enough to admit that he needed the poison of Exton's act. Bowed with sorrow over Richard's corpse, as the nation will bow with sorrow for years to come, he feels the weight of the kingly cares he took with the crown. Like Richard he has shed a kinsman's blood; like Richard he fears rebellious subjects; and like Richard he banishes the follower who was his hangman. Wretched once because he was sentenced to exile, Henry now has reason to envy Mowbray's pilgrimage to the Holy Land, and he will die still longing for the clearness he might win by leading a Crusade against the Turk.

NOTES

1. See Tillyard's excellent discussion of the medievalism of *Richard II*. *History Plays*, pp. 244-58.
2. *Shakespeare from Richard II to Henry V* (Stanford: Stanford Univ. Press, 1957), p. 17. I disagree with Traversi's assumption that the artificial-

ity of the speeches in the opening scene of *Richard II* is an indication of falsity of emotion or decadence. The artificiality of Mowbray's speeches is no greater, after all, than the artificiality of the Gardener's allegorical sentences in the later Garden scene.

3. Where Tillyard thinks "a greater sincerity of personal emotion" is the hallmark of the new political order in *Richard II* (*History Plays*, p. 259), Traversi suggests that fear is a "sign of the new order," as in York's readiness "to sacrifice his own blood for a usurper who has only used him as an instrument" (p. 45). It is difficult to think of an order of which Northumberland is a chief representative as more sincere in personal emotion than the order represented by Aumerle, Carlisle, and the Queen, who are devoted to Richard.

4. The phrase is Tillyard's, who, I think, exaggerates the aestheticism of Richard's Court: "We are in fact in a world where means matter more than ends, where it is more important to keep strictly the rules of an elaborate game than either to win or to lose it" (p. 252). On the contrary, just beneath the surface of ceremony at Richard's Court is the grim reality of political conflict conducted with ruthless purposes and effects.

5. Where Tillyard stresses the cosmic lore of *Richard II*, Ribner says, "There is a pathetic irony in Richard's proclaiming the commonplaces of Tudor political theory at the very moment when Bolingbroke is making head against him in spite of them" (*English History Play*, p. 164).

6. It seems almost certain that Shakespeare consulted both *La Chronicque de la traison et mort de Richart Deux roy Dengleterre* (edited and translated by B. Williams, *English Historical Society*, IV, 1846) and Jean Creton's *Histoire du Roy d'Angleterre Richard II* (edited and translated by John Webb in *Archaeologia*, XX, 1824). The number of verbal echoes in *Richard II* from *La Chronicque de la traison* is impressive. For example, the *Chronicque* reports that Londoners on hearing of Bolingbroke's return from exile said, "Our lives, our possessions, and all we have are at his service" (p. 187). In Shakespeare's play, Richard responds to Scroop's report of Bolingbroke's triumphal return to England, "Our lands, our lives, and all are Bolingbroke's" (III.ii.151). See note 19 for Shakespeare's borrowings from Creton.

7. There is no intimation in Daniel's poem of Richard's will to surrender to Bolingbroke. Sensibly advised by his loyal followers to accept Bolingbroke's terms at Flint Castle, Richard is treacherously captured by Northumberland in Daniel's poem—an incident Shakespeare omits from his play. When asked to surrender his crown,

Richard, according to Daniel, first tries to retain the show of majesty, then resolutely says he would sooner die than relinquish the crown, but finally is persuaded to give up the crown to save his life (*Civil Wars*, pp. 108–26).

8. Although Shakespeare begins *Richard II* at the same point at which Hall begins his Chronicle, he must have read Holinshed's account of the earlier years of Richard's reign in which Richard's manliness and courage were manifest. It is generally assumed that Shakespeare's depiction of the Cade rebellion in *2 Henry VI* was based on accounts of the Jack Straw uprising, during which the young Richard II acted with great courage. Shakespeare certainly knew Daniel's appraisal of Richard: "though weake he was, / He was not ill; nor yet so weake, but that / He shew'd much Martiall valour in his place, / Adventring oft his person for the State" (*Civil Wars*, p. 150).
9. Holinshed, *Chronicles*, II, 845.
10. See the illuminating discussion of the opening scene of *Richard II* in Palmer, *Political Characters*, pp. 124–28.
11. *Civil Wars*, p. 87. Daniel's shrewd insights into the political implications of the sentences of banishment probably cued Shakespeare's more oblique portrayal of the same events.
12. *History Plays*, p. 261.
13. Although Hall and other Chroniclers note that the accusations made against Richard at the time of his deposition strained credulity, they leave no doubt that Richard, who was accused by his contemporaries of tyranny, did trample on legality and justice. In *Woodstock*, Richard is called "wanton Tirant" by John of Gaunt, who takes the murdered Woodstock's place as defender of the common weal.
14. So evident is Richard's vicious disregard of law and his rapacity in *The Mirror* that he need not be called a tyrant: he is tyranny personified.
15. *Civil Wars*, pp. 94–95.
16. *Political Characters*, p. 134.
17. For the last time in the Garden scene, the medieval world of *Richard II* is presented to view before the deposition of Richard ushers in the new regime. Here the political allegory of the garden of the state commingles with the literary allegory of the garden as the setting for love. Thus, the poetic language of flowers speaks of political realities even as it creates a mood of lyric pathos; it defines both Richard's incompetence and the tenderness of the Queen's feeling for her "fair rose."

18. In Daniel's judgment, despite Bolingbroke's noble qualities and capacity to rule, the deposition of Richard was a grave error because it led to the civil wars of later years. Shakespeare's profounder psychological study of Richard's collapse and failure of will does not allow an audience to reach Daniel's conclusion, because the man who betrays himself the way that Richard does at Flint Castle and at the deposition is hardly fit to rule. In Shakespeare's play, Richard does not learn too late how to be king; he confesses too late his unkingliness.
19. York's description of Richard's entry into London is one of the most striking evidences of the influence of Creton, who on one page speaks of the Pilate role of the English in Richard's fall and of Richard's and Bolingbroke's entry into London. The Londoners in Creton speak of the event in precisely York's manner: "And they most devoutly gave laud and thanks to our Lord for it, saying that it was his will, and that otherwise he could not have done" (*Archaeologia*, XX, 179).
20. *History Plays*, p. 261.
21. *Political Characters*, pp. 142–43.
22. Although earnest medieval and Renaissance moralists wrote books of sage and serious advice for princes, the futility of such counseling is vividly expressed by Hythlodaye in the dialogue of Book One of More's *Utopia*.

## Ernst H. Kantorowicz

## The King's Two Bodies (1957)

> Twin-born with greatness, subject to the breadth
> Of every fool, whose sense no more can feel
> But his own wringing. What infinite heart's ease
> Must kings neglect that private men enjoy! . . .
> What kind of god art thou, that suffer'st more
> Of mortal griefs than do thy worshippers?

Such are, in Shakespeare's play, the meditations of King Henry V on the godhead and manhood of a king.[1] The king is "twin-born" not only with greatness but also with human nature, hence "subject to the breath of every fool."

It was the humanly tragic aspect of royal "gemination" which Shakespeare outlined and not the legal capacities which English lawyers assembled in the fiction of the King's Two Bodies. However, the legal jargon of the "two Bodies" scarcely belonged to the arcana of the legal guild alone. That the king "is a Corporation in himself that liveth ever" was a commonplace found in a simple dictionary of legal terms such as Dr. John Cowell's *Interpreter* (1607);[2] and even at an earlier date the gist of the concept of kingship which Plowden's *Reports* reflected had passed into the writings of Joseph Kitchin (1580)[3] and Richard Crompton (1594).[4] Moreover, related notions were carried into public when, in 1603, Francis Bacon suggested for the crowns of England and Scotland, united in James I, the name of "Great Britain" as an expression of the "perfect union of bodies, politic as well as natural."[5] That Plowden's *Reports* were widely known is certainly demonstrated by the phrase "The case is altered, quoth Plowden," which was used proverbially in England before and after 1600.[6] The suggestion that Shakespeare may have known a case (*Hales* v. *Petit*) reported by Plowden does not seem far-fetched,[7] and it gains strength on the ground that the anonymous play *Thomas of Woodstock*, of which Shakespeare "had his head full of echoes" and in which he may even have acted,[8] ends in the pun: "for I have plodded in Plowden, and can find no law."[9] Besides, it would have been very strange if Shakespeare, who mastered the lingo of almost every human trade, had been ignorant of the constitutional and judicial talk which went on around him and which the jurists of his days applied so lavishly in court. Shakespeare's familiarity with legal cases of general interest cannot be doubted, and we have other evidence of his association with the students at the Inns and his knowledge of court procedure.[10]

Admittedly, it would make little difference whether or not Shakespeare was familiar with the subtleties of legal speech. The poet's vision of the twin nature of a king is not dependent on constitutional support, since such vision would arise very naturally from a purely human stratum. It therefore may appear futile even to pose the question whether Shakespeare applied any professional idiom of the jurists of his time, or try to determine the die of Shakespeare's coinage. It seems all very trivial and irrelevant, since the image of the twinned nature of a king, or even of man in general, was most genuinely Shakespeare's own and proper vision. Nevertheless, should the poet have chanced upon the legal definitions of kingship, as probably he could not have failed to do when conversing with his friends at the Inns, it will be easily imagined how apropos the simile of the King's Two Bodies would have seemed to him. It was anyhow the live essence of his art to reveal the numerous planes active in any human being, to play them off against each other, to confuse them, or to preserve their equilibrium, depending all upon the pattern of life he bore in mind and wished to create anew. How convenient then to find those ever contending planes, as it were, legalized by the jurists' royal "christology" and readily served to him!

The legal concept of the King's Two Bodies cannot, for other reasons, be separated from Shakespeare. For if that curious image, which from modern constitutional thought has vanished

## The Historical and Political Dynamics

all but completely, still has a very real and human meaning today, this is largely due to Shakespeare. It is he who has eternalized that metaphor. He has made it not only the symbol, but indeed the very substance and essence of one of his greatest plays: *The Tragedy of King Richard II* is the tragedy of the King's Two Bodies.

Perhaps it is not superfluous to indicate that the Shakespearean Henry V, as he bemoans a king's twofold estate, immediately associates that image with King Richard II. King Henry's soliloquies precede directly that brief intermezzo in which he conjures the spirit of his father's predecessor and to the historic essence of which posterity probably owes that magnificent ex-voto known as the Wilton Diptych.[11]

> Not to-day, O Lord!
> O! not to-day, think not upon the fault
> My father made in encompassing the crown.
> I Richard's body have interr'd anew,
> And on it have bestow'd more contrite tears
> Than from it issu'd forced drops of blood.
> (IV.i.312ff.)

Musing over his own royal fate, over the king's two-natured being, Shakespeare's Henry V is disposed to recall Shakespeare's Richard II, who—at least in the poet's concept—appears as the prototype of that "kind of god that suffers more of mortal griefs than do his worshippers."

It appears relevant to the general subject of this study, and also otherwise worth our while, to inspect more closely the varieties of royal "duplications" which Shakespeare has unfolded in the three bewildering central scenes of *Richard II*.[12] The duplications, all one, and all simultaneously active, in Richard— "Thus play I in one person many people" (V.v.31)—are those potentially present in the King, the Fool, and the God. They dissolve, perforce, in the Mirror. Those three prototypes of "twin-birth" intersect and overlap and interfere with each other continuously. Yet, it may be felt that the "King" dominates in the scene on the Coast of Wales (III.ii), the "Fool" at Flint Castle (III.iii), and the "God" in the Westminster scene (IV.i), with

Man's wretchedness as a perpetual companion and antithesis at every stage. Moreover, in each one of those three scenes we encounter the same cascading: from divine kingship to kingship's "Name," and from the name to the naked misery of man.

Gradually, and only step by step, does the tragedy proper of the King's Two Bodies develop in the scene on the Welsh coast. There is as yet no split in Richard when, on his return from Ireland, he kisses the soil of his kingdom and renders that famous, almost too often quoted, account of the loftiness of his royal estate. What he expounds is, in fact, the indelible character of the king's body politic, god-like or angel-like. The balm of consecration resists the power of the elements, the "rough rude sea," since

> The breath of worldly man cannot depose
> The deputy elected by the Lord.
>
> (III.ii.54f.)

Man's breath appears to Richard as something inconsistent with kingship. Carlisle, in the Westminster scene, will emphasize once more that God's Anointed cannot be judged "by inferior breath" (IV.i.128). It will be Richard himself who "with his own breath" releases at once kingship and subjects (IV.i.210), so that finally King Henry V, after the destruction of Richard's divine kingship, could rightly complain that the king is "subject to the breath of every fool."[13]

When the scene (III.ii) begins, Richard is, in the most exalted fashion, the "deputy elected by the Lord" and "God's substitute . . . anointed in his sight" (I.ii.37f.). Still is he the one that in former days gave "good ear" to the words of his crony, John Busshy, Speaker of the Commons in 1397, who, when addressing the king, "did not attribute to him titles of honour, due and accustomed, but invented unused termes and such strange names, as were rather agreeable to the divine maiestie of God, than to any earthly potentate."[14] He still appears the one said to have asserted that the "Laws are in the King's mouth, or sometimes in his breast,"[15] and to have demanded that "if he looked at anyone, that person had to bend the knee."[16] He still is sure of himself, of his dignity, and even of the help of the celestial hosts, which are at his disposal.

# The Historical and Political Dynamics

> For every man that Bolingbroke hath press'd . . . ,
> God for his Richard hath in heavenly pay
> A glorious angel.
>
> (III.ii.60ff.)

This glorious image of kingship "By the Grace of God" does not last. It slowly fades, as the bad tidings trickle in. A curious change in Richard's attitude—as it were, a metamorphosis from "Realism" to "Nominalism"—now takes place. The Universal called "Kingship" begins to disintegrate; its transcendental "Reality," its objective truth and god-like existence, so brilliant shortly before, pales into a nothing, a *nomen*.[17] And the remaining half-reality resembles a state of amnesia or of sleep.

> I had forgot myself, am I not king?
> Awake thou coward majesty! thou sleepest,
> Is not the king's name twenty thousand names?
> *Arm, arm, my name!* a puny subject strikes
> At thy great glory.
>
> (III.ii.83ff.)

This state of half-reality, of royal oblivion and slumber, adumbrates the royal "Fool" of Flint Castle. And similarly the divine prototype of gemination, the God-man, begins to announce its presence, as Richard alludes to Judas' treason:

> Snakes, in my heart-blood warm'd, that sting my heart!
> Three Judases, each one thrice worse than Judas!
>
> (III.ii.131f.)

It is as though it has dawned upon Richard that his vicariate of the God Christ might imply also a vicariate of the man Jesus, and that he, the royal "deputy elected by the Lord," might have to follow his divine Master also in his human humiliation and take the cross.

However, neither the twin-born Fool nor the twin-born God are dominant in that scene. Only their nearness is forecast, while to the fore there steps the body natural and mortal of the king:

> Let's talk of graves, of worms and epitaphs. . . .
>
> (III.ii.145ff.)

Not only does the king's manhood prevail over the godhead of the Crown, and mortality over immortality; but, worse than that, kingship itself seems to have changed its essence. Instead of being unaffected "by Nonage or Old Age and other natural Defects and Imbecilities," kingship itself comes to mean Death, and nothing but Death. And the long procession of tortured kings passing in review before Richard's eyes is proof of that change:

> For God's sake let us sit upon the ground,
> And tell sad stories of the death of kings—
> How some have been deposed, some slain in war,
> Some haunted by the ghosts they have deposed,
> Some poisoned by their wives, some sleeping killed;
> *All murdered*—for within the hollow crown
> That rounds the mortal temples of a king,
> Keeps Death his court, and there the antic sits
> Scoffing his state and grinning at his pomp,
> Allowing him a breath, a little scene,
> To monarchize, be feared, and kill with looks,
> Infusing him with self and vain conceit,
> As if the flesh which walls about our life,
> Were brass impregnable: and humoured thus,
> Comes at the last, and with a little pin
> Bores through his castle wall, and farewell king!
> (III.ii.155ff.)

The king that "never dies" here has been replaced by the king that always dies and suffers death more cruelly than other mortals. Gone is the oneness of the body natural with the immortal body politic, "this double Body, to which no Body is equal." Gone also is the fiction of royal prerogatives of any kind, and all that remains is the feeble human nature of a king:

> mock not flesh and blood
> With solemn reverence, throw away respect,
> Tradition, form, and ceremonious duty,
> For you have but mistook me all this while:
> I live with bread like you, feel want,
> Taste grief, need friends—subjected thus,
> How can you say to me, I am a king?
> (III.ii.171ff.)

The fiction of the oneness of the double body breaks apart. Godhead and manhood of the King's Two Bodies, both clearly outlined with a few strokes, stand in contrast to each other. A first low is reached. The scene now shifts to Flint Castle.

The structure of the second great scene (III.iii) resembles the first. Richard's kingship, his body politic, has been hopelessly shaken, it is true; but still there remains, though hollowed out, the semblance of kingship. At least this might be saved. "Yet looks he like a king," states York at Flint Castle (III.iii.68); and in Richard's temper there dominates, at first, the consciousness of his royal dignity. He had made up his mind beforehand to appear a king at the Castle:

> A king, woe's slave, shall kingly woe obey.
>
> (III.iii.210)

He acts accordingly; he snorts at Northumberland who has omitted the vassal's and subject's customary genuflection before his liege lord and the deputy of God:

> We are amazed, and thus long have we stood
> To watch the fearful bending of thy knee,
> Because we thought ourself thy lawful king:
> And if we be, how dare thy joints forget
> To pay their awful duty to our presence?
>
> (III.iii.73ff.)

The "cascades" then begin to fall as they did in the first scene. The celestial hosts are called upon once more, this time avenging angels and "armies of pestilence," which God is said to muster in his clouds—"on our behalf" (III.iii.85f.). Again the "Name" of kingship plays its part:

> O, that I were as great
> As is my grief, or lesser than my *name*!
>
> (III.iii.136f.)

> Must (the king) lose
> The *name* of king? a God's *name*, let it go.
>
> (III.iii.145f.)

From the shadowy name of kingship there leads, once more, the path to new disintegration. No longer does Richard impersonate the mystic body of his subjects and the nation. It is a lonely man's miserable and mortal nature that replaces the king as King:

> I'll give my jewels for a set of beads:
> My gorgeous palace for a hermitage:
> My gay apparel for an almsman's gown:
> My figured goblets for a dish of wood:
> My sceptre for a palmer's walking-staff:
> My subjects for a pair of carved saints,
> And my large kingdom for a little grave,
> A little little grave, an obscure grave.
>
> (III.iii.147ff.)

The shiver of those anaphoric clauses is followed by a profusion of gruesome images of High-Gothic *macabresse*. However, the second scene—different from the first—does not end in those outbursts of self-pity which recall, not a Dance of Death, but a dance around one's own grave. There follows a state of even greater abjectness.

The new note, indicating a change for the worse, is struck when Northumberland demands that the king come down into the base court of the castle to meet Bolingbroke, and when Richard, whose personal badge was the "Sun emerging from a cloud," retorts in a language of confusing brightness and terrifying puns:

> Down, down I come like glist'ring Phaethon:
> Wanting the manage of unruly jades. . . .
> In the base court? Base court, where kings grow base,
> To come at traitors' calls, and do them grace.
> In the base court? Come down? Down court! down king!
> For night-owls shriek where mounting larks should sing.
>
> (III.iii.178ff.)

It has been noticed at different times how prominent a place is held in *Richard II* by the symbolism of the Sun, and occasionally a passage reads like the description of a Roman *Oriens Augusti* coin (III.ii.36–53).[18] The Sun imagery, as interwoven in Richard's answer, reflects the "splendour of the catastrophe" in a manner remindful of Breughel's *Icarus* and Lucifer's fall from the empyrean, reflecting also those "shreds of glow. . . . That round the limbs of fallen angels hover." On the other hand, the "traitor's calls" may be reminiscent of the "three Judases" in the foregoing scene. In general, however, biblical imagery is unimportant at Flint Castle: it is saved for the Westminster scene. At Flint, there is another vision which, along with foolish Phaetons and Icari, the poet now produces.

> I talk but idly, and you laugh at me,

remarks Richard (III.iii.171), growing self-conscious and embarrassed. The sudden awkwardness is noticed by Northumberland, too:

> Sorrow and grief of heart
> Makes him speak fondly like a frantic man
> 
> (III.iii.185f.)

Shakespeare, in that scene, conjures the image of another human being, the Fool, who is two-in-one and whom the poet otherwise introduces so often as counter-type of lords and kings. Richard II plays now the roles of both: fool of his royal self and fool of kingship. Therewith, he becomes somewhat less than merely "man" or (as on the Beach) "king body natural." However, only in that new role of Fool—a fool playing king, and a king playing fool—is Richard capable of greeting his victorious cousin and of playing to the end, with Bolingbroke in genuflection before him, the comedy of his brittle and dubious kingship. Again he escapes into "speaking fondly," that is, into puns:

> Fair cousin, you debase your princely knee,
> To make the base earth proud with kissing it. . . .
> Up, cousin, up—your heart is up, I know
> Thus high (*touching his own head*) at least, although your
>     knee be low.
> 
> (III.iii.190ff.)

The jurists had claimed that the king's body politic is utterly void of "natural Defects and Imbecilities." Here, however, "Imbecility" seems to hold sway. And yet, the very bottom has not been reached. Each scene, progressively, designates a new low. "King body natural" in the first scene, and "Kingly Fool" in the second: with those two twin-born beings there is associated, in the half-sacramental abdication scene, the twin-born deity as an even lower estate. For the "Fool" marks the transition from "King" to "God," and nothing could be more miserable, it seems, than the God in the wretchedness of man.

As the third scene (IV.i) opens, there prevails again—now for the third time—the image of sacramental kingship. On the Beach of Wales, Richard himself had been the herald of the loftiness of kingship by right divine; at Flint Castle, he had made it his "program" to save at least the face of a king and to justify the "Name," although the title no longer fitted his condition; at Westminster, he is incapable of expounding his kingship himself. Another person will speak for him and interpret the image of God-established royalty; and very fittingly, a bishop. The Bishop of Carlisle now plays the *logothetes*; he constrains, once more, the *rex imago Dei* to appear:

> What subject can give sentence on his king?
> And who sits here that is not Richard's subject? . . .
> And shall the figure of God's majesty,
> His captain, steward, deputy-elect,
> Anointed, crowned, planted many years,
> Be judged by subject and inferior breath,
> And he himself not present? O, forfend it, God,
> That in a Christian climate souls refined
> Should show so heinous, black, obscene a deed!
>
> (IV.i.121ff.)

Those are, in good mediaeval fashion, the features of the *vicarius Dei*. And it likewise agrees with mediaeval tradition that the Bishop of Carlisle views the present against the background of the Biblical past. True, he leaves it to Richard to draw the final conclusions and to make manifest the resemblance of the humbled king with the humbled Christ. Yet, it is the bishop who, as it were, prepares the Biblical climate by prophesying future horrors and foretelling England's Golgotha:

> Disorder, horror, fear, and mutiny
> Shall here inhabit, and this land be called
> The field of Golgotha and dead men's skulls.
>
> (IV.i.142ff.)

The bishop, for his bold speech, was promptly arrested; but into the atmosphere prepared by him there enters King Richard.

When led into Westminster Hall, he strikes the same chords as the bishop, those of Biblicism. He points to the hostile assembly, to the lords surrounding Bolingbroke:

> Did they not sometimes cry 'all hail' to me?
> So Judas did to Christ: But He, in twelve,
> Found truth in all, but one: I in twelve thousand, none.
> (IV.i.169ff.)

For the third time the name of Judas is cited to stigmatize the foes of Richard. Soon the name of Pilate will follow and make the implied parallel unequivocal. But before being delivered up to his judges and his cross, King Richard has to "un-king" himself.

The scene in which Richard "undoes his kingship" and releases his body politic into thin air leaves the spectator breathless. It is a scene of sacramental solemnity, since the ecclesiastical ritual of undoing the effects of consecration is no less solemn or of less weight than the ritual which has built up the sacramental dignity. Not to mention the rigid punctilio which was observed at the ousting of a Knight of the Garter or the Golden Fleece,[19] there had been set a famous precedent by Pope Celestine V who, in the Castel Nuovo at Naples, had "undone" himself by stripping off from his body, with his own hands, the insignia of the dignity which he resigned—ring, tiara, and purple. But whereas Pope Celestine resigned his dignity to his electors, the College of Cardinals, Richard, the hereditary king, resigned his office to God—*Deo ius suum resignavit.*[20] The Shakespearean scene in which Richard "undoes himself with hierophantic solemnity" has attracted the attention of many a critic, and Walter Pater has called it very correctly an inverted rite, a rite of degradation and a long agonizing ceremony in which the order of coronation is reversed.[21] Since none is entitled to lay finger on the Anointed of God and royal bearer of a *character indelibilis*,[22] King Richard, when defrocking himself, appears as his own celebrant:

> Am I both priest and clerk? well then, amen.
>
> (IV.i.173)

Bit by bit he deprives his body politic of the symbols of its dignity and exposes his poor body natural to the eyes of the spectators:

> Now mark me how I will undo myself:
> I give this heavy weight from off my head,
> And this unwieldy sceptre from my hand,
> The pride of kingly sway from out my heart;
> With mine own tears I wash away my balm,
> With mine own hands I give away my crown,
> With mine own tongue deny my sacred state,
> With mine own breath release all duteous oaths:
> All pomp and majesty do I foreswear. . . .
>
> (IV.i.203ff.)

Self-deprived of all his former glories, Richard seems to fly back to his old trick of Flint Castle, to the role of Fool, as he renders to his "successor" some double-edged acclamations.[23] This time, however, the fool's cap is of no avail. Richard declines to "ravel out his weaved-up follies," which his cold-efficient foe Northumberland demands him to read aloud. Nor can he shield himself behind his "Name." This, too, is gone irrevocably:

> I have no name. . . .
> And know not now what name to call myself.
>
> (IV.i.254ff.)

In a new flash of inventiveness, he tries to hide behind another screen. He creates a new split, a chink for his former glory through which to escape and thus to survive. Over against his lost outward kingship he sets an inner kingship, makes his true kingship to retire to inner man, to soul and mind and "regal thoughts":

> You may my glories and my state depose,
> But not my griefs, still am I king of those.
>
> (IV.i.192f.)

Invisible his kingship, and relegated to within: visible his flesh, and exposed to contempt and derision or to pity and mockery—

there remains but one parallel to his miserable self: the derided Son of man. Not only Northumberland, so Richard exclaims, will be found "damned in the book of heaven," but others as well:

> Nay, all of you, that stand and look upon me,
> Whilst that my wretchedness doth bait myself,
> Though some of you, with Pilate, wash your hands,
> Showing an outward pity; yet you Pilates
> Have here delivered me to my sour cross,
> And water cannot wash away your sin.
> 
> (IV.i.237ff.)

It is not at random that Shakespeare introduces here, as antitype of Richard, the image of Christ before Pilate, mocked as King of the Jews and delivered to the cross. Shakespeare's sources, contemporary with the events, had transmitted that scene in a similar light.

> At this hour did he (Bolingbroke) remind me of Pilate, who caused our Lord Jesus Christ to be scourged at the stake, and afterwards had him brought before the multitude of the Jews, saying, "Fair Sirs, behold your king!" who replied, "Let him be crucified!" Then Pilate washed his hands of it, saying, "I am innocent of the just blood." And so he delivered our Lord unto them. Much in the like manner did Duke Henry, when he gave up his rightful lord to the rabble of London, in order that, if they should put him to death, he might say, "I am innocent of this deed."[24]

The parallel of Bolingbroke-Richard and Pilate-Christ reflects a widespread feeling among the anti-Lancastrian groups. Such feeling was revived, to some extent, in Tudor times. But this is not important here; for Shakespeare, when using the biblical comparison, integrates it into the entire development of Richard's misery, of which the nadir has as yet not been reached. The Son of man, despite his humiliation and the mocking, remained the *deus absconditus*, remained the "concealed God" with regard to inner man, just as Shakespeare's Richard would trust for a moment's length in his concealed inner kingship. This inner kingship, however, dissolved too. For of a sudden Richard realizes that he, when facing his Lancastrian Pilate, is not at all like Christ, but that he himself, Richard, has his place among the Pilates and Judases, because he is no less a traitor than the others, or is even worse than they are: he is a traitor to his own immortal body politic and to kingship such as it had been to his day:

> Mine eyes are full of tears, I cannot see. . . .
> But they can see a sort of traitors here.
> Nay, if I turn mine eyes upon myself,
> I find myself a traitor with the rest:
> For I have given here my soul's consent
> T'undeck the pompous body of a king. . . .
> (IV.i.244ff.)

That is, the king body natural becomes a traitor to the king body politic, to the "pompous body of a king." It is as though Richard's self-indictment of treason anticipated the charge of 1649, the charge of high treason committed by the *k*ing against the *K*ing.

This cleavage is not yet the climax of Richard's duplications, since the splitting of his personality will be continued without mercy. Once more does there emerge that metaphor of "Sun-kingship." It appears, however, in the reverse order, when Richard breaks into that comparison of singular imagination:

> O, that I were a mockery king of snow,
> Standing before the sun of Bolingbroke,
> To melt myself away in water-drops!
> (IV.i.260ff.)

But it is not before that new Sun—symbol of divine majesty throughout the play—that Richard "melts himself away," and together with his self also the image of kingship in the early liturgical sense; it is before his own ordinary face that there dissolves both his bankrupt majesty and his nameless manhood.

The mirror scene is the climax of that tragedy of dual personality. The looking-glass has the effects of a magic mirror, and Richard himself is the wizard who, comparable to the trapped and cornered wizard in the fairy tales, is forced to set his magic art to work against himself. The physical face which the mirror reflects no longer is one with Richard's inner experience, his outer appearance, no longer identical with inner man.

# The Historical and Political Dynamics

"Was this the face?" The treble question and the answers to it reflect once more the three main facets of the double nature—King, God (Sun), and Fool:

> Was this the face
> That every day under his household roof
> Did keep ten thousand men?
> Was this the face
> That, like the sun, did make beholders wink?
> Was this the face, that faced so many follies,
> And was at last outfaced by Bolingbroke?
>
> (IV.i.281ff.)

When finally, at the "brittle glory" of his face, Richard dashes the mirror to the ground, there shatters not only Richard's past and present, but every aspect of a super-world. His catoptromancy had ended. The features as reflected by the looking-glass betray that he is stripped of every possibility of a second or super-body—of the pompous body politic of king, of the Godlikeness of the Lord's deputy elect, of the follies of the fool, and even of the most human griefs residing in inner man. The splintering mirror means, or is, the breaking apart of any possible duality. All those facets are reduced to one: to the banal face and insignificant *physis* of a miserable man, a *physis* now void of any metaphysis whatsoever. It is both less and more than Death. It is the *demise* of Richard, and the rise of a new body natural.

> *Bolingbroke*:
> Go, some of you, convey him to the Tower.
> *Richard*:
> O, good! convey? conveyors are you all,
> That rise thus nimbly by a great king's fall.
>
> (IV.i.316f.)
>
> *Plowden*:
> Demise is a word, signifying that there is a Separation of the two Bodies; and that the Body politic is conveyed over from the Body natural, now dead or removed from the Dignity royal, to another Body natural.[25]

*The Tragedy of King Richard II* has always been felt to be a political play.[26] The deposition scene, though performed scores of times after the first performance in 1595, was not printed, or not allowed to be printed, until after the death of Queen Elizabeth.[27] Historical plays in general attracted the English people, especially in the years following the destruction of the Armada; but *Richard II* attracted more than the usual attention. Not to speak of other causes, the conflict between Elizabeth and Essex appeared to Shakespeare's contemporaries in the light of the conflict between Richard and Bolingbroke. It is well known that in 1601, on the eve of his unsuccessful rebellion against the Queen, the Earl of Essex ordered a special performance of *Richard II* to be played in the Globe Theatre before his supporters and the people of London. In the course of the state trial against Essex that performance was discussed at some length by the royal judges—among them the two greatest lawyers of that age, Coke and Bacon—who could not fail to recognize the allusions to the present which the performance of that play intended.[28] It is likewise well known that Elizabeth looked upon that tragedy with most unfavorable feelings. At the time of Essex's execution she complained that "this tragedy had been played 40 times in open streets and houses," and she carried her self-identification with the title character so far as to exclaim: "I am Richard II, know ye not that?"[29]

*Richard II* remained a political play. It was suppressed under Charles II in the 1680s. The play illustrated perhaps too overtly the latest events of England's revolutionary history, the "Day of the Martyrdom of the Blessed King Charles I" as commemorated in those years in the Book of Common Prayer.[30] The Restoration avoided these and other recollections and had no liking for that tragedy which centered, not only on the concept of a Christ-like martyr king, but also on that most unpleasant idea of a violent separation of the King's Two Bodies.

It would not be surprising at all had Charles I himself thought of his tragic fate in terms of Shakespeare's *Richard II* and of the king's twin-born being. In some copies of the *Eikon Basilike* there is printed a lament, a long poem otherwise called *Majesty in Misery*, which is ascribed to Charles I and in which the unfortunate king, if really he was the poet, quite obviously alluded to the King's Two Bodies:

With my own power my majesty they wound,
In the King's name the king himself uncrowned.
So does the dust destroy the diamond.[31]

NOTES

1. *King Henry V*, IV.i.254ff.
2. Dr. John Cowell, *The Interpreter or Booke Containing the Signification of Words* (Cambridge, 1607), s.v. "King (*Rex*)," also s.v. "Prerogative," where Plowden is actually quoted. See, in general, Chrimes, "Dr. John Cowell," *EHR*, LXIV (1949), 483.
3. Joseph Kitchin, *Le Court Leete et Court Baron* (London, 1580), fol. 1$^{r-v}$, referring to the case of the Duchy of Lancaster.
4. Richard Crompton, *L'Authoritie et Jurisdiction des Courts de la Maiestie de la Roygne* (London, 1594), fol. 134$^{r-v}$, reproducing on the basis of Plowden the theory about the Two Bodies in connection with the Lancaster case.
5. See Bacon's *Brief Discourse Touching the Happy Union of the Kingdoms of England and Scotland* in J. Spedding, *Letters and Life of Francis Bacon* (London, 1861-74), III, 90ff.; see, for the print of 1603, S.T. Bindoff, "The Stuarts and Their Style," *EHR*, LX (1945), 206, n. 2, who (p. 207) quotes the passage.
6. A.P. Rossiter, *Woodstock* (London, 1946), p. 238.
7. About Shakespeare and Plowden, see C.H. Norman, "Shakespeare and the Law," *Times Literary Supplement*, June 30, 1950, p. 412, with the additional remarks by Sir Donald Somervell, *ibid.*, July 21, 1950, p. 453.
8. John Dover Wilson, in his edition of *Richard II* (below, n. 12), "Introduction," p. lxxiv; see p. xlviii ff., for Shakespeare and *Woodstock* in general.
9. *Woodstock*, V.vi.34f., ed. Rossiter, p. 169.
10. See, in general, George W. Keeton, *Shakespeare and His Legal Problems* (London, 1930); also Max Radin, "The Myth of Magna Carta," *Harvard Law Review*, LX (1947), 1086, who stresses very strongly Shakespeare's association "with the turbulent students at the Inns."
11. V.H. Galbraith, "A New Life of Richard II," *History*, XXVI (1942), 237ff.; for the artistic problems and for a full bibliography, see Erwin Panofsky, *Early Netherlandish Painting* (Cambridge, Mass., 1953), pp. 118 and 404f., n. 5, and Francis Wormald, "The Wilton Diptych," *Warburg Journal*, XVII (1954), 191-203.
12. The authoritative edition of *Richard II* is by John Dover Wilson, in the Cambridge *Works of Shakespeare* (Cambridge, 1939). Mr. Wilson's

"Introduction," pp. vii–lxxvi, is a model of literary criticism and information. I confess my indebtedness to those pages on which I have drawn more frequently than the footnotes may suggest. In the same volume is a likewise most efficient discussion by Harold Child, "The Stage-History of *Richard II*," pp. lxxvii–xcii. The political aspects of the play are treated in a stimulating fashion by John Leslie Palmer, *Political Characters of Shakespeare* (London, 1945), pp. 118ff., from whose study, too, I have profited more than my acknowledgments may show. See also Keeton, *op. cit.*, pp. 163ff. With regard to the historical Richard II, the historian finds himself in a less fortunate position. The history of this king is in the midst of a thorough revaluation of both sources and general concepts, of which the numerous studies of Professor Galbraith and others bear witness. A first effort to sum up the analytic studies of the last decades has been made by Anthony Steel, *Richard II* (Cambridge, 1941).

13. See also *King John*, III.iii.147f.:

    What earthly name to interrogatories
    Can task the free breath of a sacred king?

14. This is reported only by Holinshed; see W.G. Boswell-Stone, *Shakespeare's Holinshed* (London, 1896), p. 130; Wilson, "Introduction," p. lii. The *Rotuli Parliamentorum* do not refer to the speech of John Busshy, in 1397. To judge, however, from the customary parliamentary sermons, the speaker in 1397 may easily have gone far in applying Biblical metaphors to the king; see, e.g., Chrimes, *Const. Ideas*, pp. 165ff.

15. "Dixit expresse, vultu austero et protervo, quod leges suae erant in ore suo, et aliquotiens in pectore suo: Et quod ipse solus posset mutare et condere leges regni sui." This was one of the most famous of Richard's so-called "tyrannies" with which he was charged in 1399; see E.C. Lodge and G.A. Thornton, *English Constitutional Documents 1307–1485* (Cambridge, 1935), pp. 28f. Richard II, like the French king, merely referred to a well-known maxim of Roman and Canon Laws. Cf. C.6,23,19,1, for the maxim *Omnia iura in scrinio (pectoris) principis*, often quoted by the glossators, e.g., *Glos.ord.*, on *D*.33,10,3 v. *usum imperatorem*, or on c.16,C.25,q.2, v. *In iuris*, and quoted also by Thomas Aquinas (Tolomeo of Lucca), *De regimine principum*, II,c.8,IV,c.1. The maxim became famous through Pope Boniface VIII; see c.i,VI,1,2, ed. Emil Friedberg, *Corpus iuris canonici* (Leipzig, 1879–81), II,937: "Licet Romanus Pontifex, qui iura omnia in scrinio pectoris sui censetur habere, constitutionem condendo posteriorem, priorem . . . revocare noscatur . . ." (probably the place referred to by Richard if the cor-

rectness of the charges be granted). For the meaning of the maxim (i.e., the legislator should have the relevant laws present to his mind), see F. Gillman, "Romanus pontifex iura omnia in scrinio pectoris sui censetur habere," *AKKR*, XCII (1912), 3ff.; CVI (1926), 156ff. (also CVIII [1928], 534; CIX [1929], 249f.); also Gaines Post, "Two Notes," *Traditio*, IX (1953), 311, and "Two Laws," *Speculum*, XIX (1954), 425, n. 35. See also Steinwenter, "Nomos," pp. 256ff.; *Erg. Bd.*, p. 85; Oldradus de Ponte, *Consilia*, LII, n. i (Venice, 1571), fol. 19$^r$. The maxim occasionally was transferred also to the judge (Walter Ullman, *The Mediaeval Idea of Law as Represented by Lucas de Penna* [London, 1946], p. 107) and to the fisc (Gierke, *Gen. R.*, III, 359, n. 17) as well as to the council. For Richard's other claim (*mutare et condere leges*), the papal and imperial doctrines likewise were responsible; see Gregory VII's *Dictatus papae*, §VII, ed. Caspar (*MGH*, Epp. sel., II), p. 203; also Frederick II's *Liber aug.*, 1,38, ed. Cervone, 85, with the gloss referring to C.1,17,2,18.

16. For the genuflection, see *Eulogium Historiarum*, ed. Hayden (Rolls Series, 1863), III, 378; see Steel, *Richard II*, p. 278. The annalist mentions it in connection with "Festival Crownings" (which thus were continued during the reign of Richard) and gives an account of the king's uncanny deportment:

    In diebus solemnibus, in quibus utebatur de more regalibus, iussit sibi in camera parari thronum, in quo post prandium se ostentans sedere solebat usque ad vesperas, nulli loquens, sed singulos aspiciens. Et cum aliquem respiceret, cuiuscumque gradus fuerit, oportuit genuflectere.

17. For the body politic as a mere name, see, e.g., Pollock and Maitland, *History*, I, 490, n. 8: "le corporacion . . . n'est que un nosme, que ne poit my estre vieu, et n'est my substance." See also Gierke, *Gen.R.*, III, 281, for corporate bodies as *nomina iuris, a nomen intellectuale*, and the connections with the philosophic Nominalism.

18. For Richard's symbol of the "Rising Sun," see Paul Reyher, "Le symbole du soleil dans la tragédie de Richard II," *Revue de l'Enseignement des Langues Vivantes*, XL (1923), 254–60; for further literature on the subject, see Wilson, "Introduction," p. xii, n. 3, and for possible predecessors using that badge, John Gough Nichols, "Observations on the Heraldic Devices on the Effigies of Richard the Second and His Queen," *Archaeologia*, XXIX (1842), 47f. See for the "Sun of York" (*King Richard III*, I.i.2), also Henry Green, *Shakespeare and the Emblem Writers* (London, 1870), p. 223; and, for the *Oriens Augusti* problem, see my forthcoming study. The "sunne

arysing out of the clouds" was actually the banner borne by the Black Prince; Richard II had a sun shining carried by a white hart, whereas his standard was sprinkled with ten suns "in splendor" with a white hart lodged; see Lord Howard de Walden, *Banners, Standards, and Badges from a Tudor Manuscript in the College of Arms* (De Walden Library, 1904), figs. 4, 5, 71. I am greatly obliged to Mr. Martin Davies, of the National Gallery in London, for having called this MS to my attention.

19. The ecclesiastical *Forma degradationis* was, on the whole, faithfully observed; see the Pontifical of William Durandus (ca. 1293-95), III, c. 7, §§21-24, ed. M. Andrieu, *Le pontifical romain au moyen-age* (Studi e testi, LXXXVIII, Rome, 1940), III, 607f. and Appendix IV, pp. 680f. The person to be degraded has to appear in full pontificals; then the places of his chrismation are rubbed with some acid; finally "seriatim et sigillatim detrahit [episcopus] illi omnia insignia, sive sacra ornamenta, que in ordinum susceptione recepit, et demum exuit illum habitu clericali. . . ." See also S.W. Findlay, *Canonical Norms Governing the Deposition and Degradation of Clerics* (Washington, 1941). For knights, see Otto Cartellieri, *Am Hofe der Herzöge von Burgund* (Basel, 1926), p. 62 (with notes on p. 272); also Du Cange, *Glossarium*, s.v. "Arma reversata."

20. For Pope Celestine V, see F. Baethgen, *Der Engelpapst* (Leipzig, 1943), p. 175; for Richard, *Chronicle of Dieulacres Abbey*, ed. M.V. Clarke and V.H. Galbraith, "The Deposition of Richard II," *Bulletin of the John Rylands Library*, XIV (1930), 173, also 146.

21. Walter Pater, *Appreciations* (London, 1944), pp. 205f.; Wilson, pp. xv f.; Palmer, *Political Characters*, p. 166.

22. Cf. Chrimes, *Const. Ideas*, 7, n. 2, quoting *Annales Henrici Quarti*, ed. Riley (Rolls Series), p. 286: "Noluit renunciare spirituali honori *characteris sibi impressi* et inunctioni, quibus renunciare non potuit nec ab hiis cessare." The question as to whether or not the king, through his anointment, ever owned in a technical sense a *character indelibilis* is too complicated to be discussed here. In fact, the notion of the "sacramental character" was developed only at the time when the royal (imperial) consecrations were excluded from the number of the seven sacraments; cf. Ferdinand Brommer, *Die Lehre vom sakramentalen Charakter in der Scholastik bis Thomas von Aquino inklusive* (Forschungen zur christlichen Literatur- und Dogmengeschichte, VIII, 2) (Paderborn, 1908). A different matter is the common opinion about the sacramental character of royal anointings and the inaccurate use of the term *sacramentum*; see, for the latter, e.g., P.E. Schramm, "Der König von Navarra (1035-1512),"

ZfRG, germ. Abt., LXVIII (1951), 147, n. 72 (Pope Alexander IV referring to a royal consecration as *sacramentum*). See, in general, Eduard Eichmann, *Die Kaiserkrönung im Abendland* (Würzburg, 1942), I, 86ff., 90, 208, 279; II, 304; Philipp Oppenheim, "Die sakralen Momente in der deutschen Herrscherweihe bis zum Investiturstreit," *Ephemerides Liturgicae*, LVIII (1944), 42ff.; and, for England, the well-known utterances of Peter of Blois (*PL*, CCVII, 440D) and Grosseteste (*Ep.*, CXXIV, ed. Luard, p. 350). Actually, the lack of precision was great at all times.
23. IV.i.214ff.
24. The passage is found in the *Chronique de las Traison et Mort de Richard II*, ed. B. Williams, in: *English Historical Society*, 1846, and in Creton's French metrical *History of the Deposition of Richard II*, ed. J. Webb, in: *Royal Society of the Antiquaries* (London, 1819). A fifteenth-century English version, which has been rendered here, was edited by J. Webb, in *Archaeologia*, XX (1824), 179. See, on those sources, Wilson, "Introduction," p. lviii, cf. xvi f. and 211. The crime of treason would naturally evoke the comparison with Judas. The comparison with Pilate was likewise quite common (see, e.g., Dante, *Purg.* XX, 91), though his role was not always purely negative; see, e.g., O. Treitinger, *Die oströmische Kaiser- und Reichsidee nach ihrer Gestaltung im höfischen Zeremoniell* (Jena, 1938), p. 231, n. 104, for Pilate's inkpot in the ceremonial of the Byzantine emperor, who on Ash Wednesday symbolically "washed his hands."
25. Plowden, *Reports*, 233a.
26. Palmer, *Political Characters*, pp. 118f.
27. Wilson, "Introduction," pp. xvi ff., xlix; also Child (*ibid.*), lxxvii ff.; cf. Keeton, *Legal Problems*, p. 163.
28. Wilson, pp. xxx ff.; Keeton, pp. 166, 168.
29. Wilson, p. xxxii.
30. Wilson, p. xvii; Child, p. lxxix.
31. According to Rosemary Freeman, *English Emblem Books* (London, 1948), p. 162, n. 1, the poem was first printed in the *Eikon Basilike*, edition of 1648. Margaret Barnard Pickel, *Charles I as Patron of Poetry and Drama* (London, 1938), who prints the whole poem in Appendix C, seems to assume (p. 178) that it was first published in Bishop Burnet's *Memoirs of the Duke of Hamilton* (London, 1677), a work dedicated to Charles II. A few stanzas have been published also by F. M. G. Higham, *Charles I* (London, 1932), p. 276.

*Irving Ribner*

# Bolingbroke, a True Machiavellian (1948)

The Elizabethan manuscript translation of *The Prince*, edited by Hardin Craig,[1] calls attention to the need for investigation of a new aspect of the problem of the influence of Machiavelli upon the Elizabethan drama. Investigation of the problem has traditionally centered about the burlesque stage "Machiavel," whose genesis has been, with questionable accuracy, attributed to the *Contre-Machiavel* of Innocent Gentillet, written in 1576, translated into English by Simon Patericke in 1577, and printed in 1602, with its corrupted version of the Florentine's philosophy.[2] The wide influence of the "Machiavelli legend" in England may be seen in the traditional "Machiavels" of the Elizabethan stage—the Iagos, Aarons, Gloucesters, and Edmunds of Shakespeare's plays—whom Edward Meyer,[3] Mario Praz,[4] and others have treated. But an English translation of *The Prince*, which must have been in existence as early as 1585, though it be in manuscript form, reminds us that the text of Machiavelli's own work was known also, and that it exerted an influence independent of such corruptions as that of Gentillet.

Nor are manuscript translations the only evidence we have. Lewis Einstein many years ago argued that the political career of Thomas Cromwell was modeled closely upon the philosophy of Machiavelli.[5] The story of how John Wolfe, a London printer, published the original Italian of Machiavelli's works in England with false Italian title-page inscriptions, from 1584 to 1588, is well known. Italian editions of *The Prince* must also have been brought back to England by the many travelers to Italy, and a Latin translation was available by 1560.

A manifestation upon the Elizabethan stage of the actual Machiavellian philosophy in *The Prince* may perhaps be seen in Shakespeare's Bolingbroke, both in *Richard II* and in the Henry IV plays. Henry IV's political career, as Shakespeare presents it, coincides strongly with what Machiavelli saw as necessary for the new prince who would unify and strengthen Italy at a time when the Florentine republic had fallen and Medici despotism seemed inevitable.

When we think of Bolingbroke and Machiavelli, we are immediately struck by the similarity between the chaotic England of the one and the chaotic Italy of the other. Italy, writes Machiavelli, is "brought down to her present position, to be more a slave than the Hebrews, more a servant than the Persians, more scattered than the Athenians; without head, without government; defeated, plundered, torn asunder, overrun; subject to every sort of disaster."[6]

And Bolingbroke's England, in the dying words of John of Gaunt,

> Is now leas'd out (I die pronouncing it)
> Like to a tenement or pelting farm.
> England, bound in with the triumphant sea,
> Whose rocky shore beats back the envious siege
> Of wat'ry Neptune, is now bound in with shame,
> With inky blots and rotten parchment bonds.
> That England that was wont to conquer others
> Hath made a shameful conquest of itself.[7]

Machiavelli, writing *The Prince* in a time of political chaos and corruption, is calling for a governor who will lead Italy out of bondage and restore it to prosperity, and in his book, he sets down the formula by which such a leader may accomplish that end.

> So Italy remains without life and awaits the man, whoever he may be, who is to heal her wounds, put an end to the plundering of Lombardy and the tribute laid on Tuscany and the kingdom of Naples, and cure her of those sores that have long been suppurating. She may be seen praying God to send some one to redeem her from these cruel and barbarous insults.[8]

## The Historical and Political Dynamics

Shakespeare's Bolingbroke appears to be just such a leader.[9] Coming into power at a similar moment in the history of England, his handling of that power, when it is his, follows closely the formula set down by Machiavelli.

As the curtain rises on *Richard II*, we find Bolingbroke in a typical application of that philosophy. Bolingbroke, in his accusation of Mowbray, is covertly attacking the government of Richard, of which Mowbray is a part. Bolingbroke knows that Richard is as responsible for the murder of Gloucester as is Mowbray,[10] and all of his passionate speeches are merely the rhetoric of a politician assuming a pose.

This deception for political purposes is completely in line with Machiavelli's words on dissimulation and the keeping of faith, contained in Chapter 18 of *The Prince*. "To those who see and hear him," he writes, "he should seem all compassion, all faith, all honesty, all humanity, all religion." Bolingbroke, to his hearers, seems all of that, but he need only seem, for as Machiavelli says, "It is not necessary, then, for a prince really to have all the virtues mentioned above, but it is very necessary to seem to have them." Bolingbroke is the "prudent" man who "cannot and should not observe faith when such observance is to his disadvantage."[11] The solemn oath he takes to Richard when he is banished, he breaks with ease. Honesty and trust mean nothing to Bolingbroke when his own advantage is involved.

In Chapter 4 of *The Prince*, Machiavelli says that in the type of principality to which England belongs, where "there are a prince and barons, and the latter hold their positions not through the grace of their lord but through the antiquity of their blood,"[12] a usurping prince must have a tool among the barons. "You can enter them easily, if you win to your side some baron of the kingdom, because there are always some lords who are discontented and desire revolution; these, for the reasons given, can open you the way to control of the country and make victory easy for you."[13] Such a tool Bolingbroke finds in Northumberland. Note his courtship of the young Percy:

> I thank thee, Gentle Percy; and be sure
> I count myself in nothing else so happy
> As in a soul remembering my good friends;

> And as my fortune ripens with thy love,
> It shall be still my true love's recompense.
> My heart this covenant makes, my hand thus seals it.[14]

Here we have a statement of sworn friendship, but it is a lying and a deceitful statement, for, as becomes a follower of Machiavelli, a new prince must remember the Florentine's warning that one will not be "able to keep as friends those who have placed you there, because you cannot satisfy them in the manner they have been looking forward to, and you cannot use strong medicine against them because you are under obligation to them."[15] Bolingbroke knows that he will have to get rid of the "ladder wherewithal he mounts the throne" as soon as he is king, and this he does in *1 Henry IV*. This pledge of friendship to the Percys is an excellent example of calculated Machiavellian deceit.

Bolingbroke from the very beginning enlists the good will of the common people upon his side, and here also he is following to the letter a basic precept of Machiavelli. In *The Prince*, we find:

> He who becomes ruler with the aid of the great maintains himself with more difficulty than he who becomes ruler with the aid of the people, because the first is in the position of a prince with a good many subjects whom he regards as his equals, and for this reason cannot direct them as he wishes to. But he who becomes prince with popular favor stands alone, and has no subjects, or at most only a few, who are not ready to obey him. Further, one cannot satisfy the upper class with honor and without injury to others, but it is possible to satisfy the people in that way, because the purpose of the people is more just than that of the upper class, since the latter wish to oppress and the former not to be oppressed. Besides, when the people are unfriendly the prince never can make himself secure, for he has too many against him. . . .[16]

And further:

> But a man who becomes prince in opposition to the people and with the favor of the upper classes, ought to endeavor before everything else to gain the support of the people. . . .[17]

And finally:

> I shall conclude merely that it is necessary for a prince to have the friendship of the people; otherwise he has no resource in adversity.[18]

This is a strongly emphasized point in Machiavelli's philosophy, and it is strongly emphasized in Shakespeare's depiction of Bolingbroke. In the first act of *Richard II*, the king says of him:

> Ourself and Bushy, Bagot here, and Green
> Observ'd his courtship to the common people;
> How he did seem to dive into their hearts
> With humble and familiar courtesy;
> What reverence he did throw away on slaves,
> Wooing poor craftsmen with the craft of smiles
> And patient underbearing of his fortune,
> As 'twere to banish their affects with him.
> Off goes his bonnet to an oyster-wench;
> A brace of draymen bid God speed him well
> And had the tribute of his supple knee,
> With 'Thanks, my countrymen, my loving friends';
> As were our England in reversion his,
> And he our subjects' next degree in hope.[19]

How successful Bolingbroke's wooing of the people is, can be seen in the Duke of York's description of his triumphal march through London:

> Then, as I said, the Duke, great Bolingbroke,
> Mounted upon a hot and fiery steed
> Which his aspiring rider seem'd to know,
> With slow and stately pace kept on his course,
> Whilst all tongues cried 'God save thee, Bolingbroke.'
> . . . . . . . . . . . . . . . . . . . . . . . . . . . . . . . . . . . . .
> Whilst he, from the one side to the other turning,
> Bareheaded, lower than his proud steed's neck,
> Bespake them thus, 'I thank you, countrymen.'
> And thus still doing, thus he pass'd along.[20]

Contrast this with the crowd's reception of Richard, whom he has supplanted. Bolingbroke, in true Machiavellian fashion, had wooed the common people and won them to his side.

In the magnificent deposition scene in *Richard II*, Henry is as Machiavellian as ever. To the crowd, he paints himself as a man of virtue, coming in submission to kingly authority, merely to plead a just cause:

> Henry Bolingbroke
> On both his knees does kiss King Richard's hand
> And sends allegiance and true faith of heart
> To his most royal person; hither come
> Even at his feet to lay my arms and power. . . .[21]

But at the end of the scene, Richard is in Henry's power, and is conveyed to London by him, as a king only in name. Here again Bolingbroke is accomplishing his own unjust ends and, at the same time, giving his act the appearance of justice for the sake of the crowd. "He should strive in all his actions," says Machiavelli, giving his formula for the efficient ruler, "to give evident signs of greatness, spirit, gravity, and fortitude."[22] Bolingbroke is here giving the appearance of having those virtues which Machiavelli says he should pretend to, but need not have.

The first act which Bolingbroke performs upon coming into power is to destroy Bushy, Bagot, Green, and the Earl of Wilshire, the faithful supporters of Richard. Now, one of the most important of Machiavelli's principles, contained in Chapter 3 of *The Prince*, is that when a new prince has come into power, all those who supported the old prince must be destroyed. There is a "natural and normal necessity," he writes, "which makes it always necessary for a new ruler to harm those over whom he places himself," even to the extent of wiping out the race of the old prince.[23] Further confirmation comes from Bolingbroke's immediate arrest of the Bishop of Carlisle, although he is a member of the clergy, when he speaks against the dethronement of Richard.[24]

Another of the basic principles in the philosophy of Machiavelli is that of legality in the maintenance of a kingdom, and particularly of hereditary legality:

> I say, then, that hereditary states, being accustomed to the family of their prince, are maintained with fewer difficulties than new ones, because it is enough for the hereditary ruler merely not to go beyond the customs of his ancestors,

and otherwise to deal with accidents by moving slowly and cautiously. This is so true that if such a prince is of ordinary diligence, he will always maintain himself in his position, unless some extraordinary and excessive force deprives him of it; and even if he is deprived of it, he will get it back whenever the conqueror falls into misfortune.[25]

Throughout the plays, Bolingbroke is concerned with the legality of his title. He knows that he has no hereditary right to the throne, and it is to him a constant source of anxiety. In Act IV of *Richard II*, when Richard sends in word that he is ready to give up the crown, Henry says:

> Fetch hither Richard, that in common view
> He may surrender. So we shall proceed
> Without suspicion.[26]

He wants no doubt cast upon the legality of the transaction. And in *2 Henry IV*, on his deathbed, he speaks of the question with his son:

> God knows, my son,
> By what bypaths and indirect crook'd ways
> I met this crown; and I myself know well
> How troublesome it sat upon my head.
> To thee it shall descend with better quiet,
> Better opinion, better confirmation;
> For all the soil of the achievement goes
> With me into the earth. . . .
>              And now my death
> Changes the mood; for what in me was purchas'd
> Falls upon thee in a more fairer sort;
> So thou the garland wear'st successively.[27]

Bolingbroke's dying consolation is that his son, Henry V, will wear the crown with hereditary right to bolster it, as Machiavelli said it should be bolstered.[28] This preoccupation with the importance of title makes necessary the murder of Richard II. While Richard lives, Henry's title to the throne is open to question; so Richard must not live.

According to another principle of Machiavelli, the deposed ruler must always be destroyed.

> But afterwards if you wish to maintain your conquest, these conditions will cause you innumerable difficulties, both with those who have aided you and with those you have overcome. Nor is it enough for you to exterminate the family of the prince, because the nobles will still be left to take the lead in new rebellions. . . .[29]

Bolingbroke, therefore, must destroy both Richard and Northumberland. Richard is destroyed immediately and Northumberland at the first opportunity that arises. That the murder of Richard is an act of extreme cruelty does not dismay Bolingbroke in the least. If his title is to be made secure, and the nation strengthened and united, Richard must be murdered. Machiavelli says:

> Hence a prince ought not to be troubled by the stigma of cruelty, acquired in keeping his subjects united and faithful. By giving a very few examples of cruelty he can be more truly compassionate than those who through too much compassion allow disturbances to continue, from which arise murders or acts of plunder. Lawless acts are injurious to a large group, but the executions ordered by the prince injure a single person. The new prince, above all other princes, cannot possibly avoid the name of cruel, because new states are full of perils.[30]

As a disciple of the Machiavellian philosophy, Bolingbroke cannot do the killing himself. "Princes should have things that will bring them hatred done by their agents," says Machiavelli,[31] and Bolingbroke accordingly employs Pierce of Exton.

Bolingbroke's last statement in *Richard II* is one in the Machiavellian vein. "I'll make a voyage to the Holy Land," he says.[32] Machiavelli maintains throughout that the good ruler must appear pious in the eyes of his people.

The political activity of Bolingbroke in Shakespeare's *Richard II* closely adheres to Machiavelli's political philosophy as contained in *The Prince*. There are a few incidents where Bolingbroke does not follow Machiavelli to the letter, the most noteworthy of these being his failure to destroy Aumerle; but these incidents, in relation to the whole, are minor. In almost every important act, from his quarrel with Mowbray in the opening scene, to his projected pilgrimage to Jerusalem in the closing, the underlying philosophy of Machiavelli can be seen.

If we accept this thesis as true, many problems arise. Was this parallel accidental, or was it intentional? Had Shakespeare read *The Prince* in one of the Elizabethan manuscript translations or in the Italian, or had he perhaps studied the career of Thomas Cromwell? There is no doubt that he was familiar with the Machiavel that came to him with the heritage of the Elizabethan stage; we find it in his plays. But whether or not Shakespeare, as a student of political theory, was familiar with the actual ideas of Machiavelli is another matter, and one which presents a subject for further study.

NOTES

1. Niccolò Machiavelli, *The Prince: An Elizabethan Translation*, edited by Hardin Craig (Chapel Hill, 1944). The Furthman MS. which Dr. Craig edited, is the best of seven extant manuscripts containing three distinct translations of *The Prince*, each entirely unrelated to the 1640 translation of Edward Dacres. For a description of the remaining six manuscripts see Napoleone Orsini, *Studi sul Rinascimento in Inghilterra* (Firenze: Sansoni, 1937), pp. 1-19.
2. The classic presentation of this thesis is Edward Meyer, *Machiavelli and the Elizabethan Drama* (Weimar: Emil Felber, 1897). Others include Piero Rebora, *L'Italia nel Dramma Inglese (1558-1642)* (Milan: Modernissima, 1925), pp. 165-94.
3. Meyer, *op cit.*
4. Mario Praz, "Machiavelli and the Elizabethans," *Proceedings of the British Academy*, XIV (1928), 49-97.
5. Lewis Einstein, *The Italian Renaissance in England* (New York, 1902), p. 292. The story of Cardinal Reginald Pole's reading *The Prince* in manuscript in 1527, upon the instigation of Cromwell who had brought it with him from Italy, is an old one that has been told many times. See, for instance, Grattan Freyer, "The Reputation of Machiavelli," *Hermathema*, LVI (1940), 154.
6. Niccolò Machiavelli, *The Prince*, translated and edited by Allen H. Gilbert, University Classics (Chicago, 1941), p. 177. All future references to Machiavelli in this paper will be to this edition.
7. William Shakespeare, *Richard II*, II.i.59-66. Shakespearean refer-

ences are to *Complete Works of Shakespeare*, edited by George Lyman Kittredge (Boston, 1936).
8. *The Prince*, p. 177.
9. See discussion of his cause by the nobles in *Richard II*, II.i.221-300.
10. This is made clear in Act I, Scene ii, lines 37ff., in which John of Gaunt, speaking of Gloucester's murder, says:

> God's is the quarrel; for God's substitute,
> His deputy anointed in his sight,
> Hath caus'd his death. . . .

thus making Richard's guilt clear. For further evidence, see also *Richard II*, II.i.126-32.
11. *The Prince*, pp. 148-50.
12. *Ibid.*, p. 104.
13. *Ibid.*, p. 105.
14. *Richard II*, II.iii.45-50.
15. *The Prince*, p. 97.
16. *Ibid.*, p. 123.
17. *Ibid.*, p. 124.
18. *Idem*.
19. *Richard II*, I.iv.23-36.
20. *Ibid.*, V.ii.7-21.
21. *Ibid.*, III.iii.35-39.
22. *The Prince*, p. 151.
23. *The Prince*, pp. 97-98.
24. *Richard II*, IV.i.103-106.
25. *The Prince*, p. 96.
26. *Richard II*, IV.i.155-57.
27. *2 Henry IV*, IV.v.184-91, 199-202.
28. *The Prince*, p. 96.
29. *Ibid.*, p. 105.
30. *Ibid.*, p. 145.
31. *Ibid.*, p. 153.
32. *Richard II*, V.vi.49.

# PART II
*RICHARD II*
The Theatre

C.E. Montague

# F.R. Benson's Richard II (1899)

Mr. Benson, whom nothing seems to tire, played Richard II on Saturday afternoon and Petruchio in the evening. Of the latter one need not at this time of day say much. Like his Hamlet—of which by a misprint we were made to say the other day that it was one of his "least known" instead of one of his "best known" pieces of acting,—it is familiar to every Manchester playgoer. It is unconventional, and in that sense contentious; when it was seen in London ten years ago those of the critics who hold a brief for the conventions of the moment were scandalized at the notion that anything Shakespearean or partly Shakespearean should be played in a vein so boisterous. By this time one would hope that Mr. Benson must have brought it home to everybody that the play is itself a roaring extravaganza, only to be carried off at all upon the stage by a sustained rush of high spirits that leaves no time to think. It is full of legible notices to this effect—the burlesque bidding for Bianca, for instance, and the "my horse, my ox, my ass" speech, and endless others. Mr. Benson's gusty and tearing Petruchio, with a lyrical touch of romance in the voice and look here and there in his delivery of lines like

> Such wind as scatters young men through the world,
> To seek their fortunes further than at home,
> Where small experience grows,

strikes us as not only the best Petruchio we have seen but the only reading of the part that will hold water. The play, too, furnishes Mrs. Benson with, we think, her best part in Katharine and Mr. Weir with a very good one in Grumio, both played in the same key of vehement and fantastical humor as Mr. Benson's Petruchio. It does one good to see a play so well understood and so courageously and consistently played on that understanding. It was played with infinite zest and spirit on Saturday night to a very full house, which it kept in almost continuous laughter.

The chief interest of the day, however, attached to Mr. Benson's Richard II, a piece of acting which is much less known here, and to whose chief interest we do not think that critical justice has ever been done. An actor faulty in some other ways, but always picturesque, romantic, and inventive, with a fine sensibility to beauty in words and situations and a voice that gives this sensibility its due, Mr. Benson brings out admirably that half of the character which criticism seems almost always to have taken pains to obscure—the capable and faithful artist in the same skin as the incapable and unfaithful King. With a quite choice and pointed infelicity, Professor Dowden has called Shakespeare's Richard II, "an amateur in living, not an artist"; Mr. Boas, generally one of the most suggestive of recent writers on Shakespeare, has called his grace of fancy "puerile" and its products "pseudo-poetic." The general judgment on the play reads as if the critics felt they would be "only encouraging" kings like the Richard of this play if they did not assure him throughout the ages that his poetry was sad stuff at the best. "It's no excuse," one seems to hear them say, and "Serve you right, you and your poetry." It is our critical way to fall thus upon the wicked or weak in books and leave him half-dead, after taking from him even the good side that he hath. Still it is well to see what Shakespeare meant us to, and we wonder whether any one who hears Mr. Benson in this part with an open mind can doubt that Shakespeare meant to draw in Richard not only a rake and muff on a throne and falling off it but, in the same person, an exquisite poet; to show with one hand how kingdoms are lost and with the other how the creative imagination goes about its work; to fill the same man with the attributes of a feckless wastrel in high place and with the quite distinct but not incompatible attributes of a typical, a consummate artist.

"But," it will be asked by persons justly tired of sloppy talk about art, "What *is* an artist; what, exactly, is it in a man that makes an artist of him?" Well, first a proneness in his mind to

# The Theatre

revel and bask in its own sense of fact; not in the use of fact—that is for the men of affairs, the Bolingbrokes; nor in the explanation of fact—that is for the men of science; but simply in his own quick and glowing apprehension of what is about him, of all that is done on the earth or goes on in the sky, of dying and being born, of the sun, clouds, and storms, of great deeds and failures, the changes of the seasons, and the strange events of men's lives. To mix with the day's diet of gifts and sounds the man of this type seems to bring a wine of his own that lights a fire in his blood while he takes the meal. What the finest minds of other types eschew he does, and takes pains to do. To shun the dry light, to drench all he sees with himself, his own temperament, the humours of his own moods—this is not his dread but his wish, as well as his bent. "The eye sees what the eye brings the means of seeing." "A fool sees not the same tree that a wise man sees." "You shall see the world in a grain of sand and heaven in a wild flower." This heightened and delighted personal sense of fact, a knack of seeing visions at the instance of seen things, is the basis of art.

Only the basis, though. For that art may come a man must add to it a veritable passion for arresting and defining in words or lines and colors or notes of music, not each or any thing that he sees, nor anybody else's sense of that thing, nor yet the greatest common measure of many trained or untrained minds' senses of it, but his own unique sense of it, the precise quality and degree of emotion that the spectacle of it breeds in him and nobody else, the net result of its contact with whatever in his own temperament he has not in common with other men. That is the truth of art, to be true less to facts without you than to yourself as stirred by facts. And truth it must be with a vengeance. To find a glove-fit of words for your sense of "the glory and the freshness of a dream," to model the very form and pressure of an inward vision to the millionth of a hair's breadth —the vocabulary of mensuration ludicrously fails to describe those infinitesimal niceties of adjustment between the inward feeling and the means of its presentment. And indeed it is only half true to speak as if feeling and its expression were separable at all. In a sense the former implies the latter. The simplest feeling is itself changed by issuing in a cry. Attaining a kind of completeness, given, as it were, its rights, it is not the same feeling after the cry that it was before. It has become not merely feeling interpreted by something outside it and separable from it, but fuller feeling, a feeling with more in it, feeling pushed one stage further in definiteness and intensity, an arch of feeling crowned at last. So, too, all artistic expression, if one thinks the matter out, is seen to be not merely a transcription of the artist's sense of fact but a perfecting of that sense itself; and the experience which never attains expression, the experience which is loosely said to be unexpressed, is really an unfinished, imperfect experience and one which, in the mind of an artist, passionately craves for its own completion through adequate expression. "There are no beautiful thoughts," a fastidious artist has said, "without beautiful forms." The perfect expression *is* the completed emotion. So the artist is incessantly preoccupied in leading his sense of fact up to the point at which it achieves not merely expression but its own completion in the one word, phrase, line, stanza that can make it, simply as a feeling of his own, all that it has in it to be. He may be said to write or paint because there is a point beyond which the joy of tasting the world about him cannot go unless he does so; and his life passes in a series of moments at which thought and expression, the sense of fact and the consummate presentation of that sense, rush together like Blake's "soul and body united," to be indistinguishably fused together in a whole in which, alone, each can attain its own perfection.

We have drawn out this tedious description of the typical artist because the further it goes the more close a description does it become of the Richard whom Mr. Benson shows us in the last three acts. In him every other feeling is mastered, except at a few passing moments, by a passion of interest in the exercise of his gift of exquisite responsiveness to the appeal made to his artistic sensibility by whatever life throws for the moment in his way. Lamb said it was worthwhile to have been cheated of the legacy so as not to miss "the idea of" the rogue who did it. That, on a little scale, is the kind of aesthetic disinterestedness which in Shakespeare's Richard, rightly presented by Mr. Benson, passes all bounds. The "idea of" a King's fall, the "idea of" a wife and husband torn apart, the "idea of" a very crucifixion of indignities—as each new idea comes he revels in his own warmed and lighted apprehension of it as freely as in his apprehension of the majesty and mystery of the idea of a kingship by divine right. He runs out to meet the thought of a lower fall or a new shame as a man might go to his door to see a sunset or a storm. It has been called the aim of artistic culture to witness things with appropriate emotions. That is this Richard's aim. Good news or bad news, the first thing with him is to put himself in the right vein for getting the fullest and most poignant sense of its contents. Is ruin the word—his mind runs to steep itself in relevant pathos with which in turn to saturate the object put before it; he will "talk of graves and epitaphs," "talk of wills," "tell sad stories of the death of kings." Once in the vein, he rejoices like a good artist who has caught the spirit of his subject. The very sense of the loss of hope becomes "that sweet way I was in to despair." To his wife at their last meeting he bequeaths, as one imaginative writer might bequeath to another some treasure of possibilities of tragic effect, "the lamentable tale of me." And to this intoxicating sense of the beauty or poignancy of what is next him he joins the true passion of concern for its perfect expression. At the height of that preoccupation enmities, fears, mortifications, the very presence of onlookers are as if they were not. At the climax of the agony of the abdication scene Shakespeare, with a magnificent boldness of truth, makes the artist's mind, in travail with the lovely poetical figure of the mirror, snatch at the possibility of help at the birth of the beautiful thing, even from the bitterest enemy,—

> say that again;
> The shadows of my sorrow; ha, let's see.

And nothing in Mr. Benson's performance was finer than the King's air, during the mirror soliloquy, as of a man going about his mind's engrossing business in a solitude of its own making. He gave their full value, again, to all those passages, so enigmatic, if not ludicrous, to strictly prosaic minds, in which Richard's craving for finished expression issues in a joining of words with figurative action to point and eke them out; as where he gives away the crown in the simile of the well, inviting his enemy, with the same artistic neutrality as in the passage of the mirror, to collaborate manually in an effort to give perfect expression to the situation. With Aumerle Richard is full of these little symbolic inventions, turning them over lovingly as a writer fondles a phrase that tells. "Would not this ill do well," he says of one of them, like a poet showing a threnody to a friend.

There was just one point—perhaps it was a mere slip—at which Mr. Benson seemed to us to fail. In the beginning of the scene at Pomfret what one may call the artistic heroism of this man, so craven in everything but art, reaches its climax. Ruined, weary, with death waiting in the next room, he is shown still toiling at the attainment of a perfect, because perfectly expressed, apprehension of such sad dregs as are left him of life, still following passionately on the old quest of the ideal world, the unique image, the one perfect way of saying the one thing.

> I cannot do it; yet I'll hammer it out.

Everybody knows that cry of the artist wrestling with the angel in the dark for the word it will not give, of Balzac "plying the pick for dear life, like an entombed miner," of our own Stevenson, of Flaubert "sick, irritated, the prey a thousand times a day of cruel pain" but "continuing my labor like a true working man, who, with sleeves turned up, in the sweat of his brow, beats away at his anvil, whether it rain or blow, hail or thunder." That "yet I'll hammer it out" is the gem of the whole passage, yet on Saturday Mr. Benson, by some strange mischance, left the words clean out. He made amends with a beautiful little piece of insight at the close, where, after the lines

> Mount, mount, my soul! Thy seat is up on high,
> Whilst my gross flesh sinks downward, here to die,

uttered much as any other man might utter them under the first shock of the imminence of death, he half rises from the ground with a brightened face and repeats the two last words with a sudden return of animation and interest, the eager spirit leaping up, with a last flicker before it goes quite out, to seize on this new "idea of" the death of the body. Greater love of art could no man have than this, and it was a brilliant thought of Mr. Benson's to end on such a note. But indeed the whole performance, but for the slip we have mentioned, was brilliant in its equal grasp of the two sides of the character, the one which everybody sees well enough and the one which nearly everybody seems to shun seeing, and in the value which it rendered to the almost continuous flow of genuine and magnificent poetry from Richard to the descant on morality in kings, for instance, and the exquisite greeting to English soil and the gorgeous rhetoric of the speeches on divine right in kings. Of Mr. Benson's achievements as an actor his Richard II strikes us as decidedly the most memorable.

## William Butler Yeats

# At Stratford-on-Avon (1901)

I

I have been hearing Shakespeare, as the traveller in *News from Nowhere* might have heard him, had he not been hurried back into our noisy time. One passes through quiet streets, where gabled and red-tiled houses remember the Middle Age, to a theatre that has been made not to make money, but for the pleasure of making it, like the market houses that set the traveller chuckling; nor does one find it among hurrying cabs and ringing pavements, but in a green garden by a river side. Inside I have to be content for a while with a chair, for I am unexpected, and there is not an empty seat but this; and yet there is no one who has come merely because one must go somewhere after dinner. All day, too, one does not hear or see an incongruous or noisy thing, but spends the hours reading the plays, and the wise and foolish things men have said of them, in the library of the theatre, with its oak-panelled walls and leaded windows of tinted glass; or one rows by reedy banks and by old farmhouses, and by old churches among great trees. It is certainly one's fault if one opens a newspaper, for Mr. Benson gives one a new play every night and one need talk of nothing but the play in the inn-parlor under the oak beams blackened by time and showing the mark of the adze that shaped them. I have seen this week *King John*, *Richard II*, the second part of *Henry IV*, *Henry V*, the second part of *Henry VI*, and *Richard III* played in their right order, with all the links that bind play to play unbroken; and partly because of a spirit in the place, and partly because of the way play supports play, the theatre has moved me as it has never done before. That strange procession of kings and queens, of warring nobles, of insurgent crowds, of courtiers, and of people of the gutter has been to me almost too visible, too audible, too full of an unearthly energy. I have felt as I have sometimes felt on grey days on the Galway shore, when a faint mist has hung over the grey sea and the grey stones, as if the world might suddenly vanish and leave nothing behind, not even a little dust under one's feet. The people my mind's eye has seen have too much of the extravagance of dreams, like all the inventions of art before our crowded life had brought moderation and compromise, to seem more than a dream, and yet all else has grown dim before them.

In London the first man one meets puts any high dream out of one's head, for he will talk to one of something at once vapid and exciting, some one of those many subjects of thought that build up our social unity. But here he gives back one's dream like a mirror. If we do not talk of the plays, we talk of the theatre, and how more people may be got to come, and our isolation from common things makes the future become grandiose and important. One man tells how the theatre and the library were at their foundation but part of a scheme the future is to fulfill. To them will be added a school where speech, and gesture, and fencing, and all else that an actor needs will be taught, and the council, which will have enlarged its Festivals to some six weeks, will engage all the chief players of Shakespeare, and perhaps of other great dramatists in this and other countries. These chief players will need to bring but few of their supporters, for the school will be able to fill all the lesser parts with players who are slowly recovering the lost tradition of musical speech. Another man is certain that the Festival, even without the school, which would require a new endowment, will grow in importance year by year, and that it may become with favoring chance the supreme dramatic event of the world; and when I suggest that it may help to break the evil prestige of London he becomes enthusiastic.

Surely a bitter hatred of London is becoming a mark of those that love the arts, and all that have this hatred should help anything that looks like a beginning of a center of art elsewhere. The easiness of travel, which is always growing, began by emptying the country, but it may end by filling it; for adventures like this of Stratford-on-Avon show that people are ready to journey from all parts of England and Scotland and Ireland, and even from America, to live with their favorite art as shut away from the world as though they were "in retreat," as Catholics say. Nobody but an impressionist painter, who hides it in light and mist, even pretends to love a street for its own sake; and could we meet our friends and hear music and poetry in the country, none of us that are not captive would ever leave the thrushes. In London, we hear something that we like some twice or thrice in a winter, and among people who are thinking the while of a music-hall singer or of a member of parliament, but there we would hear it and see it among people who liked it well enough to have travelled some few hours to find it; and because those who care for the arts have few near friendships among those that do not, we would hear and see it among near friends. We would escape, too, from those artificial tastes and interests we cultivate, that we may have something to talk about among people we meet for a few minutes and not again, and the arts would grow serious as the Ten Commandments.

## II

I do not think there is anything I disliked in Stratford, beside certain new houses, but the shape of the theatre; and as a larger theatre must be built sooner or later, that would be no great matter if one could put a wiser shape into somebody's head. I cannot think there is any excuse for a half-round theatre, where land is not expensive, or no very great audience to be seated within earshot of the stage; or that it was adopted for a better reason than because it has come down to us, though from a time when the art of the stage was a different art. The Elizabethan theatre was a half-round, because the players were content to speak their lines on a platform, as if they were speakers at a public meeting, and we go on building in the same shape, although our art of the stage is the art of making a succession of pictures. Were our theatres of the shape of a half-closed fan, like Wagner's theatre, where the audience sit on seats that rise towards the broad end while the play is played at the narrow end, their pictures could be composed for eyes at a small number of points of view, instead of for eyes at many points of view, above and below and at the sides, and what is no better than a trade might become an art. With the eyes watching from the sides of a half-round, on the floor and in the boxes and galleries, would go the solid-built houses and the flat trees that shake with every breath of air; and we could make our pictures with robes that contrasted with great masses of color in the back cloth and such severe or decorative forms of hills and trees and houses as would not overwhelm, as our naturalistic scenery does, the idealistic art of the poet, and all at a little price. Naturalistic scene-painting is not an art, but a trade, because it is, at best, an attempt to copy the more obvious effects of nature by the methods of the ordinary landscape-painter, and by his methods made coarse and summary. It is but flashy landscape-painting and lowers the taste it appeals to, for the taste it appeals to has been formed by a more delicate art. Decorative scene-painting would be, on the other hand, as inseparable from the movements as from the robes of the players and from the falling of the light; and being in itself a grave and quiet thing it would mingle with the tones of the voices and with the sentiment of the play, without overwhelming them under an alien interest. It would be a new and legitimate art appealing to a taste formed by itself and copying nothing but itself. Mr. Gordon Craig used scenery of this kind at the Purcell Society performance the other day, and despite some marring of his effects by the half-round shape of the theatre, it was the first beautiful scenery our stage has seen. He created an ideal country where everything was possible, even speaking in verse, or speaking in music, or the expression of the whole of life in a dance, and I would like to see Stratford-on-Avon decorate its Shakespeare with like scenery. As we cannot, it seems, go back to the platform and the curtain, and the argument for doing so is not without weight, we can only get rid of the sense of unreality, which most of us feel when we listen to the conventional speech of Shakespeare, by making scenery as conventional. Time after time his people use at some moment of deep emotion an elaborate or deliberate metaphor, or do some improbable thing which breaks an emotion of reality we have imposed upon him by an art that is not his, nor in the spirit of his. It also is an essential part of his method to give slight or obscure motives of many actions that our attention may dwell on what is of chief importance, and we set these cloudy actions among solid-looking houses, and what we hope are solid-looking trees, and illusion comes to an end, slain by our desire to increase it. In his art, as in all the older art of the world, there was much make-believe, and our scenery, too, should remember the time when, as my nurse used to tell me, herons built their nests in old men's beards! Mr. Benson did not venture to play the scene in *Richard III* where the ghosts walk, as Shakespeare wrote it, but had his scenery been as simple as Mr. Gordon Craig's purple back cloth that made Dido and Aeneas seem wandering on the edge of eternity, he would have found nothing absurd in pitching the tents of Richard and Richmond side by side. Goethe has said, "Art is art, because it is not nature!" It brings us near to the archetypal ideas themselves, and away from nature, which is but their looking-glass.

## III

In *La Peau de Chagrin* Balzac spends many pages in describing a coquette, who seems the image of heartlessness, and then invents an improbable incident that her chief victim may discover how beautifully she can sing. Nobody had ever heard her sing, and yet in her singing, and in her chatter with her maid, Balzac tells us, was her true self. He would have us understand that behind the momentary self, which acts and lives in the world, and is subject to the judgment of the world, there is that which cannot be called before any mortal Judgment seat, even though a great poet, or novelist, or philosopher be sitting upon it. Great literature has always been written in a like spirit, and is, indeed, the Forgiveness of Sin, and when we find it becoming the Accusation of Sin, as in George Eliot, who plucks her Tito in pieces with as much assurance as if he had been clockwork, literature has begun to change into something else. George Eliot had a fierceness one hardly finds but in a woman turned argumentative, but the habit of mind her fierceness gave its life to was characteristic of her century, and is the habit of mind of the Shakespearean critics. They and she grew up in a century of utilitarianism, when nothing about a man seemed important except his utility to the State, and nothing so useful to the State as the actions whose effect can be weighed by the reason. The deeds of Coriolanus, Hamlet, Timon, Richard II had no obvious use, were, indeed, no more than the expression of their personalities, and so it was thought Shakespeare was accusing them, and telling us to be careful lest we deserve the like accusations. It did not occur to the critics that you cannot know a man from his actions, because you cannot watch him in every kind of circumstance, and that men are made useless to the State as often by abundance as by emptiness, and that a man's business may at times be revelation, and not reformation. Fortinbras was, it is likely enough, a better King than Hamlet would have been, Aufidius was a more reasonable man than Coriolanus, Henry V was a better man-at-arms than Richard II, but after all, were not those others who changed nothing for the better and many things for the worse greater in the Divine Hierarchies? Blake has said that "the roaring of lions, the howling of wolves, the raging of the stormy sea, and the destructive sword are portions of Eternity, too great for the eye of man," but Blake belonged by right to the ages of Faith, and thought the State of less moment than the Divine Hierarchies. Because reason can only discover completely the use of those obvious actions which everybody admires, and because every character was to be judged by efficiency in action, Shakespearean criticism became a vulgar worshipper of Success. I have turned over many books in the library at Stratford-on-Avon, and I have found in nearly all an antithesis, which grew in clearness and violence as the century grew older, between two types, whose representatives were Richard II, "sentimental," "weak," "selfish," "insincere," and Henry V, "Shakespeare's only hero." These books took the same delight in abasing Richard II that schoolboys do in persecuting some boy of fine temperament, who has weak muscles and a distaste for school games. And they had the admiration for Henry V that school-boys have for the sailor or soldier hero of a romance in some boys' paper. I cannot claim any minute knowledge of these books, but I think that these emotions began among the German critics, who perhaps saw something French and Latin in Richard II, and I know that Professor Dowden, whose book I once read carefully, first made these emotions eloquent and plausible. He lived in Ireland, where everything has failed, and he meditated frequently upon the perfection of character which had, he thought, made England successful, for, as we say, "cows beyond the water have long horns." He forgot that England, as Gordon has said, was made by her adventurers, by her people of wildness and imagination and eccentricity; and thought that Henry V, who only seemed to be these things because he had some commonplace vices, was not only the typical Anglo-Saxon, but the model Shakespeare held up before England; and he even thought it worth while pointing out that Shakespeare himself was making a large fortune while he was writing about Henry's victories. In Professor Dowden's successors this apotheosis went further; and it reached its height at a moment of imperialistic enthusiasm, of ever-deepening conviction that the commonplace shall inherit the earth, when somebody of reputation, whose name I cannot remember, wrote that Shakespeare admired this one character alone out of all his characters. The Accusation of Sin produced its necessary fruit, hatred of all that was abundant, extravagant, exuberant, of all that sets a sail for shipwreck, and flattery of the commonplace emotions and conventional ideals of the mob, the chief Paymaster of accusation.

## IV

I cannot believe that Shakespeare looked on his Richard II with any but sympathetic eyes, understanding indeed how ill-fitted he was to be King, at a certain moment of history, but understanding that he was lovable and full of capricious fancy, "a wild creature" as Pater has called him. The man on whom Shakespeare modelled him had been full of French elegancies, as he knew from Hollingshead, and had given life a new luxury, a new splendor, and been "too friendly" to his friends, "too favorable" to his enemies. And certainly Shakespeare had these things in his head when he made his King fail, a little because he lacked some qualities that were doubtless common among his scullions, but more because he had certain qualities that are uncommon in all ages. To suppose that Shakespeare preferred the men who deposed his King is to suppose that Shakespeare judged men with the eyes of a Municipal Councillor weighing the merits of a Town Clerk; and that had he been by when Verlaine cried out from his bed, "Sir, you have been made by the stroke of a pen, but I have been made by the breath of God," he would have thought the Hospital Superintendent the better man. He saw indeed, as I think, in Richard II the defeat that awaits all, whether they be Artist or Saint, who find themselves where men ask of them a rough energy and have nothing to give but some contemplative virtue, whether lyrical phantasy, or sweetness of temper, or dreamy dignity, or love of God, or love of His creatures. He saw that such a man through sheer bewilderment and impatience can become as unjust or as violent as any common man, any Bolingbroke or Prince John, and yet remain "that sweet lovely rose." The courtly and saintly ideals of the Middle Ages were fading, and the practical ideals of the modern age had begun to threaten the unuseful dome of the sky; Merry England was fading, and yet it was not so faded that the Poets could not watch the procession of the world with that untroubled sympathy for men as they are, as apart from all they do and seem, which is the substance of tragic irony.

Shakespeare cared little for the State, the source of all our judgments, apart from its shows and splendors, its turmoils and battles, its flamings out of the uncivilized heart. He did indeed think it wrong to overturn a King, and thereby to swamp peace in civil war, and the historical plays from *Henry IV* to *Richard III*, that monstrous birth and last sign of the wrath of Heaven, are a fulfillment of the prophecy of the Bishop of Carlisle, who was "raised up by God" to make it; but he had no nice sense of utilities, no ready balance to measure deeds, like that fine instrument, with all the latest improvements, Gervinus and Professor Dowden handle so skillfully. He meditated as Solomon, not as Bentham meditated, upon blind ambitions, untoward accidents, and capricious passions, and the world was almost as empty in his eyes as it must be in the eyes of God.

> Tired with all these, for restful death I cry;—
>   As, to behold desert a beggar born,
> And needy nothing trimm'd in jollity,
>   And purest faith unhappily forsworn,
> And gilded honour shamefully misplaced,
>   And maiden virtue rudely strumpeted,
> And right perfection wrongfully disgrac'd,
>   And strength by limping sway disabled,
> And Art made tongue-tied by authority,
>   And folly, doctor-like, controlling skill,
> And simple truth miscalled simplicity,
>   And captive good attending captain ill:
> Tired with all these, from these would I begone
> Save that, to die, I leave my love alone.

# V

The Greeks, a certain scholar has told me, considered that myths are the activities of the Daemons, and that the Daemons shape our characters and our lives. I have often had the fancy that there is some one Myth for every man, which, if we but knew it, would make us understand all he did and thought. Shakespeare's Myth, it may be, describes a wise man who was blind from very wisdom, and an empty man who thrust him from his place, and saw all that could be seen from very emptiness. It is in the story of Hamlet, who saw too great issues everywhere to play the trivial game of life, and of Fortinbras, who came from fighting battles about "a little patch of ground" so poor that one of his Captains would not give "six ducats" to "farm it," and who was yet acclaimed by Hamlet and by all as the only befitting King. And it is in the story of Richard II, that unripened Hamlet, and of Henry V, that ripened Fortinbras. To poise character against character was an element in Shakespeare's art, and scarcely a play is lacking in characters that are the complement of one another, and so, having made the vessel of porcelain Richard II, he had to make the vessel of clay Henry V. He makes him the reverse of all that Richard was. He has the gross vices, the coarse nerves, of one who is to rule among violent people, and he is so little "too friendly" to his friends that he bundles them out of doors when their time is over. He is as remorseless and undistinguished as some natural force, and the finest thing in his play is the way his old companions fall out of it broken-hearted or on their way to the gallows; and instead of that lyricism which rose out of Richard's mind like the jet of a fountain to fall again where it had risen, instead of that phantasy too enfolded in its own sincerity to make any thought the hour had need of, Shakespeare has given him a resounding rhetoric that moves men, as a leading article does to-day. His purposes are so intelligible to everybody that everybody talks of him as if he succeeded, although he fails in the end, as all men great and little fail in Shakespeare, and yet his conquests abroad are made nothing by a woman turned warrior, and that boy he and Katherine were to "compound," "half French, half English," "that" was to "go to Constantinople and take the Turk by the beard," turns out a Saint, and loses all his father had built up at home and his own life.

Shakespeare watched Henry V not indeed as he watched the greater souls in the visionary procession, but cheerfully, as one watches some handsome spirited horse, and he spoke his tale, as he spoke all tales, with tragic irony.

## VI

The five plays, that are but one play, have, when played one after another, something extravagant and superhuman, something almost mythological. Those nobles with their indifference to death and their immense energy seem at times no nearer the common stature of men than do the Gods and the heroes of Greek plays. Had there been no Renaissance and no Italian influence to bring in the stories of other lands English history would, it may be, have become as important to the English imagination as the Greek Myths to the Greek imagination; and many plays by many poets would have woven it into a single story whose contours, vast as those of Greek myth, would have made living men and women seem like swallows building their nests under the architrave of some Temple of the Giants. English literature, because it would have grown out of itself, might have had the simplicity and unity of Greek literature, for I can never get out of my head that no man, even though he be Shakespeare, can write perfectly when his web is woven to threads that have been spun in many lands. And yet, could those foreign tales have come in if the great famine, the sinking down of popular imagination, the dying out of traditional phantasy, the ebbing out of the energy of race, had not made them necessary? The metaphors and language of Euphuism, compounded of the natural history and mythology of the classics, were doubtless a necessity also, that something might be poured into the emptiness. Yet how they injured the simplicity and unity of the speech! Shakespeare wrote at a time when solitary great men were gathering to themselves the fire that had once flowed hither and thither among all men, when individualism in work and thought and emotion was breaking up the old rhythms of life, when the common people, no longer uplifted by the myths of Christianity and of still older faiths, were sinking into the earth.

The people of Stratford-on-Avon have remembered little about him, and invented no legend to his glory. They have remembered a drinking-bout of his, and invented some bad verses for him, and that is about all. Had he been some hard-drinking, hard-living, hard-riding, loud-blaspheming Squire they would have enlarged his fame by a legend of his dealings with the devil; but in his day the glory of a Poet, like that of all other imaginative powers, had ceased, or almost ceased outside a narrow class. The poor Gaelic rhymer leaves a nobler memory among his neighbors, who will talk of Angels standing like flames about his death-bed, and of voices speaking out of bramble-bushes that he may have the wisdom of the world. The Puritanism that drove the theatres into Surrey was but part of an inexplicable movement that was trampling out the minds of all but some few thousands born to cultivated ease.

# T.C. Worsley

## Shakespeare's Histories at Stratford, 1951 (1952)

When we conceive of *Richard II* as the prologue to the cycle we have to adjust our feelings about it radically. It becomes less the tragedy of Richard himself and more the Rise of Bolingbroke. Politically it represents the struggle between a new and an old conception of Kingship, and this struggle is dramatized in a personal struggle between Bolingbroke and Richard. The drama is only strengthened by the fact that the upholder of the old conception is weak and the upholder of the new strong.

The importance of the first two acts is very great in setting the scene, placing the factions and rivalries and displaying the currents of opinions that are dividing hearts and loyalties. Some of these differences are pointed at the very opening in distinctions of dress and of bearing. The play opens in the king's palace where a council of state has been summoned. The first to enter are the nobles who talk among themselves, until the king and his entourage come in. The king takes up the orb and sceptre, and mounts the spot-lighted throne with his followers grouped around him. The elegance of the royal party now calls attention to the fact that the nobles, by contrast, are plain men, plainly dressed in russets and dull reds and green: dressed plainly, but not meanly. It is, in fact, the kind of plainness of which plain men are proud. While the epicene king and his followers are dandies, dressed in pastel pinks, light blues and golds. They parade their jewelry; they are frenchified. The plain men's plainness may easily be imagined to be a kind of unspoken protest against this frippery.

The king speaks in an affected mince. Gaunt, whom he first calls out, answers him in an unaffected regional accent. Accidents of casting will not allow the regional accent to be accurate: and Gaunt's Welsh may at first strike strangely on the ear. But it soon ceases to, and the point—a very good one—remains (it is to be underlined later): the speech of the nobles in their different local pronunciations reminds us that at this time they lived away in their own provinces retaining the manners and customs and individuality of their own localities. They come to London, most of them, only when they are summoned on affairs of State, as they are now in this matter of the quarrel between Mowbray and young Bolingbroke. These two, as they now take the center of the stage, particularize a little further these generalizations. Thomas Mowbray is a soldier, not a courtier, simple, sincere, direct and plain. But Bolingbroke—and we may have noticed the same of Gaunt—being of the blood royal, is less plain than the plain men, though not gaudy like the king's followers. He is of the court, but not of *this* court. Spiritually he belongs with the plain men—is a young man of the old virtues. He has their nobility without their plainness; and out of it he despises the king.

For already in the first scenes the nature of the personal antagonism between these two is foreshadowed. It is lightly stressed in Bolingbroke's first words to the king:

> Many years of happy days befall
> My gracious sovereign, my most loving liege.

There is an easily discernible irony in the emphasis Mr. Harry Andrews puts on that "most loving." And this irony Richard returns later in giving Mowbray leave to speak:

> Were he my brother, nay, my kingdom's heir,
> As he is but my father's brother's son,

the last line pointed directly at Bolingbroke. Our sympathy in these early scenes can hardly but be with the noble virile figure Mr. Harry Andrews presents as the young Bolingbroke. There is, it is true, a touch of arrogance, but it is youthful arrogance, justifiable in view of the treatment he receives from the king. This treatment is worse than unjust, it is frivolous. For while Mowbray and Bolingbroke are opposed in a quarrel that concerns not only their honor but their very lives, Richard would, if he could, smile the whole thing away:

> Forget, forgive, conclude and be agreed:
> Our doctors say this is no month to bleed.

And the entourage sycophantically laugh at these inadequate little pleasantries.

Yet behind the personal struggle there is, equally important, a political struggle on foot. The principle of Kingship as a sacred inalienable function is what Richard stands upon. "Lions make leopards tame." It is the divine right that makes Richard a lion and he remains a lion by virtue of that even if he proves in his own person a feeble one. It is the principle itself that is now to be attacked and, by the end of the play, overthrown. Here at the beginning this principle is not even challenged from the outside, though it is threatened from within. A lion, to remain a lion, must act the lion. It is no good merely to roar:

> We were not born to sue but to command.

if the moment after you admit:

> Which since we cannot do. . . .

The principle, in fact, is to be betrayed through the weakness of its chief officer, and it is this which is to make the drama. Yet, still at this time there is enough common goodwill behind that principle for it to have been maintained if Richard had been strong. In the little scene which follows this, the old Duchess of Gloucester is rebuked—when she cries out for individual vengeance against Richard—by Gaunt who has as much reason as she to fight the king on personal grounds, but who stands for the old values:

> God's is the quarrel: for God's substitute,
> His deputy anointed in His sight,
> Hath caused his death: the which if wrongfully
> Let heaven revenge: for I may never lift
> An angry arm against His minister.

The king is God's substitute, His minister; his orders and acts have the authority of the divine. To oppose him is to oppose God.

The sacred principle is not directly challenged until Bolingbroke's return from exile. In the scene at the lists—when the fight is stopped by the king throwing down his warder and the king descends and pronounces sentence—his authority is still not questioned. Bolingbroke accepts his sentence with the same contemptuous irony he has displayed earlier. For at least the lion has acted, has asserted his lionship, and no one as yet directly questions his authority. Even Mowbray feels that the struggle is on a purely personal level—as in one aspect it is—and his prophecy when he throws back Bolingbroke's last accusation in his face, lingers in the mind long later:

> But what thou art, God, thou and I do know;
> And all too soon, I fear, the king shall rue.

The issue is forced by the king's recklessly flippant behavior over John of Gaunt's death. Gaunt on his deathbed felt justified in attacking the king with a violence that he never dared use before. But it is the king's behavior that he attacks: not his kingship. That the old order cannot question. Gaunt's brother, York, now at Gaunt's death the last surviving of the Black Prince's sons, is left to carry this principle on shoulders all too weak to support it. Richard's immediate seizure of Gaunt's property at the moment of the announcement of his death is almost more than he can bear. He takes the trimmer's course, "I'll not be by the while"; but he can't escape his responsibility by turning his head away, and with a fine stroke of ironic humor Richard fixes it more firmly on him by creating him Lord Governor during his absence in Ireland.

All this time standing by, solid, immovable, expressionless, has been the most representative imaginable of the plain men from the distant provinces, Northumberland. He has said almost nothing. He has watched the tantrums of the childish king with all the plain man's scorn for the neurotic. He has not intervened. But he *has* decided. The middle generation of the older order has made up its mind in him. The principle of Divine Right is no longer sovereign. This king, this representative of it, has made it impossible. When the king and his followers go out, the plotting begins.

Such, in outline, was the impression which the production of these first two acts conveyed to us. A number of slight shifts of emphasis brought them forward as the introduction not just to this play but to the whole cycle. Notably, the principle at stake was always underlined so that it made a clear impact unobscured by the personalities in the foreground. The pageantry of the court was particularly dignified and solemn to reinforce upon us that the king as person is only incidental to the king as function. The one direct personal clash, that between the king and Gaunt, —beautifully produced to a mounting climax—remained lucidly a *personal* clash. The majesty of the king as king, and the respect paid to his sovereignty, were carefully emphasized, however wilfully and childishly Richard himself behaved. This childishness of the king—his tears of temper and his bored impatience with York's reminiscences of the Black Prince—was played up unsparingly by Mr. Redgrave; and its alternation with moments of regal dignity and command suggested exactly the right combination of instability and regality to contrast with the even dignity of Mr. Andrews' youthful Bolingbroke. A few touches of production for him—like the solemn lengthening of his exit line:

> Where'er I wander, boast of this I can,
> Though banished, yet a true born Englishman

—establish him firmly in our sympathy and prepare us for his taking a central position from now on.

For in the grand sweep it is Bolingbroke who is the main character, not Richard; and we must be persuaded to watch him no less intently for the rest of this play than we watch Richard himself. How Bolingbroke rises to his situation is as important as how Richard falls to his. So it is Bolingbroke who opens the second part, a Bolingbroke who we notice at once has grown, physically and spiritually, in the years of exile. There is a greater weight about him now. The chin has put on a beard and the youthful arrogance has become dignity. Foremost among his followers is that same proud Northumberland. He is a little less plain now than he was before. He has learned to flatter his new master, though he doesn't do it very well. Or is there now a slight irony in *his* tone, foreshadowing the change in him? From the political point of view this scene where Bolingbroke finds Richard with only a handful of followers in Flint castle is the center of the play. It is here that the cause is lost, the old principle of kingship destroyed by the vacillation of its last champion. And the production, rightly for its purpose, plays the scene with exaggerated weight and deliberation. For at the outset it seems as if the principle can be maintained if only Richard will believe in it himself. But the disasters that have befallen him one after the other seem to have unmanned him and by now this principle is only a kind of literary fancy with which to bemuse himself:

> Not all the water in the rough rude sea
> Can wash the balm from an anointed king . . .
> God for his Richard hath in heavenly pay
> A glorious angel. . . .

The phrases are fine but (Mr. Redgrave manages to convey in his style of delivering them) the power has leaked out of them. He uses them as conjurations:

> I had forget myself: am I not king?
> Awake thou coward majesty. . . .

and they conjure nothing but disaster. If they still really meant anything to him, they might still work. For this meeting between Bolingbroke and the king is the final test of their validity. The issue is still theoretically open. Bolingbroke and his followers still claim that they come only for their due. The imperturbable Northumberland, it is true, regards the whole thing with a certain contempt, as play acting. When he goes forward to bear the king a greeting from Bolingbroke and is chidden by Richard for not kneeling to the sacred majesty, he doesn't drop to his knee, he just stands there insolently, immovably, and lets the gush of words flow past him. Not so, though, Bolingbroke. By another fine stroke of production he, when Richard descends, tells his followers to show all due respect to the king, and he himself performs a wonderfully elaborate triple obeisance in front of the man who still must be regarded as his liege lord. And the exchange that follows between them is made to carry an enormous weight as if it were two or three times longer than the single page of text which is all it really is.

> *Bol.*: My gracious Lord I come but for my own.
> *K. Rich.*: Your own is yours, and I am yours and all.
> *Bol.*: So far be mine, my most redoubted Lord
>   As my true service shall deserve your love.
> *K. Rich.*: Well you deserve: they well deserve to have
>   That know the strong'st and surest way to get. . . .
>   What you will have, I'll give and willing too
>   For do we must what force will have us do.

The change in Bolingbroke is now pronounced. The arrogance has gone and the contempt with it. He is almost gentle with the king. The irony is now all on Richard's side—an irony, Mr. Redgrave makes us feel, that springs from self-pity. But the great impression of this scene is that we are made to feel that Richard might still up to the last words gain something out of the wreck, if he had any longer the will. It is that he lacks. He puts his own defeat into Bolingbroke's mouth:

> *K. Rich.*: Set on towards London, cousin, is it so?
> *Bol.*: Yea, my good Lord.
> *K. Rich.*: Then I must not say no.

That scene is the turning point. Bolingbroke has now seized power: and from now on through the rest of this play and into the two parts of *Henry IV* we shall watch him reaping the results of his breaking of the ancient principle, to which process, in the longer view, the deposition and murder of Richard is only incidental. Crime, accusation and counter-accusation, plot and counter-plot. The play began with this and Bolingbroke's reign is to begin with it. Bolingbroke ascends the throne as Henry IV, but even as he does so he knows that he steps into a louring world of enmity:

> Little are we beholding to your love,
> And little looked for at your helping hands.

If the deposition scene belongs largely and rightly to Richard, all the same Bolingbroke is never allowed to sink back into unimportance. So decidedly and impressively has he been built up for us that we are conscious throughout Richard's eloquent dramatics of Bolingbroke *growing* there on the throne, as, without speaking, his eyes follow the deposed king's every action. The other central character, Northumberland, has also grown meanwhile; but where Bolingbroke grows in nobility and stature, Northumberland grows only in arrogance, as if power were almost visibly rising to his head. The mastery with which these two characters have been built up for us is indicated by the force with which the respective adjectives Richard applies to them strike us when they come. "Mark, *silent* king," he says to Bolingbroke. "No lord of thine, thou *haught insulting* man," he cries at Northumberland. And in each case—it is the result of careful preparation of course, as if these epithets had been taken from the first as key phrases and scene by scene been built up to—the description comes as a kind of confirmatory seal on what we have been feeling about them.

This is only another way of saying that for the special purposes of this production Northumberland and especially Bolingbroke—subsidiary roles, ordinarily speaking—have to be kept, and are kept, in the center of the picture. The emphasis cannot be allowed to come down too heavily on Richard, for he here makes his last appearance while the others go on. This is the main difference between a production of the cycle and a production of the play by itself. And here the success with which the producer achieved this shift of emphasis is demonstrated by the fact that he did it in spite of a drastic cut which worked against his idea. The whole of the sub-plot describing Aumerle's treachery and his arrival at his father's house, York's discovery of the plot and the scene where he with his Duchess and Aumerle plead with Bolingbroke—this scene, which would have helped to reinforce the weight on Bolingbroke, was sacrificed. The result might easily have been to tip the balance dangerously at the end toward the interior drama of the play, with Richard's long prison scene coming so close after deposition. But in fact this did not happen. Careful production, together with the very great weight and dignity which Mr. Andrews put into Bolingbroke, established him sufficiently for his final rejection of Piers Exton, short though it is, to make a full effect and to leave Bolingbroke at the end of the play a lonely and noble figure in the forefront of our minds. . . .

## Harley Granville-Barker

# Letter to John Gielgud (Oct. 15, 1937)

... But I'll now tumble out my impressions of *Richard II* for you, and if you pick anything useful out of them for a future time, good. Remember, though, that I haven't looked at the play's print for a fairly long time and my memory is a sieve.

I applauded you at first sight for so unselfishly hiding yourself in a corner. But I fear you were wrong to do so. I fancy W.S. thought of the scene as a meeting of the Privy Council—Richard presiding (the P.C. and the Star Chamber, the King absent, were the courts of the day for State affairs) probably raised on a dais at the end or centre of the table, formally presiding. And after letting the discussion rip—and actually, I dare say, playing cup-and-ball or reading Froissart or the *New Yorker* during the dull parts. But the point is that while W.S. doesn't begin to *write Richard* till he comes back from Ireland (till he becomes himself, a *man* and not merely a King), he does keep one guessing and wondering what sort of a man he is up to that point, and what the devil he will do next, and the more we see of his cryptic face the better. You got that admirably during the Lists scene—as good a piece of Shakespeare staging as I can remember. But I'd like it done from the beginning. Richard, of course, carries too much sail for his keel and so swings violently from side to side at any puff of wind. But his stillness and silence in between—which W.S. intended, I think, though he had not yet discovered how to make such things positively effective (as Othello's silences are)—show us the poet who is not really living in this practical world at all, but in one of his own imagination.

All the "plastique" of this part of the production and the blending of the scene (but not a word of the D. of Gloucester could I hear. I fancy she was getting her emphasis all wrong) all that scenic invention excellent. Gaunt's death scene particularly, and the colloquy afterwards (though damn all that crossing and genuflection and *Dies Irae*) first-rate.

. . . I understand you not stressing the sexual-pervert part of Bushy-Bagot-Green—though of course the suggestion is there: but very delicately done by Shakespeare, an *ex post facto* one, only brought in at their dying moment, cf. Gaveston in *Edward II* by a man who wasn't a sensitive dramatist—but I think they might be more gorgeously dressed than the others, to show that they are the caterpillars of the Commonwealth, whereas Bolingbroke and Mowbray and Aumerle should be "rich not gaudy." But why is the poor D. of Y. (who is by the way rather a Polonius—a first study for him?—your man lacks distinction) so shabby?

But my chief grouse is about the verse. It is a lyrical play. W.S. has not yet learned to express anything except in speech. There is nothing much, I mean, in between the lines, as there is in *Macbeth* (for an extreme example). Therefore—I am preaching; forgive me—everything the actor does must be done *within the frame* of the verse. Whatever impression of action or thought he can get within this frame without disturbance of *cadence* or *flow*, he may. But there must be nothing, no trick, no check, beyond an honest pause or so at the end of a sentence or speech. And I believe you'll seldom find that the cadence and emphasis—the mere right scansion of the verse does not give you the meaning without much of any further effort on the actor's part. The *pace* you may vary all you like. Clarity there must be, of course. But here, it is really the breaking of the rhythm which destroys it, for, as I said, Shakespeare has written one tune and his words are playing that in the treble (say); if one tries to play another tune with them in the bass—naturally we can't understand the thing.

Variety of pace—tone—colour of speech; yes, as much as possible, but within the *frame*. You must not turn W.S.'s quavers into crotchets or semibreves—or semiquavers for that matter. And I think each character ought to have his own speech. I thought during the first half of the play they were imitating each other; then I found they were imitating *you* and your taste for sadder *sforzandi*; good enough for Richard and clearly indicated for "Down—down I come—" and "No lord of thine, thou haught insulting man—" appropriate to him but quite wrong for Augustus Caesar-Bolingbroke or Mowbray or the "Tenor" gallantry of Aumerle.

The thing got—I began to swear—more and more hung up as it went on, and you began to play more and more astride the verse instead of in it. The scenic invention of the deposition scene was again admirable. B. on the throne, you wandering about below like a lost creature—admirable (but oh, if you'd have let the marvellous and sweet music of that verse just *carry you along with it*). The *tune* of that "bucket and well" bit (again the business admirable) and even more of the "No deeper wrinkles yet . . ." It is like an *andante* of Mozart. Shakespeare has done it for you. Why not let him?

Yes, scenic invention here again admirable, but I fancy that this is meant to be a scenic repetition of the opening, with B. taking his place on the very throne on which we saw Richard sitting then.

*And* your holding up the whole play (progressively so) obliged you to cut the Aumerle conspiracy, the dramatic point of which is merely that it is a swift and excited interlude between the *slow* (this good again, I thought) farewell between Richard and the Queen and the slow, philosophical death scene. "I have been wondering how I may compare . . . etc.," the pace of which is changed by the arrival of the groom and goes to the rapidity of the death—but that ought to be a hell of a fight. Note that for all the action suggested in the play there has been no single stroke of violence till then. It has all been done by politics—B. finessing the old D. of G. and taking you without a struggle, to when at the end that politician gets his dirty work *done* for him—it should be very dirty.

Then he comes in—the hypocrite—and condemns Exton. He feels in a sense what he says. But this is why the B.'s of this world are successful; they can feel that way.

# John Gielgud

## Stage Directions (1963)

*Richard the Second* is a ceremonial play. In spite of its long list of characters only a few are of the first importance, and most of these are very broadly treated, especially in the early scenes. The young King himself, though his personal beauty and the subservient manner in which he is treated, as he sits idly on his throne, must draw all eyes to him immediately, is only lightly sketched at first in a few rather enigmatic strokes. It is not until after his return from Ireland, almost halfway through the play, that his inner character begins to be developed in a series of exquisite cadenzas and variations. In these later scenes, the subtleties of his speeches are capable of endless shades and nuances, but (as is nearly always the case in Shakespeare) the actor's vocal efforts must be contrived within the framework of the verse, and not outside it. Too many pauses and striking variations of tempo will tend to hold up the action disastrously and so ruin the pattern and symmetry of the text.

The actor of Richard cannot hope at any time during the action to be wholly sympathetic to the audience. Indeed he must use the early scenes to create an impression of slyness, petty vanity, and callous indifference. But he must also show himself to be innately well-bred, sensitive to beauty (as *he* understands it, though he cannot himself see the beauty of the dying Gaunt), lonely in his remote position of Kingship, young, headstrong, frivolous, and entirely out of sympathy with the older men who try so vainly to advise him and control his whims.

In the later scenes, however, the lovely lines he has to speak can hardly fail to win a certain sympathy for him, and he gradually becomes more understandable and so more pitiable.

But owing to his utter lack of humor and his constant egotism and self-posturing, there is always a risk that he may become tedious and irritating to the audience unless the finer shades of his character are very subtly portrayed.

It is essential for an actor playing Richard to find the exact line of his disintegration. First, by grading the successive scenes as they follow one another, with their shifting changes of mood expressed in a continually minor key, and then by developing the detail and constructive pattern of the speeches as they become more elaborate and involved.

Richard is one of the rare parts in which the actor may indulge himself, luxuriating in the language he has to speak, and attitudinizing in consciously graceful poses. Yet the man must seem, too, to be ever physically on his guard, shielding himself, both in words and movement, from the dreaded impact of the unknown circumstances which, he feels, are always lying in wait to strike him down. He is torn between the intrinsic weakness of his nature and the pride and fastidiousness of his quality and breeding. He strives continually to retain his kingly dignity, to gain time by holding it up to the light before his enemies (as he will actually hold up the mirror later on in the deposition scene), while he prepares inwardly to face the shock of the next humiliation. Finally, cast out into the empty darkness of his prison, he is forced to realize at last that neither his personal beauty nor the divine right of kingship can save him from inevitable horror, as he is forced to contemplate his private doom.

Thus the actor has a dual responsibility. He must present the external action as the King suffers his defeats—the news of his favorites' deaths, the surrender to Bolingbroke at Flint, the defiant shame of the deposition scene and the agonies of farewell to his Queen. Yet he must somehow contrive at the same time to execute the poetic intricacies of the text with a full appreciation of its musical intention, using a completely lucid (and possibly stylized) method of vocal and plastic interpretation. The speaking of blank verse can only be projected, so as to hold an audience, by artificial and technical means—tone, emphasis and modulation. The task may seem an impossibly difficult one—to play, as it were, in two different styles at once, just as a singer has to do in opera. But this is actually a question of technique. A good actor experiences emotion at rehearsal—or imagines the experience of it vividly, which is not quite the same thing—and then selects, through trial and error, what he wishes to convey at each given moment of his performance. So he has always a double task—that of living in his role and at the same time judging his own effects in relation to his fellow players and the audience, so as to present an apparently spontaneous, living being, in a pattern carefully devised beforehand, but capable of infinite shades of color and tempo, and bound to vary slightly at every performance. The actor is, after all, a kind of conjuror, and in a part like Richard he will find infinite opportunities to put his skill into practice, playing, as Richard himself plays, on the feelings of an audience until they are at one with the complicated nature of the character; then, even when they cannot condone his actions or sympathize with his misfortunes, they come at length to understand his intricate nature and can share in his unique experience.

Whether the scenes of the Aumerle conspiracy in the fourth act should be retained or omitted in the theatre is a difficult question to decide. Many people think that they are not by Shakespeare, and that they may have been cobbled together by another hand to pad out the necessary playing time, when the deposition scene, owing to its dangerous political implications, was omitted in Elizabeth's day. Certainly the rhyming couplets in these scenes have a strong flavor of fustian melodrama, and many of the lines can seem ridiculous unless they are delivered with consummate power and tact. Also they make the play considerably longer. On the other hand they are of value to vary the somewhat monotonous tone and style of the main part of the text, and they serve to make a break in style, dividing the two great scenes of Richard's grief (the deposition scene and the farewell to the Queen) from his final soliloquy and fight to death in the prison. These episodes gain considerably in their effect if the King has been absent from the stage for two scenes beforehand. Also, of course, the Aumerle scenes contain the celebrated passage between York and his Duchess, describing Richard's entry into London in the power of Bolingbroke, and the first references to the wildness of Prince Hal.

The opening scene of the play, though dramatically effective in reading, always presents considerable difficulties for a modern audience. The implications of the King's complicity in the murder of Gloucester (which has taken place before the action begins) are not easy to understand. Most of us are less familiar with history than the Elizabethans, who seem to have had a curiously detailed knowledge of the intricate topical events of the times chronicled by Holinshed and so faithfully followed in the Histories of Shakespeare. The opening quarrel between Mowbray and Bolingbroke is repeated with greater elaboration and formality in the tournament scene at Coventry, with only the short duologue between the Duchess of Gloucester and Gaunt to separate them. This intermediate scene also refers back almost exclusively to the murder of Gloucester, and it is difficult to make it interesting, since the Duchess appears without any introduction and is to have no further part in the action, though the account of her death some scenes later makes an effective moment for old York. In all this early part of the play the action is formalized and lacking in progression. The King's motives seem to be deliberately understated, while the characters of his Queen and various lords and favorites are very baldly indicated. Ceremony and fine speaking must combine to hold the interest of the audience. The vocal effects must be carefully orchestrated: Mowbray's fine tenor speeches, Bolingbroke's strong blustering tones, and the deep bass warning voice of Gaunt.

Unfortunately, throughout the tragedy, the verse seems to be too evenly distributed, and often with more music than sense of character. Everyone speaks in images, parentheses, and elaborate similes, whether gardeners, exquisites, or tough realistic nobles, and though this richness of metaphor gives, in reading, a beautiful, tapestried, somewhat Gothic effect (like an illuminated missal or a Book of Hours), the continually artificial style tends to become somewhat indigestible on the stage, and stands between the audience and their desire to get on more intimate terms with the characters and situations. It is therefore especially important to have actors for the chief parts who are strongly contrasted individual types as well as skilled speakers of verse.

The more simply the characters are played on broad, conventional (but not too melodramatic) lines, the scenes appearing to flow smoothly and swiftly with the correct stress and phrasing, but without too much elaboration, either of action, grouping, or pauses, the better will the beauty of the general pattern emerge and the interest of the audience be sustained. The actor of Richard may then be allowed, like the solo violin in a concerto, to take certain liberties with his cadenzas, developing their intricacies legitimately in an almost unlimited variety of pace and detail, in contrast to the more plodding ground bass of Bolingbroke, Northumberland and the other nobles.

Many of the shorter scenes in the play can produce an exquisite effect; especially the famous episode of the Queen with the gardeners at Langley, for example, and the little duologue between the Welsh captain and Salisbury (which has something of the same sensitive yet sinister effect as the little scene in *Macbeth* in which the murderers wait for Banquo on the lonely heath). These passages should have a romantic, simple expressiveness in contrast to the formality of the great scenes which precede and follow them.

There are several difficult links in the action. The scene between Ross, Willoughby and Northumberland after Gaunt's death, and the passage when the three favorites part for the last time on hearing of Bolingbroke's return, seem almost like choral exercises for three voices, and should, perhaps, be directed mainly from this point of view. The quarrel of the peers, before the entrance of Richard in the deposition scene, is difficult to stage without a dangerous risk of seeming ridiculous (the throwing down and picking up of gloves and so on), and it is advisable to make some discreet cuts to avoid bathos both here and in the Aumerle conspiracy scenes, if they are included. The character of York, used by Shakespeare as a kind of wavering chorus throughout the play, touching yet sometimes absurd, can be of great value, provided that the actor and director can contrive between them a tactful compromise between comedy and dramatic effect. To make him a purely farcical character (as has sometimes been attempted) weakens the play, and is quite opposed, it seems to me, to the intention of the dramatist. The women in the cast are very lightly drawn, and they are difficult parts for actresses to clothe with flesh and blood, though vocally and pictorially they can make a considerable effect—the two Duchesses old and proud, the little Queen so young and helpless—in the somewhat conventional episodes allotted to them.

Most of the characters, except Gaunt, York, Carlisle and the two Duchesses, seem to be young and full of life, and there should be something of the same impetuous brilliance that is so wonderfully vivid in *Romeo and Juliet* in the way they glitter and struggle and hurl themselves toward their fates. *Richard the Second* is a play, above all, which must in performance be finely orchestrated, melodious, youthful, headlong, violent and vivid. It must not be heavy or dragging, and the actors must know where they are going in their long speeches. Every effort must be made to contrast scene against scene. At first we must be made aware of the lightness of Richard's character, his fatal, obstinate frivolity, unchecked by the baleful warnings and implacable nobility of Gaunt. Then, as we reach the heart of the play, and the King's own heart and soul are gradually revealed to us by Shakespeare, we must see him forced, by the realization of his favorites' deaths and the desertion of his countrymen, reluctantly beginning to abandon his contemplative poetic fantasies, to face the brutal reality of Northumberland's hostility and the grim determination of the ruthless Bolingbroke.

The great problem, as in all Shakespearean plays, is to achieve a straightforward musical rendering of the verse, and yet to combine this with a sense of exciting actuality in the action. The events of the play must really seem to happen, and yet, as in an opera, the music of the lines must be neither slurred, dragged nor unduly hurried. In short, the technical brilliance of the poetic writing must be correctly balanced and simply executed, with the added color of character and personality, while at the same time the shock of the actual events presented must appear to be spontaneous and realistically convincing. The poetry must be welded imperceptibly into the dramatic action to a point where the audience will accept the two together—and, if successfully managed, the two styles should support one another to create a complete harmony of effect.

## John Russell Brown

## Shakespeare's Plays in Performance (1966)

So far I have considered the actor's contribution to performance, but relationships between performances, shifts of interest from one character to another, the effects of movement and changing modes of illusion have already drawn our attention. Now the stage-picture must come to the forefront. As a play is performed, a dramatist is controlling the audience's view of its action, now towards a single character, now a group, now a dead body, or an empty throne, or nothing.

An audience is aware of the physical objects displayed before it, as well as the words it hears. Shape, size, color; contrasts, numbers, distance; movement, organization and lack of organization are all influencing the audience's response. There are moments when a number of figures seem to stand within a realistic perspective in calculated relationship to each other, and moments when they form a two-dimensional frieze (no figure more important than another), or when a small eccentric detail dominates the whole, or when an empty space is more impressive than the rest of a crowded stage. We need to speak of the changing picture on the stage as of a composition, as we might speak of the formal characteristics of a painting. This deployment is part of the performed play and strongly affects what it does to an audience; it is part of the theatrical language which Shakespeare developed during the course of his career.

Two warnings are needed. First it will not be sufficient to list the contents of the stage-picture and their relationships. We must try to describe how the audience perceives that picture. In a picture gallery we recognize that there is an appropriate way of looking at any picture. It would be absurd to stand all the time within a foot or two of a French impressionist painting, a Monet or a Degas. That would be appropriate only if we were considering the painter's technique. In order to see the effect that his picture is able to transmit, we would automatically step back a few paces and so become aware of the relationship of the brush-strokes to each other, of the whole effect of light, color, movement and space. The picture is made for such a wide focus. Other pictures—some Dutch realists for example—invite, and require, a minute scrutiny: one needs to step up close to the canvas. So it is in the theatre: the right focus, be it wide or intense, is necessary for seeing the masterpiece. Without this adaptation we may see only what appears to be incompetent brush-work, or an inability to give distinction or emphasis.

In watching a play in a theatre—any play, in any theatre—we sometimes sit forward in our chair, head forward and eyes intent on one particular point in the arena or picture which is the stage; this kind of dramatic focus is intense, concentrated. We observe or watch for the minutest action or word; we often see only one particular person or hear only one particular sound, even though the stage may be crowded or noisy, or disorderly. The opposite extreme is a wide dramatic focus. Instead of sitting forward we are sometimes relaxed, sitting back, and responsive to the whole picture. At such a time no one person or sound, or action dominates the impression we receive; we are sitting back and "taking it all in"; we are conscious of the overall effect, of the interweaving of pattern and the range of color. It is a wide focus. We can become aware of a changing dramatic focus by marking these two extremes.

We must also remember constantly that the play exists in time; the stage-picture is always developing from one form to another and at varying speeds. One momentary grouping may gain emphasis or meaning because it echoes an earlier grouping, in a different setting or with another dominating figure. A single figure may be more eloquent of loneliness because just before the stage had been crowded and animated. The changing visual impressions are also modified by narrative. So a sudden liveliness may appear to be little more than a meaningless disturbance, because the audience is wholly unprepared for it and so it shocks rather than elucidates. When narrative expectation

# The Theatre

is thwarted by a movement to some other part of the fable, an apparently static, formal scene may lose its impression of stability, or a brief descriptive scene take on an unusual air of deliberation. The stage picture is always changing and the audience's reaction to it can be controlled by dramatic narrative and response to character and situation.

The stage picture cannot be assessed easily; but if we do not discover the appropriate focus for each moment we may misread the dramatic text—and that is done all too easily.

I shall consider first, *Richard II*: an early play, written, for the most part, in a particularly lucid style.

It begins with the stage set formally. Richard is enthroned and surrounded, as the Quarto edition of 1597 says, with *"nobles and attendants."* Richard commands the center of the stage, but he is seen as a king in relationship to his subjects, rather than as a person interesting in his own right. He speaks in set fashion to his uncle, John of Gaunt, and requires precise, official answer. When Gaunt's son, Henry Bolingbroke, and Thomas Mowbray, Duke of Norfolk, are called to the King's presence, they bitterly accuse each other of treason. Richard fails to reconcile their demands of honor and appoints a day for trial by combat at Coventry. The whole stage empties at once, and on the outcome of that future event the audience's attention will wait.

So the first scene would appear if it were played on its own merits, with each word spoken as simply as possible. But if the audience has some previous knowledge of Richard's history, or if the actors try to give consistent portrayals of their roles, there will be further and conflicting impressions. Richard's formal protestation of impartiality, his "Forget, forgive; conclude and be agreed," and his comments on "bold" Bolingbroke, may carry subtextual impressions of irony, apprehension or antagonism. Bolingbroke's accusations may seem aimed at the King rather than Mowbray, and Mowbray's confidence to stem from royal support rather than his own innocence. But even if these impressions are missed, the audience will be made to question the scene's textual and visual impressions by the simple dialogue of the next scene. Mowbray has been accused of murdering Thomas, Duke of Gloucester, a son of Edward III and so Bolingbroke's uncle and the King's, but now, in contrast to the visual elaboration of the first formal picture, a quiet, still, intimate scene shows Thomas' widowed Duchess appealing for revenge, and his brother, John of Gaunt, refusing because:

> correction lieth in those hands
> Which made the fault.

The King and judge of the first scene had been responsible for Mowbray's murdering Gloucester, a fact to which no overt allusion has hitherto been made. Now the audience must question the earlier picture in retrospect, or find their unease strengthened. The new information is given unemphatically, for Gaunt does not have to persuade his hearer of its truth, but just before the audience's interest is redirected to the lists at Coventry, the Duchess is shown alone, believing that she goes to die.

For the third scene, at Coventry, the full stage is again "set" (as the Quarto has it) formally. The King enters in procession to the sound of trumpets, and personal feelings are subdued within the larger gestures and more fluent responses of public ceremonial. But now the focus is changed, for the audience will watch both sides closely, and "God's substitute" also, as he stands as judge on a higher level of the stage. The excitement of the duel itself is quenched before it begins, when Richard, with a simple movement of his hand, stops proceedings. This is unexpected and so draws all the alerted attention to the King who holds attention by wise words about civil strife and his own duties, and then pronounces the judgment which he and his council have agreed upon: Bolingbroke is to be banished for ten years and Mowbray for life. But this is not all: the newly watchful audience may discern a brief sign of complicity or shame as Richard with "some unwillingness" passes sentence on Mowbray, and a covert accusation as the banished man claims a "dearer merit": a single hesitation can now sharpen the audience's perception of signs of subtextual motivation. Bolingbroke's submission with:

> Your will be done. This must my comfort be,
> That sun that warms you here, shall shine on me. . . .

may seem to veil a rivalry with the King himself. Richard dominates the stage as he gives judgment, but at the close of the scene Bolingbroke is left alone with his friends and, as he fails to acknowledge their farewells, the course of the drama waits upon the expression of his personal and private feelings. So a newly clarified interest is balanced between Richard and Bolingbroke.

To sum up the visual effects so far, we can say that Shakespeare has introduced the action with a wide focus so that the audience is made aware of the patterns of the King's relationship to nobles and officials, and of father to son and fatherless nephew. But a more intimate focus is then induced with a short scene which adds notably, but quietly, to the exposition, and so when the next crowded, formal scene follows there are momentary intensifications of focus; but these never lead to direct narrative statement. Sometimes the audience's curiosity is aroused by some action or speech after it has been completed; or one character, by his words, provokes a closer scrutiny of another, or of relationships between several other characters. So the moments of close interest are sporadic and always lead back to a comprehensive view of the stage, or to a quick review of the preceding action. The audience's intense interest is not engaged for any single character or event, and yet, since the wider issues have been resolved in judgment and banishment, it is these insights which arouse most of the audience's expectation of further development. We can say that the stage-picture is at once comprehensive and subtle, that the focus is potentially intense over a wide design.

More informal scenes follow which complicate the audience's view, extending their interest and knowledge without coordinating individual impressions. While the splendors and properties are still alive in the memory, Richard is seen disrobed and at ease with his intimates. Now he is sarcastic about "High Hereford" and answers the national threat of rebellion in Ireland by deciding to lease his royal estates and exact subscriptions from wealthy subjects. When news comes that Gaunt is sick, Richard wishes his uncle were dead so that he might seize his possessions, and then goes to visit him: "Pray God we may make haste, and come too late," he says, and "Amen" respond his companions. In all this the pious and responsible solemnities of the first regal scenes are mocked: is this erratic informality a truer picture of Richard and of his country?

In a solemn, static scene that follows, the dying Gaunt speaks of the "scepter'd isle" of England with a reiterative eloquence that lends fire to patriotic commonplaces and has made the speech famous out of its context: this is a self-contained, largely verbal episode. Next Richard enters, and Gaunt denounces his husbandry and openly accuses him of the murder of Gloucester. Gaunt leaves the royal presence and, as York tries to placate the king, his death is announced. Immediately Richard confiscates Gaunt's possessions and York is no longer patient but denounces Richard as Gaunt had done: his remonstrance is breathless, not so imposing but more pitiful than Gaunt's, yet the King does not listen; rather, with surprising decision, he makes York governor in England during his own absence in Ireland, and then again hurries from the scene. As Gaunt and York have taken the center of the stage in denunciation, Shakespeare has ensured that the King prevents a prolonged close focus by jests and rapid decisions and movements. Verbally the situation is clearer, but the focus is still predominantly wide; it has only become more insecure, more uncertain and more frequently disturbed by momentary clarifications and intensities.

As soon as Richard has left the stage, the Earl of Northumberland and the lords, Ross and Willoughby, agree together that the King "is not himself" but transformed by his flatterers, and then they hasten to join Bolingbroke newly returned at the head of an army to redress all wrongs. Here is a simpler, stronger interest in the narrative development, but before the audience is allowed to follow it, there is a quiet moment in which the Queen mourns the absence of her "sweet Richard"— an entirely new reaction to this baffling figure. When she hears of Bolingbroke's arrival she despairs and York is unable to reassure her: "Comfort's in heaven," he warns, "and we are on the earth." He has little confidence in his resources or decisions: and, as he leaves with the Queen, the audience sees Richard's lesser friends count their chances and promptly decide to save their own skins, two fleeing to Bristol and one to Ireland. So from this gentle and then hesitating and shifting scene, the audience will turn with relief to Bolingbroke who now appears confident in arms and attended by Northumberland. They are joined by other nobles and all speak courteously, as if in homage to the new central figure. Bolingbroke's speeches are both strong and relaxed, so that the stage picture is at last ordered and assured (as it had *seemed* to be at the beginning), and the action steadily developing. York enters to denounce the rebel, but then declares himself neutral. There is a brief scene recounting the dispersal of the King's Welsh army on hearing rumors of his death, and then the action moves to Bristol where Bolingbroke, now accompanied by York as well, condemns to death Bushy and Green, Richard's cowardly friends. He takes charge of the realm as if he were the king of it, and holds the center of the stage; again echoing the first "set" scene.

The narrative encourages the audience to expect the uneasy focus to settle on the opposition of two main figures, two potential centers of the stage. But when Richard returns as from Ireland with Aumerle and the Bishop of Carlisle, after being absent for some four hundred and sixty lines (over one-sixth of the whole play), he does not meet Bolingbroke at once. The scene of his return (III.ii) is antithetical to that of Bolingbroke's: Richard is joined by other friends, as his rival had been, but they bring bad news and not an easy courtesy; and, whereas the rebel's course was clear, the King's is makeshift. Yet from this point to his death the dramatic focus grows more and more intent upon Richard for his own sake, whenever he appears; the audience sees progressively deeper into his consciousness. Sometimes the more stable Bolingbroke is a potential rival for attention in the center of a crowded stage, but after his opponent has surrendered he says very little: he assumes the crown, but never mentions his intention to do so; he deposes Richard, but leaves most of the business and persuasion to Northumberland and York. The audience is continually aware of Bolingbroke's presence, but he seems to stand further away from them than Richard, or than he himself had done formerly. Such is the cunning perspective of the stage picture.

The focus is intensified on Richard by huge transitions of thought and feeling, and by silences. He easily dominates the stage on his return because all the ill-tidings are known to the audience before they are told to him, and so there is no competitive narrative interest. Moreover he is eloquent and the other characters dependent upon him. But the focus is so narrowly intense because of his silences: it seems as if the extremes of his spoken despair and hope are impelled by some unexpressed fear, some knowledge or state of being which he cannot escape and cannot fully meet. He tries many ways to hope or despair, to some stable and "true" reaction: at first plain fantasy, then affirmation of trust in God, then meditation on the oblivion of death, then renunciation of his duties. But his friends on stage cannot believe or join in any of them, and silence always follows —as if none of his words were valid the moment after they have been spoken. Richard himself is aware of this ineffectiveness and directs attention to it verbally: he thinks he will be mocked for "senseless conjuration" and that he has been "mistaken all this while."

At the end of the scene he discharges his army and hurries off-stage, "From Richard's night, to Bolingbroke's fair day," and forbids anyone to speak further. He seems to know that it is from the expression of his own thoughts that he tries to escape at the end, rather than from physical or political danger. Between the rhetoric and the silences, the audience's attention is drawn toward Richard at the center of the stage and towards the unexpressed insecurity and suffering at the center of his being.

The scene in which Richard confronts Bolingbroke's army provides a wide stage-picture organized, for the first time, on two opposing centers. As Richard speaks and looks royally, claiming the power of "God omnipotent" and prophesying war as the result of Bolingbroke's treason, he seems once more to justify his position on the upper level of the stage at the center of the picture. Yet when Northumberland promises that the rebel claims only his own inheritance, Richard suddenly changes and agrees to meet his demands: it is as if the focal point of the composition suddenly lost its substance. As his message is carried back, Richard acknowledges:

> O that I were as great
> As is my grief, or lesser than my name!

> Or that I could forget what I have been!
> Or not remember what I must be now!
>
> (III.iii.136-39)

Then again his insecurity is made apparent by the extremity and variety of his reactions: he speaks openly and fluently of future defeat, a life of pious poverty and an obscure death. As Aumerle weeps, Richard retreats still further into the fantasy of "two kinsmen" digging "their graves with weeping eyes." Mildly he submits to Northumberland's request that he should meet Bolingbroke in the base court; but before he descends from his dominating position in the picture, his mind flashes to his former power and glory:

> Down, down I come, like glist'ring Phaethon,
> Wanting the manage of unruly jades.

To his enemies it seems that:

> Sorrow and grief of heart
> Makes him speak fondly [foolishly], like a frantic [mad] man;
> Yet he is come.

The visual submission is criticized, as it were, by Richard's words, which he cannot wholly control. He cuts short all argument by placing himself in the enemy's power before that is demanded of him; and, as before, he hurries to conclude the scene. From now on, the picture will tend to be dominated by Bolingbroke and his agents, but the focus is still intent upon Richard whenever he speaks or moves. Borrowing phrases from the criticism of paintings, we may say that the whole composition is static, at rest; but it is disturbed by the figure of Richard which is mobile and restless.

A wholly static interlude follows, of wide focus. It is set in a garden where Richard's Queen overhears two gardeners talk of affairs of state. They speak solemnly and pityingly of the "wasteful king" who has not "trimm'd and dress'd his land" as they their garden, and repeat the news that he is to be deposed. They are not Shakespeare's usual comic characters impressing their own personalities or points of view. Their quaint, slow-moving dialogue acts as a fixed point of reference like Gaunt's talk of a "sceptred isle," an unequivocal statement of the widest dramatic issues from outside Richard's personal dilemma.

Then the action moves to London, with Bolingbroke in full control. The Bishop of Carlisle boldly denounces the rebel and prophesies "Disorder, horror, fear, and mutiny" to future generations. He is arrested by Northumberland and at this tense moment Richard is brought on to the stage. He has already decided to resign the crown—Shakespeare does not use this incident to argue about political issues—and now gives effect to his decision step by step, as if obeying instructions or as if seeking to re-create the ceremonial solemnity of the early scenes. But he is now aware that his words and actions do not reflect his inward nature, neither his "regal thoughts" nor his deep sorrow. And his audience, both on stage and in the auditorium, is made aware of this disparity. When he cries "God save the king," no one dares respond "Amen," and when he calls Bolingbroke to stand opposite him with one hand on the crown he is forced to protest that he cannot resign his cares with the resignation of his office. As he tries to speak of this, his words have a new authority: they do not express conflicting extremes and do not issue from nervous silences. The man who submits now dominates the scene: he draws all attention to himself and, within the pattern or ordained events, he controls the nature of the action and denounces his enemies. Yet this new strength derives from weakness: he speaks more firmly and steadily because he now knows he *cannot* speak of his own crimes nor alleviate his grief; he cannot tell "what name to call himself." It is at this point that Shakespeare introduced an incident for which his sources gave not the slightest suggestion: Richard calls for a looking glass and when he sees few signs of his suffering in it, he dashes it to pieces. The true image of Richard is not in his appearance, nor his words. Again the scene is quickly finished: he asks for leave to go and is conveyed to the Tower. Shakespeare has at once presented a wide picture and led the audience's interest intently toward a single figure standing to one side of the composition; and as the focus intensifies the drama becomes abruptly disturbed by subtextual realities and the whole wide picture is disturbed and rapidly dissolved.

There is a brief scene as the Queen greets her husband on

his way to prison, not recognizing the royal lion in his meek submission. There is no nervous alternation of mood now, nor anxious silence. They exchange short rhymed speeches, and then part with a kiss, in accepted silence. But the audience whose interest has been so intensified upon Richard may see the very fluency of the scene as a deliberately external manner of valediction; Richard communicates his inward grief by trying to conceal it, and in performance the dialogue can sound tender and precarious, as well as controlled. Richard yet again hurries from the stage, lest they "make woe wanton with this fond delay"; he is still afraid of what he might say; for all the verbal formalism of this scene, the center of the picture is still mysterious, still lacking a defined and static quality.

The audience hears of further indignities that Richard is made to suffer, but it has to wait through two bustling, half-comic scenes before he is presented again. Then—and this is for the first time in the play—he appears alone. In soliloquy the audience's attention is drawn wholly to him. The focus is now undeniably intense, and yet Shakespeare introduces a considered, reflective, almost literary tone:

> I have been studying how I may compare
> The prison where I live unto the world. . . .
> 
> (V.v.1–2)

In due order Richard now describes his disordered thoughts—religious, ambitious, flattering—and acknowledges that he is content in none of them. As music is played off-stage, he speaks of "wasting" his "time," and of his recompense in being "wasted" by time and being forced to "mark the time" of Bolingbroke's progress. Grief, folly, faults, defeat and insecurity are all acknowledged; he no longer tries to escape from such thoughts but seeks to tame them by expressing them thoughtfully. The tone is almost unvaried and the pace almost steady: not quite, for still the balance is not easy. The change has left him helpless, expecting that:

> Nor I, nor any man that but man is,
> With nothing shall be pleas'd till he be eas'd
> With being nothing.

Yet music, played out of time, threatens this composure. Only when he remembers that it is meant for his comfort and is a sign of love, can he bear that too, and the scene is once more composed. Then comes a quickening of interest in an unexpected entry: he is hailed as "royal Prince!," and Richard answers the visitor quickly with a sharply ironic "Thanks, noble peer!" He is a groom of his stable, and tells Richard of his horse, the roan Barbary, and of this creature's pride in bearing Bolingbroke in triumph. Richard curses the horse, but then stops to consider: because the animal was "created to be aw'd by man" he begs its forgiveness, and remembers that he himself has been forced to bear a burden and submit as if he were an animal. Immediately a warder enters with food and orders the groom away; the focus is sharpened by the unknown, and by an attendant sense of immediate danger. Richard, however, thinks of his servant—"If thou love me, 'tis time thou wert away"—and a silence can be held in performance, despite the excitement, by an undefined and unexpressed sympathy between master and groom. The latter replies: "What my tongue dares not, that my heart shall say." Such a silence does not require utterance; momentarily there is intimacy and understanding, and even, perhaps, a deep peace.

After this intensely focused moment, Shakespeare returned to his primary sources with the warder's harsh words asking Richard to eat. The warder refuses to taste the food to guard against poison, saying that Bolingbroke's order forbids this, and then Richard leaps at him with:

> The devil take Henry of Lancaster and thee!
> Patience is stale, and I am weary of it.

There are cries for help and Exton and his assistants rush in. Action is violent and general: Richard kills two men, and then is overpowered by numbers and struck down. Suddenly the stage is fully alive with his anger, authority and physical strength, with a struggle and then defeat—all in an instant. The deep, necessarily static focus has been broken, and then when the violence is past—violence can sustain interest in the theatre only for comparatively short times—Richard speaks his last, presumably faint, words (again wholly Shakespeare's invention) that are all the more impressive by contrast with the tumult:

> Mount, mount, my soul! thy seat is up on high;
> Whilst my gross flesh sinks downward, here to die.

Richard had often longed for death because it would bring oblivion and perhaps pity, but as he faces assassination he finds new aspiration: royal anger and, then, hope in a world beyond death and change, spring from his deepest being.

Shakespeare's Richard talks a great deal about himself—some critics have called him a poet rather than a king—but an understanding of his part in the play cannot be found by simply analyzing what he says, weighing the word against the word; his stage reality depends also on subtext, and on the changing picture as it directs the audience's attention progressively towards the thoughts behind the words and the thoughts of silence, and towards his last unthinking, physical reactions. By simple quotation it can be shown that Richard is a man who talks "too idly," one "who wastes time" and is then "wasted by it"; or that he is a king who must uncrown himself and yet cannot escape the cares that "tend the crown." But such formulae do not embrace the whole experience the play provides in a theatre.

In a tragedy, after death there is always more to say. If only the eyes are closed and pious ceremonies performed in silence, the audience is shown that death affects other people besides the protagonist. A hushed drum, a bowed head, or a moment without sound or motion is enough to establish death as a fact for others' comprehension; the hero may have unpacked his heart with words but this must still be presented, his death must have this consequence. Many dramatists have made the further communication explicitly, in a chorus which tells the men and women of Thebes that no one can be called happy until he has died in peace, that there is always an end to tears, that wisdom is taught by suffering. Some authors, more busily, have recounted death's manifold implications through a group of women tidying their thoughts aloud; others have announced a long-kept secret through the mouth of some wise, experienced man—how he who has died had been true to his heritage, or had been struck down by some hidden guilt. Authors who prefer to maintain a full dramatic illusion have presented retaliation or submission, praise or blame, in continued action, or have concluded with a prayer that begs some god to appease man's misery and remorse. In Shakespeare's day the standard procedure was explicit comment, a statement of the play's meaning or significance. Elizabethan tragedy usually drew a firm line after the death of the hero, and then totalled up good deeds and bad. In this play, Shakespeare's method is to give another scene, another picture with different figures: after the death of Richard, when the focus has been more intense than ever before, Shakespeare transferred attention to Bolingbroke seated in Richard's throne; a formal "set" scene, with a predominantly wide focus.

The transference is, however, long prepared for: the wide focus of the early scenes had not been invoked needlessly. The first stage-pictures with Richard as judge of Mowbray and Bolingbroke were repeated half-way through when Bolingbroke stood as judge of Bushy and Green, and then of Aumerle and Surrey against the charges of Bagot, Fitzwater and others. In his second judgment Bolingbroke dealt with the same offence as had concerned Richard: the murder of Thomas, Duke of Gloucester. But there were significant differences: the contestants were more numerous and more quick-tempered; the judge said far less than his predecessor, his most arresting contributions being his silence, his repeal of Mowbray and then, on hearing of this old enemy's death after fighting in the crusades, his praise and prayer for him. All these scenes are echoed in the last formal scene, and so strengthen it; once the momentary surprise has passed, it seems the inevitable close to the play as a whole.

Again, between Richard's farewell to his Queen and his last appearance, Shakespeare elaborated on accounts in his sources by introducing two scenes showing the Duke of York's discovery that his son, Aumerle, is engaged in conspiracy against Bolingbroke. The audience need not know these events in order to follow Richard's story—indeed, almost invariably the scenes are cut from modern productions—so Shakespeare must have had other reasons for inventing them. Firstly they demonstrate the effects of revolution; and, secondly, their comic details of calling for boots to a loquacious wife provide a release from the tension of following Richard's story. And they also affect the dramatic focus. By introducing these scenes Bolingbroke is again seated as judge. At first he seems well able to manage the danger to his person, reducing the stature of both Aumerle and his mother with an ironic: "My dangerous cousin, let your mother in" (V.iii.81). But, as the Duchess kneels in supplication and refuses to obey Bolingbroke's thrice repeated "Rise up, good aunt" until he has promised, and doubly promised, pardon for her son's life, the audience is shown both the new king's power and his subject's tendency to doubt the effect of his commanding words of friendship and forgiveness. The irony touches Bolingbroke closely, for as the suppliant rises she cries (and this is all she says): "A God on earth thou art"—the rebel, the silent king, has to hear himself called a god by those he favors. To this salutation he answers nothing: but his tone changes and, ignoring the agonized and flustered woman, he speaks directly of tracking down other conspirators and swears that all of them shall die. The episode ends when the Duchess leaves with her pardoned son and places such revolutions of fortune in another perspective: "Come my old son; I pray God make thee new."

I have dwelt so long on this scene because the final scene of the play is again, for the fourth time, Bolingbroke enthroned as king and judge. The picture including its central figure is now quite familiar, so that despite its wide focus the audience may give particular attention to small points of difference, or imprecision. York, Northumberland and Fitzwater bring news that his enemies are defeated and slain; only the Bishop of Carlisle is brought a prisoner before him, and he—strangely perhaps—is pardoned because Bolingbroke has seen "sparks of honour" in this implacable enemy. Then there follows another, more impressive entry into the royal presence: Sir Pierce of Exton with Richard's body in a coffin. At least four men are needed to bear this burden on to the stage, and they must move more slowly and ceremonially than the eager messengers who have preceded them. Bolingbroke does not speak, but as the coffin is deliberately placed before him, Exton announces:

> Great King, within this coffin I present
> Thy buried fear.

The answer is:

> Exton, I thank thee not; for thou hast wrought
> A deed of slander with thy fatal hand
> Upon my head and all this famous land.
> . . . Though I did wish him dead,
> I hate the murderer, love him murdered.
> The guilt of conscience take thou for thy labour,
> But neither my good word nor princely favour;
> With Cain go wander thorough shades of night,
> And never show thy head by day nor light.

He turns from Exton, to address his silent, watching noblemen:

> Lord, I protest my soul is full of woe
> That blood should sprinkle me to make me grow.

And the play ends with self-assumed penance:

> Come, mourn with me for what I do lament,
> And put on sullen black incontinent:
> I'll make a voyage to the Holy Land,
> To wash this blood off from my guilty hand.

A reader of the play might claim that Bolingbroke's last words are prompted by his practiced political intelligence: to dash Exton's hopes, or to announce new business to employ the energies of fractious nobles (following such counsel as, in *Henry IV*, Shakespeare was to put in Bolingbroke's own mouth). But in performance such interpretations are not fully satisfying, for the picture, the visual impression, qualifies the words. On the crowded stage all are silent and intent upon their king, so that if he attempted dissimulation he would scarcely be content with the continued silence which is the only response to his words (compare Prince John and the Lord Chief Justice talking together after Henry V has made a similar announcement of foreign wars at the end of *2 Henry IV*). Moreover this moral note has been heard before where it could serve no political purpose: as Bolingbroke prayed for Mowbray, as he spoke of his son's irresponsibility hanging like a plague over him, and perhaps as he pardoned Aumerle "as God shall pardon me," and as he pardoned the Bishop of Carlisle. Possibly Bolingbroke's silence when he heard his subjects accuse each other of treason and when he heard the Bishop denounce his assumption of the throne should be viewed as earlier attempts to conceal a subtextual guilt. These moments passed quickly and without emphasis, but the repetition of the picture of a king crowned and surrounded by his nobles directs the audience's attention progressively upon variations and movement: slight tensions beneath formal poses can thus become impressive.

As at the end of a sonnet, the last line can send the reader back to the first, till the experience which the sonnet gives is viewed whole and complete, contained and understood, so at the end of this tragedy, the audience's visual sense will retravel to its beginning, to a group of ambitious, striving, related and insecure human beings. To ensure this response the awakening of a new Richard in his death scene has been presented so briefly; Bolingbroke has been held uncommunicative within the wide picture of the drama while the intense focus was directed more and more upon Richard; and the early scenes were allowed no single dominant interest. Instead of concentrating the drama upon a hero's story, Shakespeare has presented a man in isolation and defeat who overcomes fear and learns to recognize guilt, responsibility and courage in himself; and has off-set this with a man who knows little of fear and recognizes guilt only when he assumes the responsibility he has continually sought. The last scene presents Bolingbroke in a new way, verbally: and Richard is there in his coffin, eloquent of his own story, visually.

Both Bolingbroke's and Richard's last words are about their souls, and of Heaven or the Holy Land; and this also completes a series of scenes, still moments when an isolated figure appeals to a state of being outside the world of the stage. In the second scene, the Duchess of Gloucester is told to "complain" to "God, the widow's champion and defence," and this resource is again invoked by the unexpected report of the banished Mowbray fighting in the crusades, by York reminding the distressed Queen that "Comfort's in heaven, and we are on the earth," and his warning to Bolingbroke:

> Take not, good cousin, further than you should,
> Lest you mistake. The heavens are over our heads.

The last scene, in a moment of piety, lightly draws these moments together too.

The surest and most comprehensive effects of the conclusion are carried by the stage-picture: viewing the wide picture the audience may see deeply into the characters and the society portrayed, and even into a timeless perspective associated with traditional religion. This visual and formal language is not so precise as words, but it can affect the audience subtly and without its conscious knowledge; it can suggest vast implications and sensitive psychological reactions; it can awaken a response without limiting it by definition, declaration or propaganda.

*Stanley Wells*

# John Barton's *Richard II* (1976)

John Barton's production of *Richard II* has already received a good deal of academic attention. The designer, Timothy O'Brien, published an article about his designs in *Shakespeare Jahrbuch*, in 1975.[1] A student of mine, Mr. J.E. Stredder, wrote an M.A. thesis on the production,[2] and an article by him based on his thesis will appear in the *Shakespeare Jahrbuch* for 1976. Dr. James Tulip, of the University of Sydney, has also published an essay partly concerned with the production.[3] I am, of course, anxious not to duplicate their work, and especially not to appear simply to be cribbing from my own student's thesis. So I feel that I should vary my approach in this lecture, and that I might most usefully talk about the play in terms of the production rather than present a descriptive account of the performance.

The amount of academic attention that this production has already received reflects some of its characteristics. It was in some respects the most strongly interpretative production of a Shakespeare play that I have ever seen. It was also exceptionally stylized. Its most strikingly unusual feature was that two actors, Richard Pasco and Ian Richardson, played the roles of Richard and Bolingbroke alternately. They are perhaps the best equipped classical actors of their generation. Both of them are splendid verse-speakers, experienced actors with grace of movement, expressive gestures, and great capacity to sway and hold an audience. They are also interestingly different from one another. Pasco, taller and of bigger build, has the more obviously "committed" acting style. He is an emotional actor; his large eyes easily command pathos, his rich, vibrant voice, with a wide tonal range, can be both thrilling and moving. Ian Richardson, slighter in build, is more obviously intellectual. He excels in high comedy and sardonic wit, as may be suggested by the fact that one of his best roles was Vindice in *The Revenger's Tragedy*. He can convey a sense of detachment from the role, a haughty aloofness. His voice is less resonant, but his speaking is brilliantly incisive, calculated and completely controlled. He has enormous technical accomplishment and, perhaps, a more natural bent for comedy than for tragedy.

To see each of these actors within a short space of time as both Richard and Bolingbroke in the same production afforded a fascinating opportunity to consider the contribution of the actor's personality to the role he plays. Bolingbroke is often given to a player of the second rank, and it was interesting to see the part played by a leading actor. But the decision to cast these performers in both roles also had interpretative implications. It has often been said that Richard II is an actor, and, as I shall hope to show, the production explored this aspect of the character. There was also a very strong attempt to show close spiritual resemblances between Richard and Bolingbroke, and this, too, may have been helped by the casting.

The production had numerous other unusual features. It was played on a largely bare stage. At its first appearance, in 1973, there was a narrow, escalator-like structure, receding as it rose higher, on each side of the stage. A platform or bridge spanning the two staircases was normally high above the stage but could ascend or descend. Before the performance began, a pyramid of golden steps was set in the center of the stage. On it was a kind of scarecrow on which hung the King's robe, surmounted by a mask and a crown. It was at the same time both a symbol of the play's concerns and a declaration of the symbolic method by which they were to be presented. When the production was revived in 1974, the staircase and bridge were no longer used. The stage was cleared, and a golden cloak hung high above the stage as a sun symbol. At the end of the scene, which coincided with the interval, the cloak was released and fluttered down to the stage. There were other alterations, too, most of them reducing the number of symbolic staging devices.

Hobby-horses—that is, costumes which made the actors appear to be riding horses—were used from time to time. They were particularly appropriate for the scene of the lists (I.iii), giving an impression of the pageantry associated with formal jousts and tournaments. Like real horses, they had to be carefully handled. The actors occasionally introduced humanizing touches of comedy by making the horses appear to be restive, and patting their heads to quiet them. I mentioned the platform or bridge which, when the production was first given, spanned the two staircases, and which could ascend and descend. On it Richard could rise and fall, so that, in these performances, "Down, down I came, like glistering Phaëthon," referred to a mechanical rather than a human descent. Richard wore a splendid coat of pleated gold in which, as he spread his arms, he made of himself a visual image of the sun. (In 1974 Richard's descent was made down the steps of the central dais.)

The director originally intended that all the characters in the play except the king should wear masks. Timothy O'Brien writes that the idea was to create a sense of the king's isolation, but that it "ran so counter to all that the actors had been taught about the expressive face being the focus of their performances, and so perturbed Bolingbroke, that masks in the end were only used at moments of portent" (p. 117). Even though the consistent use of masks was abandoned, Mr. O'Brien writes that "their depersonalizing influence was at rehearsals and contributed to the intended formality of behavior on the stage in the end" (pp. 117–18). This remark points to another special feature of the production. There was a very conscious stylization of acting method; many speeches were delivered directly at the audience rather than as part of a dialogue among the characters on stage. This created occasional problems. For example, at a dramatic moment in the scene of the lists, the Lord Marshal has to say: "The King hath thrown his warder down" (I.iii.118). The actor told me that if he spoke this line while staring straight at the audience, he roused laughter. The information was obviously redundant. Here, a personal reaction was necessary. He had to turn to watch the king's action, then wheel to face the audience to express his surprise, for the line to be plausible.

In these, and other ways, this was, then, a strongly stylized and symbolical production. It imposed strains upon its audiences. They had to respond to unfamiliar production techniques, and to try to see the point of deliberately unnatural methods of performances which might easily have seemed ludicrous and pretentious. My account so far of the director's methods may suggest tricksiness and gimmickry. The production was accused of these faults. Nevertheless, it was highly successful and was given many performances. It created its own audiences, I think. Though certain aspects of it were strange and initially puzzling, its impact was great and repaid a degree of intellectual and imaginative effort in its audiences. It represented a very serious and intelligent effort to find theatrical correlatives to various features of Shakespeare's playwriting techniques in this early play, and it is in these terms that I should like to consider it. Let me first attempt to characterize some of Shakespeare's aims in writing the play.

Though he worked basically from Raphael Holinshed's massive chronicle history of England, he seems also to have read around the subject a good deal; and he selected from and rearranged historical facts with some freedom. The general tendency of his alterations is to universalize his subject: to tell the story of the reign of Richard II in a manner that brings it into touch with general ideas, and that suggests matters of fundamental significance behind the particular events that the play dramatizes. The play is much concerned with kingship, with the problems that face an ordinary human being who has to adopt the semi-divine role of king, to try to live up to its responsibilities and make proper use of its privileges. This concern was stressed in the program note that Mrs. Barton wrote for her husband's production. It is headed *The King's Two Bodies*, which is the title of an important book by the historian Ernst Kantorowicz,[4] to which Mrs. Barton refers. This book studies the medieval and Elizabethan doctrine that a king has two bodies, or natures, one "flawless, abstract and immortal," the other "fallible, individual and subject to death and time." This dual nature creates great problems for the man who has to bear it. He is, as it were, an imperfect human being in a guise of perfection, a flawed face behind an idealized mask. As Mrs. Barton wrote, "the Richard of the early scenes is often callous, greedy, frivolous, self-indulgent and unjust. . . . A private face that should remain hidden not only manifests itself but contradicts the impersonal mask of kingship by which it should be overlaid." It is clear why the mask was an important symbol in this production.

Another major concern of the play is the relationship between the king and his country, and the plight of a country that is weakly governed. In this of course it reflects contemporary concerns. When Shakespeare wrote it, his Virgin Queen was in her 60s with no obvious heir. It was feared that whoever succeeded to the throne might not match up to the demands of the office, and some of Elizabeth's subjects were even moved to question the validity of the hereditary principle. The queen's susceptibility to influence by favorites provoked direct comparison with Richard II. There were strong movements to depose her. It is interesting that the scene of Richard's deposition was omitted from the three editions of the play published while the queen was still alive. The play must have been thought relevant to the political situation, and eventually it was actually used as a weapon in the political campaign. The Earl of Essex's supporters hired Shakespeare's company of actors to present it as a gesture of support and defiance on the eve of Essex's rebellion. Obviously it was felt, in spite of its historical basis, to deal with live issues. It is especially interesting that Shakespeare and his company were not punished for this special performance. This, surely, is a measure of the extent to which Shakespeare had transcended topicality and presented historical events in a manner that could be regarded as poetical and philosophical rather than political and topical. The relationship between the king and his country is an aspect of this, for the land is seen in the play both as the source of Richard's glory, his "large kingdom," and as the "little grave" which eventually will swallow him. Mr. Barton symbolized the land by a chalice of earth placed centrally to the front of the stage. Several characters took up earth from it at significant points. The gardener planted a sprig in it, when he said of the queen:

> Here did she fall a tear. Here in this place
> I'll set a bank of rue, sour herb of grace.
> Rue even for truth here shortly shall be seen
> In the remembrance of a weeping Queen.
>
> (III.iv.104–107)

And Richard placed his hand close to the chalice on his return from Ireland at the words: "Dear earth, I do salute thee with my hand."

Before starting to write *Richard II*, Shakespeare made a decision of fundamental importance. He decided to write this play entirely in verse. It was a decision he had made three times before, always in history plays: two of the three parts of *Henry VI*, and *King John*. He was never to make the same decision again. Partly this must be the result of the rapid evolution of dramatic styles during the 1590s. *Richard II* must have seemed old-fashioned soon after it was written. Perhaps this is why in 1601—only about six years after its composition—the actors were able to complain that it was "so old and so long out of use as that they should have small or no company at it."[5] Presumably when he wrote it, Shakespeare was more subservient to the requirements of historical-tragical decorum than he was soon to become. These included the convention that high-ranking characters spoke in verse, and low-ranking ones in prose. In this play, even characters and episodes which might, in a different context, have been represented in prose are given the dignity of verse. This implies, obviously, a degree of stylization and artificiality in the language, and one result of this is that a number of the characters are so lacking in individuality that they seem mainly or entirely choric in function. A partial example is provided by the Duchess of Gloucester. She has only one scene (I.ii). There is some personal force behind her statements as she pleads for revenge against her husband's murderers, yet we feel that the main reason for her presence in the play is as a spokesman of the old order and as a mouthpiece for the conveying of necessary background information. Mr. Barton appropriately presented her in stylized fashion. In 1973 she emerged from a trapdoor, holding a skull above her head and crying "Blood!" to John of Gaunt in tones that were electronically echoed. This created a melodramatic impression which exemplified the dangers of stylization, and in 1974 she simply entered from the wings and spoke quietly, though she still carried the skull.

A similar character is the Welsh Captain, in Act Two, Scene

Four. He has a purely choric speech about the state of the country:

> The bay trees in our country are all withered,
> And meteors fright the fixèd stars of heaven.
> The pale-faced moon looks bloody on the earth,
> And lean-looked prophets whisper fearful change. . . .

In the note on this scene in my New Penguin edition of the play, which was used for this production, I say that the captain "is important rather for his representative quality than for any personal characteristics." It is an obvious enough comment; I quote it because John Barton's handling of the scene represented a translation into theatrical terms of this kind of critical comment. The captain's speech was spoken not by one man but by eight of them; each of the additional seven was given one line. They stood in a row across the stage in a low light and with their backs to the audience. There was an accompaniment of plaintive horn music. Thus all suggestion of individuality was eliminated, and their choric function was made abundantly plain.

The most obviously choric scene of all is that of the gardeners (III.iv). As gardeners, they have no reality whatever. They are gardeners simply because this is part of the metaphor that Shakespeare also employs in their language. England has already on a number of occasions been compared to a garden, and now the metaphor is fully expanded and developed:

> Our sea-walled garden, the whole land,
> Is full of weeds, her fairest flowers choked up,
> Her fruit trees all unpruned, her hedges ruined,
> Her knots disordered, and her wholesome herbs
> Swarming with caterpillars.

As a literary expression of the state of the kingdom, that is eloquent. It would be entirely at home in an Elizabethan narrative poem. But this is a play, not a poem; and these lines of beautifully controlled, measured blank verse have to be spoken by someone in the guise of a gardener. What usually happens is that actors seek comic effect, dressing and speaking like the gravediggers in *Hamlet* (who, of course, speak prose), and thus draw attention to themselves, or to the characters they are playing, and away from the meaning of the scene. This is obviously wrong; but to play them as exceptionally well-bred and literate gentlemen who just happen to have taken up gardening as a profession has the equally unsatisfactory effect of sacrificing any sense of reality of the speakers as people. When I was editing the play I did some research into the gardeners of great Elizabethan estates, thinking they might perhaps have been roughly the equivalent of modern professors of botany, or directors of Agricultural Research Stations, but I was not too convinced by what I found. So I thought John Barton hit upon a brilliantly ingenious solution in making them monks, intelligent and literate people who might nevertheless be also full-time gardeners. Quiet organ music was heard in the first part of the scene, with the queen and her ladies; the gardeners sang softly as they entered from the back of the stage. Music accompanied the head gardener's final speech as he took a sprig of rue from his sleeve and planted it in the chalice of earth.

The gardeners' scene represents at an extreme level a procedure which can be observed throughout this play, and which is very much bound up with Shakespeare's decision to write entirely in verse, and in verse of a predominantly plangent, lyrical, elegiac kind that seems almost to have been created for this play. Constantly action as well as language is stylized. Shakespeare seems to be taking the representation of people and events, as of speech, as far away from a naturalistic mode as he dares, rigorously subordinating credibility of immediate effect to the patterns of thought and image that carry the play's truest meanings. Consider for example the way that characters in some of his other plays react to the news that they have been banished. Here is Romeo:

> Ha, banishment! Be merciful, say "death";
> For exile hath more terror in his look,
> Much more than death. Do not say "banishment."
>
> (III.ii.12–14)

Here is Kent in *King Lear*:

> Fare thee well, King. Sith thus thou wilt appear,
> Freedom lives hence, and banishment is here.
> 
> (I.i.180-81)

You will remember Coriolanus:

> You common cry of curs, whose breath I hate
> As reek o' th' rotten fens, whose loves I prize
> As the dead carcasses of unburied men
> That do corrupt my air. I banish you.
> 
> (III.iii.121-25)

And now here is Mowbray, in *Richard II*:

> A heavy sentence, my most sovereign liege,
> And all unlooked for from your highness' mouth.
> A dearer merit, not so deep a maim
> As to be cast forth in the common air
> Have I deservèd at your highness' hands.
> The language I have learnt these forty years,
> My native English, now I must forgo,
> And now my tongue's use is to me no more
> Than an unstringèd viol or a harp,
> Or like a cunning instrument cased up—
> Or being open, put into his hands
> That knows no touch to tune the harmony.
> 
> (I.iii.154-65)

Romeo's reaction is directly related to his feelings for Juliet. He would rather die than be away from her. Kent's is an idiosyncratic expression of his blunt nature and his capacity to make the best of a bad job. Coriolanus's is a wonderfully vivid expression of personal hatred and defiance. But Mowbray's is a meditation on the idea that in a foreign country his language will be of no use to him—not an entirely implausible reaction, but far more important as one in a sequence of passages concerned with the function and power of words, especially a sovereign's words, than as a personal reaction from Mowbray himself. Similarly only a little later, when Bolingbroke and his father, John of Gaunt, discuss the sentence that has been passed, their conversation soon becomes a philosophical discussion on the power of the imagination which is deeply relevant to one of the play's overriding concerns—for the king rules largely by his power over people's imaginations—but far from a naturalistic representation of a talk between an old father and his newly banished son.

Such stress in the play's language on the symbolic aspects of the situations portrayed is paralleled by similarly calculated stylization of action. Take for instance Act Three, Scene Two, in which Richard has just returned from Ireland. He speaks his most confident affirmation of the power of kingship:

> Not all the water in the rough rude sea
> Can wash the balm off from an anointed king.
> The breath of worldy men cannot depose
> The deputy elected by the Lord.
> For every man that Bolingbroke hath pressed
> To lift shrewd steel against our golden crown,
> God for his Richard hath in heavenly pay
> A glorious angel. Then if angels fight,
> Weak men must fall; for heaven still guards the right.

Salisbury enters and reports that the Welsh army has defected to Bolingbroke. Richard consoles himself with the thought, "Is not the King's name twenty thousand names?" Immediately Scroop enters and reports Bolingbroke's success in raising troops in England. Richard calls for Bushy, Bagot, and Green and learns that they are dead. And Richard speaks his great meditation on the mortality of kings. The action here is, of course, unhistorical. Shakespeare has compressed events that happened over a period of time at two different places, Barkloughly and Conway. But the reality of the situation is not what matters. There is just enough truth in the happenings to form a structure for Shakespeare's poetic exploration of the polarities of Richard's confidence and despair.

Mr. Barton found several ways of reflecting Shakespeare's dramatic technique in the staging. Richard entered on horseback: not a hobby-horse this time, but a large representation of Roan Barbary, a mythical horse with a unicorn's horn, propelled on skis. Richard looked splendid, with a great plume of feathers above his regal helmet. He dismounted to salute his land. He was all confidence in the opening of the scene, and took a cross from the Bishop of Carlisle as he said:

> For every man that Bolingbroke hath pressed
> To lift shrewd steel against our golden crown,
> God for his Richard hath in heavenly pay
> A glorious angel.

But he let it fall back into Carlisle's hands as he heard of the defection of the Welsh army. After Aumerle's words of encouragement, he remounted the horse. But learning of the deaths of his friends, he let his sword clatter to the ground and himself dismounted, speaking his great lament in a spotlight to the front of the stage. Minor characters spoke most of their lines straight out to the audience, and were symmetrically grouped. Richard left the stage quietly and on foot. The patterning of the action was reflected in the varying symmetries of the stage-picture.

The dramatic method illustrated in this scene, and generally characteristic of the play, throws an emphasis on ideas and their poetical expression rather than on credibility of action and psychologically plausible portrayal of individual personalities. Even characters with quite lengthy roles in this play are formed on similar bases. I have already referred to the Duchess of Gloucester, who has only one scene, which is in effect part of the play's exposition. Richard's queen has an important part to play, but it is not because of anything strongly individual in her personality; indeed, at times she seems almost like an emblematic embodiment of grief. John of Gaunt makes an impact because of his best-known speech, on England—"This royal throne of kings; this seat of Mars"—one of those speeches where the actor's main problem lies in making sure that the audience does not sing along with him. Tony Church delivered it directly to the audience, as a public rather than a private utterance, appropriately since Gaunt is primarily a mouthpiece for certain ideals of kingship and national pride.

These characteristics of the play help to explain and justify the method that John Barton adopted of portraying many of the play's characters. His actors nobly quelled the natural temptation to humanize and round out the outlines of a part. They acted as elements in a somewhat abstract design, not as if each of them was the center of the design. Sometimes, indeed,

Mr. Barton manipulated the play in ways that created an even greater degree of symbolism in character portrayal. The most striking example was the presentation of the Earl of Northumberland's relationship with Bolingbroke. Northumberland was made to seem the active agent in Bolingbroke's rise to the throne. He was unrealistically presented. Towards the end of Act Two, Scene One, he appeared, along with Ross and Willoughby, in a long black robe concealing buskins, high boots which increased his height. In Act Two, Scene Three he rode a big black horse. His power over Bolingbroke was shown to be gradually increasing; correspondingly, Bolingbroke's responsibility seemed less. Northumberland was in charge of the off-stage executions of Bushy and Bagot, and wore black plumes in his helmet. In the episode of Richard's parting from his queen, Northumberland appeared at his most unreal, seeming now a ruthless embodiment of menace and totalitarian power. We heard that he had been spoken of in rehearsals as a "Himmler-figure," a characteristic attempt both to generalize and to find a modern equivalent. The individual was lost in his costume resembling a bird of prey, and towered ominously over the dejected king and queen. Richard was now "down" indeed. The stylization of costuming extended to the faceless figures on each side of him, riding black hobby-horses, each with a rope attached to one of Richard's arms.

You will perhaps have noticed that there are two distinct processes in the production methods that I have been describing. One is an effort to devise methods that will find appropriate theatrical conventions to mirror the particular dramatic conventions of this play. The other is one that may be said to build still further upon these theatrical conventions. In his presentation of the relationship between Northumberland and Bolingbroke, the director was creating a simplified pattern from Shakespeare's multiplicity of suggestiveness. Partly he was reinforcing structural patterns that are present in Shakespeare's text; partly he was distorting them. These processes were observable elsewhere. At times they resulted in clear improvements. The scene of the gages, for example, has often caused embarrassment in the theatre. Bagot accuses Aumerle of responsibility for Gloucester's death. Aumerle rejects the accusation, throwing down his glove as a challenge. Fitzwater repeats the accusation and throws down his glove. Percy does the same; so does another, anonymous Lord. The Duke of Surrey throws *his* glove down, taking Aumerle's part. Finally Aumerle borrows another glove and throws *that* down as another challenge. The highly patterned action is obviously calculated, but, as gloves gradually pile up on the stage, it is in danger of seeming ludicrous. In performance this scene has usually been shortened or omitted. If you had smuggled a text into the Royal Shakespeare Theatre, you would have found that though the episode was included, Mr. Barton had so rearranged the lines and reassigned the speeches that he had virtually rewritten the scene. It came over powerfully, with no hint of comedy.

Other scenes that have often been omitted are those concerned with Aumerle's conspiracy and his mother's attempts to save him from its consequences. The scenes are, I think, not completely successful. Shakespeare is trying, not quite successfully, to achieve a subtle fusion of seriousness and comedy for which he cannot command the necessary technical resources, so that the comedy tends to submerge the seriousness. But there are good reasons for including the scenes, and the awkwardness in the writing can be mitigated by tactful acting. Sir John Gielgud wrote in an introduction to the play: "The character of York . . . can be of great value, provided that the actor and director can contrive between them a tactful compromise between comedy and dramatic effect."[6] John Barton had good actors in the roles, and he wisely permitted here a more naturalistic, personal style of acting. By relaxing the stylization evident elsewhere, he was facing up to the problems of the episode and making the best of it, rather than evading the issue by the drastic cutting to which many directors have resorted in desperation of making the scenes work.

Although, as I have insisted, many of the lesser characters in this play are important rather as elements in a design than as individual human beings; nevertheless, at the center of the design is one supremely important figure, and another who is scarcely less so. Richard and Bolingbroke are rather like the figures on a weather clock. As one goes in, the other comes out; and, it would seem, with almost as little exercise of their own will-power. This see-saw element in the play became the mainspring of the production, though not without textual manipulation and distortion, to some of which I have already referred. In her program note, Mrs. Barton wrote: "Like the two buckets filling one another that Richard imagines in the deposition scene, buckets which take a contrary course within the deep well of the crown, Richard's journey from king to man is balanced by Bolingbroke's progress from a single to a twin-natured being. Both movements involve a gain and a loss. Each, in its own way, is tragic."

As a generalized critical statement, that is acceptable. But as such it is inevitably a simplification. There are implications of tragedy in the portrayal of Bolingbroke, especially if we read his part in this play in the light of the extended portrait of him given in Parts One and Two of *Henry IV*; but I should find it difficult to argue, and I do not suppose that Mrs. Barton would argue, that the Bolingbroke of *Richard II* is a fully realized tragic figure. The suggestion of equivalence between Richard and Bolingbroke which Mr. Barton's production undoubtedly gave required the importation of lines from *2 Henry IV* and the transference of an important passage in *Richard II* to Bolingbroke from another character. Latent in the casting, it was made in the production even before the first words were spoken; and it was linked with an image to which I have already referred. Mrs. Barton pointed to Shakespeare's exploration of "the latent parallel between the King and that other twin-natured being, the Actor. Like kings, actors are accustomed to perform before an audience. Like kings, they are required to submerge their own individuality within a role and, for both, the incarnation is temporary and perilous. Like the two kings in *Richard II*, their feelings towards their roles are often ambiguous, a mixture of exhilaration and disgust. And . . . Richard is intensely conscious, in the early scenes, of kingship as a role to be acted." An introductory mime impressed this parallel upon us.

Before the house lights dimmed there appeared a figure resembling Shakespeare, carrying a book resembling the First Folio, printed seven years after he died. He contemplated the robed scarecrow, opened the book, and signalled for the appearance of the actors. They filed on in two columns, one headed by

Ian Richardson, the other by Richard Pasco. They all wore rehearsal costume. The leaders of the company joined Shakespeare at the dais, each holding one side of the book. Shakespeare mounted the pyramid, took from the scarecrow the crown and the mask, and placed them on the open book. The two actors held the crown and mask high between them; Shakespeare bowed to the actor who was to play Richard at that performance, and gradually the actors took on their costumes and wigs, in view of the audience, assuming the appearance of the characters they were to play. The robing of Richard was a kind of coronation ritual; the court knelt to him, chanting words not in the text: "God save the King! Long live the King! May the King live forever!" Richard faced the audience, echoed "May the King live forever!" and removed his mask.

Thus the director prefigured the play's concern with the inevitable tension between the demands made by the office of kingship, of being God's deputy on earth, and the capacities of the human being who has to try to fill a role that is inevitably too big for him. And, even more important to this production, he associated this with the idea of the actor assuming the role that he had to play on stage. The human being who has to play the king in real life was paralleled with the actor who has to play the role of king in the theatre.

Although *Richard II* is more thoroughly poetic and verbalized than some of Shakespeare's later plays, it still leaves quite a lot to the actors. Richard does not say very much in the earlier part of the play; Bolingbroke does not say much in the later. The actors must decide how to interpret their silences. Richard, in his first scene, is visually dominant but says little. Should the actor attempt thus early to suggest anything positive about Richard's personality, or should he hold back? In the past, actors have added business here to create a more positive impact. Beerbohm Tree and F.R. Benson are famous for having had Richard caress and feed hounds in bored indifference; later in the play, one of the hounds was seen to have transferred allegiance to Bolingbroke. Gielgud suggests that the actor "must use the early scenes to create an impression of slyness, petty vanity, and callous indifference." Yet the quarrel between Bolingbroke and Mowbray is about a matter in which the King is deeply implicated—the murder of the Duke of Gloucester. Both of Mr. Barton's actors, quite rightly, showed Richard's silence as the reverse of indifference, rather a careful keeping silent in the knowledge that Richard might at any moment be directly accused.

Richard's behavior in the first part of the play becomes progressively worse, culminating in his brutal treatment of John of Gaunt, whose speech about what England ought to be serves as a measure of Richard's personal disqualifications for the kingly office. But it would not be disputed, I think, that after his return from Ireland, as the tide of fortune turns against him, Shakespeare gradually reinstates him in the audience's favor. An interpretative problem arises over the presentation of Richard's relations with his favorites, Bushy and Green. In Act Three, Scene One, Bolingbroke accuses them of having

> Made a divorce betwixt his [Richard's] Queen and him,
> Broke the possession of a royal bed.

Some critics and actors have interpreted this as an accusation against Richard of homosexuality. This belief can color an actor's entire interpretation of the role. But the portrayal of Richard's relationship with his queen in the rest of the play does nothing to support the accusation. I do not think we can say precisely what Shakespeare had in mind; but in Mr. Barton's production, the suggestion was not merely avoided but actively negated. When the Duke of York heard the accusation he reacted with incredulity, in a way that suggested it reflected discredit on whoever made it rather than on Richard, against whom it is made. Even before his return from Ireland, then, Richard was rising in the audience's sympathy.

One important symbol in this production was a mirror. Shakespeare himself calls for it, but Mr. Barton made much more extensive use of it than the text requires. The actors as actors used a mirror in the introductory mime, as they put on their costumes. Richard used the mirror more than once in the scene of the lists; indeed, he decided to go to Ireland only when he realized "how splendid he will look in armour (he holds his plumed helmet in the crook of his arm and reviews himself in the mirror)" (Stredder, p. 51). The mirror was thus established as a symbol of Richard's vanity before he called for it in the deposition scene (IV.i). In describing some of the techniques of the production, I have said little of the acting, but I should like to pay tribute, particularly, to Richard Pasco's treatment of this passage. We had a powerful sense of impotent and frustrated rage as he dashed his hand through the glass. Peter Thomson described the sequel[7] with a perceptive sense of its symbolism: "When Richard had punched out the glass, Bolingbroke lifted the empty ring-frame and placed it over Richard's head deliberately enough for us to see it pass from halo to crown, and from crown to noose to the enormously stressed accompaniment of"

> The shadow of your sorrow hath destroy'd
> The shadow of your face.
>
> (IV.i.292-93)

These lines were repeated, chanted in chorus, by the attendant lords. There was self-pity in Richard's action, perhaps, but there was strength, too; the strength of a man who, though he had been stripped of both the fantasies and the realities of monarchy—he now wore a simple gown—still had the strength to seek to know the truth about himself. For me, this was the emotional climax of the performance. Richard wore the empty frame of the mirror round his neck in the scene with his queen on the way to the Tower, and it was still there for the opening of his soliloquy shortly before his death in Pomfret Castle.

Whereas the growth of sympathy for Richard grows naturally from the text of the play, Bolingbroke's position in this respect is more problematical. The mere fact that he takes the place of the deposed King may turn us against his sinister, largely silent presence. "As he assumes the King's role," Mrs. Barton wrote, he "becomes silent, impersonal and remote: his thoughts and emotions concealed behind a mask." We are shown little of his inner feelings. Shakespeare gives him no soliloquy.

But in the production, much was different. Mr. Barton clarified, strengthened, and simplified Bolingbroke's role. The idea of becoming king was shown to have occurred to him earlier than in Shakespeare's text. After his banishment, his father, John of Gaunt, bidding him farewell, drew the shape of a crown in the air over his head—quite improperly, I thought, considering Gaunt's steadfast allegiance to the old order. In the same episode, the director added to Bolingbroke's final speech the line: "Now must I serve a long apprenticehood." This adapts Bolingbroke's words, "Must I not serve a long apprenticehood / To foreign passages" (I.iii.271-72), but the inescapable implication was that he would be apprenticed to the monarchy. I have described already the symbolical presentation of Northumberland as a way of minimizing Bolingbroke's guilt. In the trial of Bushy and Green, Bolingbroke did not speak the charges as from himself, but read them with obvious distaste from a document which Northumberland handed to him. The clear implication was that they were trumped-up charges.

Mr. Barton even gave Bolingbroke the soliloquy that Shakespeare failed to provide. It came at the beginning of Act Five, Scene Three, in which Shakespeare himself shows the new king unhappy at the absence of his son and experiencing some of the trials and tribulations of kingship. Mr. Barton inserted a speech which began with an abbreviated version of the same character's lament on his sleeplessness from *2 Henry IV* (III.i.4-9, 12-14), continued with four-and-a-half lines spoken by Warwick in the same play (III.i.80-84), four-and-a-half lines already spoken by Richard in *Richard II* (V.i.55-59), and three-and-a-half lines based on more of Henry's speeches in *2 Henry IV* (IV.v.185, 197-98; III.i.30-31). The gist of this extraordinary piece of cobbling was a meditation on royal sleeplessness, and awareness on Henry's part that he has been placed where he is by Northumberland, and that civil war will ensue. The soliloquy ended with words from *2 Henry IV*:

> Happy low, lie down!
> Uneasy lies the head that wears the [sic] crown!

On the last line, a group of lords came out of the shadows behind Henry, echoing the line, and a bridge passage was concocted from the lines following this in *2 Henry IV*. In the final scene, too, a skillful series of readjustments of emphasis drew sympathy for Bolingbroke at Northumberland's expense. The heads of the executed noblemen were brought in by Northumberland's men, impaled on pikes, whereas in the text they are merely mentioned. Richard's [sic; the intended name is Henry's] disgust at this brutality was clear. Harry Percy's accusation against the Bishop of Carlisle was reassigned to his father, Northumberland, and Bolingbroke's forgiveness of Carlisle became a calculatedly rebellious revulsion against Northumberland's domination.

The manipulation of Bolingbroke's role, and the additions to it, were clearly designed to increase sympathy for him, to suggest in him an awareness of a cyclical element in human history, and to bring him closer to Richard. This design was completed in the prison scene.

At the end of Richard's soliloquy, a groom enters to him. He has with some difficulty got permission to come to visit his old master, whom he saddens with the story of how Richard's horse, Roan Barbary, carried the usurper, Bolingbroke, to his coronation. This tiny but striking episode has its place in the design of the play. The common people have few representatives in *Richard II*. The groom is one of them, and his final allegiance helps to bind us to Richard in his last moments. He was played as a hooded figure with a rustic accent. When Richard had said,

> I was not made a horse,
> And yet I bear a burden like an ass,
> Spurred, galled, and tired by jauncing Bolingbroke
>                                                          (V.v.92-94)

he suddenly recognized the man before him. The groom threw back his hood and revealed himself as Bolingbroke in disguise. Richard took from his own neck the frame of the mirror and held it between them, so that each saw the other as if he were a reflection of himself. The director seemed intent on suggesting a recognition on Bolingbroke's part that both he and Richard have been the playthings of fortune, both finally united in a Wilfred Owen-like "strange meeting" in which their shared experience of the hollowness of the kingly crown draws them together more powerfully than their former rivalry sets them apart. Here we saw them as themselves, neither needing to act a part. They knelt for a moment in this pose before Bolingbroke left on the line: "What my tongue dares not, that my heart shall say."

It was a theatrically impressive moment, and represented an extension of something that is genuinely present in the play as Shakespeare wrote it. I confess all the same that I found it strained. Mr. Barton said during a public discussion at which I took the chair that he intended it as "a subliminal moment, so that though it is meaningful to Richard, he cannot actually tell whether it was dream or reality." And Mr. O'Brien writes: "Was it the King's eyes that gave to the groom the face of Bolingbroke?" (p. 119). This uncertainty might have been conveyable in the cinema by some kind of superimposition of images, but in the theatre we could not help identifying the actor as Bolingbroke. The confrontation seemed to demand an explanation that was not provided by the dialogue, and it conflicted with the line Richard has to say only a few moments later, when he attacks the keeper with the words, "The devil take Henry of Lancaster and thee," a line which surely denies the implication that there is explicit fellow-feeling between the two men. It illustrates a danger of Mr. Barton's production-methods; that, at their extremes, they were directing their audience what to think, instead of stimulating their imaginations to think it.

Here, it seemed to me, the director achieved theatrical effectiveness at the expense of our credulity. It was not a cheap theatricality, because it epitomized one aspect of the director's interpretation of the play; but it labored the point. I had, however, nothing but admiration for a piece of theatrical trickery at the end of the performance. The play had begun with the investiture of an actor as King Richard II. It seemed about to end with the final investiture, following Richard's death, of Bolingbroke as King Henry IV. Exton entered with the coffin of Richard, whom he had brutally murdered. Ian Richardson, when he played Bolingbroke, fell upon the coffin with a great cry of anguish, as if for his dearest friend. Mournful music sounded, and on the play's last line the coffin descended, as if into a vault. Coronation music returned, and the figure of Shakespeare, seen at the beginning of the play, appeared as if to crown Bolingbroke, who turned towards him, his back to the audience. Drums rolled powerfully in crescendo. Courtiers gathered around Bolingbroke. He was invested with the golden robe of kingship. All but two of his courtiers fell away, the music reached a climax, and the king turned to us. The drums suddenly ceased, and the courtiers beside Bolingbroke threw back their hoods and revealed themselves, one as the actor who had been playing Richard, the other as the actor who had been playing Bolingbroke. The robes between them, though glittering, were empty. The face was not that of King Richard, nor of King Henry. It was the face of the eternal king who keeps his court within the "mortal temples of a king." It was the face of death.

## NOTES

1. "Designing a Shakespeare Play: *Richard II*," *Shakespeare Jahrbuch* (West/ 1974), pp. 111-20.
2. "'Richard II' at Stratford, 1973"; M.A. in Shakespeare Studies, University of Birmingham, 1973.
3. "Dramatic Representation in Shakespeare's *Richard II*," *Sydney Studies in English* 1 (1975-76), pp. 32-45.
4. *The King's Two Bodies: A Study in Medieval Political Theology* (Princeton, 1957).
5. Testimony of Augustine Phillips, 18 February 1600, quoted in E.K. Chambers, *William Shakespeare*, 2 vols. (Oxford, 1930), II,325.
6. *King Richard the Second*, Folio Society, 1958; reprinted in *Stage Directions* (London, 1963), pp. 28-35; quotation from p. 33.
7. "Shakespeare Straight and Crooked: A Review of the 1973 Season at Stratford," *Shakespeare Survey* 27 (1974), pp. 143-54; quotation from p. 153.

# PART III
## *RICHARD II*
## The Psychology of Its Characters

## Samuel Taylor Coleridge

# Lectures on Shakespeare and Milton (1812)

Having said thus much on the, often falsely supposed, blemishes of our poet—blemishes which are said to prevail in *Richard II* especially,—I will now advert to the character of the King. He is represented as a man not deficient in immediate courage, which displays itself at his assassination; or in powers of mind, as appears by the foresight he exhibits throughout the play: still, he is weak, variable, and womanish, and possesses feelings, which, amiable in a female, are misplaced in a man, and altogether unfit for a king. In prosperity he is insolent and presumptuous, and in adversity, if we are to believe Dr. Johnson, he is humane and pious. I cannot admit the latter epithet, because I perceive the utmost consistency of character in Richard: what he was at first, he is at last, excepting as far as he yields to circumstances: what he shewed himself at the commencement of the play, he shews himself at the end of it. Dr. Johnson assigns to him rather the virtue of a confessor than that of a king.

True it is, that he may be said to be overwhelmed by the earliest misfortune that befalls him; but, so far from his feelings or disposition being changed or subdued, the very first glimpse of the returning sunshine of hope reanimates his spirits, and exalts him to as strange and unbecoming a degree of elevation, as he was before sunk in mental depression: the mention of those in his misfortunes, who had contributed to his downfall, but who had before been his nearest friends and favourites, calls forth from him expressions of the bitterest hatred and revenge. Thus, where Richard asks:

> Where is the Earl of Wiltshire? Where is Bagot?
> What is become of Bushy? Where is Green?
> That they have let the dangerous enemy
> Measure our confines with such peaceful steps?
> If we prevail, their heads shall pay for it.
> I warrant they have made peace with Bolingbroke.
>                                                    Act III, Scene 2.

Scroop answers:

> Peace have they made with him, indeed, my lord.

Upon which Richard, without hearing more, breaks out:

> O villains! vipers, damn'd without redemption!
> Dogs, easily won to fawn on any man!
> Snakes, in my heart-blood warm'd, that sting my heart!
> Three Judases, each one thrice worse than Judas!
> Would they make peace? terrible hell make war
> Upon their spotted souls for this offence!

Scroop observes upon this change, and tells the King how they had made their peace:

> Sweet love, I see, changing his property
> Turns to the sourest and most deadly hate.
> Again uncurse their souls: their peace is made
> With heads and not with hands: those whom you curse
> Have felt the worst of death's destroying wound,
> And lie full low, grav'd in the hollow ground.

Richard receiving at first an equivocal answer,—"Peace have they made with him, indeed, my lord,"—takes it in the worst sense: his promptness to suspect those who had been his friends turns his love to hate, and calls forth the most tremendous execrations.

From the beginning to the end of the play he pours out all the peculiarities and powers of his mind: he catches at new hope, and seeks new friends, is disappointed, despairs, and at length makes a merit of his resignation. He scatters himself into a multitude of images, and in conclusion endeavours to shelter himself from that which is around him by a cloud of his own thoughts. Throughout his whole career may be noticed the most rapid transitions—from the highest insolence to the lowest humility—from hope to despair, from the extravagance of love to the agonies of resentment, and from pretended resignation to the bitterest reproaches. The whole is joined with the utmost richness and copiousness of thought, and were there an actor capable of representing Richard, the part would delight us more than any other of Shakespeare's master-pieces,—with, perhaps, the single exception of King Lear. I know of no character drawn by our great poet with such unequalled skill as that of Richard II.

Next we come to Henry Bolingbroke, the rival of Richard II. He appears as a man of dauntless courage, and of ambition equal to that of Richard III; but, as I have stated, the difference between the two is most admirably conceived and preserved. In Richard III all that surrounds him is only dear as it feeds his inward sense of superiority: he is no vulgar tyrant—no Nero or Caligula: he has always an end in view, and vast fertility of means to accomplish that end. On the other hand, in Bolingbroke we find a man who in the outset has been sorely injured: then, we see him encouraged by the grievances of his country, and by the strange mismanagement of the government, yet at the same time scarcely daring to look at his own views, or to acknowledge them as designs. He comes home under the pretence of claiming his dukedom, and he professes that to be his object almost to the last: but, at the last, he avows his purpose to its full extent, of which he was himself unconscious in the earlier stages.

This is proved by so many passages, that I will only select one of them; and I take it the rather, because out of the many octavo volumes of text and notes, the page on which it occurs is, I believe, the only one left naked by the commentators. It is where Bolingbroke approaches the castle in which the unfortunate King has taken shelter: York is in Bolingbroke's company—the same York who is still contented with speaking the truth, but doing nothing for the sake of the truth,—drawing back after he has spoken, and becoming merely passive when he ought to display activity. Northumberland says:

> The news is very fair and good, my lord:
> Richard not far from hence hath hid his head.
> Act III, Scene 2.

York rebukes him thus:

> It would beseem the Lord Northumberland
> To say King Richard:—Alack, the heavy day,
> When such a sacred king should hide his head!

Northumberland replies:

> Your grace mistakes me: only to be brief
> Left I his title out.

To which York rejoins:

> The time hath been,
> Would you have been so brief with him, he would
> Have been so brief with you, to shorten you,
> For taking so the head, your whole head's length.

Bolingbroke observes,

> Mistake not, uncle, farther than you should;

And York answers, with a play upon the words "take" and "mistake":

> Take not, good cousin, farther than you should,
> Lest you mistake. The heavens are o'er our heads.

Here, give me leave to remark in passing, that the play upon words is perfectly natural, and quite in character: the answer is in unison with the tone of passion, and seems connected with some phrase then in popular use. Bolingbroke tells York:

> I know it, uncle, and oppose not myself
> Against their will.

Just afterwards, Bolingbroke thus addresses himself to Northumberland:

> Noble lord,
> Go to the rude ribs of that ancient castle;
> Through brazen trumpet send the breath of parle
> Into his ruin'd ears, and thus deliver.

Here, in the phrase "into his ruin'd ears," I have no doubt that Shakespeare purposely used the personal pronoun, "his," to shew, that although Bolingbroke was only speaking of the castle, his thoughts dwelt on the king. In Milton the pronoun, "her" is employed, in relation to "form," in a manner somewhat similar. Bolingbroke had an equivocation in his mind, and was thinking of the king, while speaking of the castle. He goes on to tell Northumberland what to say, beginning:

> Henry Bolingbroke,

which is almost the only instance in which a name forms the whole line; Shakespeare meant it to convey Bolingbroke's opinion of his own importance:—

> Henry Bolingbroke
> On both his knees doth kiss King Richard's hand,
> And sends allegiance and true faith of heart
> To his most royal person; hither come
> Even at his feet to lay my arms and power,
> Provided that, my banishment repealed,
> And lands restor'd again, be freely granted.
> If not, I'll use th' advantage of my power,
> And lay the summer's dust with showers of blood,
> Rain'd from the wounds of slaughter'd Englishmen.

At this point Bolingbroke seems to have been checked by the eye of York, and thus proceeds in consequence:

> The which, how far off from the mind of Bolingbroke
> It is, such crimson tempest should bedrench
> The fresh green lap of fair King Richard's land,
> My stooping duty tenderly shall show.

He passes suddenly from insolence to humility, owing to the silent reproof he received from his uncle. This change of tone would not have taken place, had Bolingbroke been allowed to proceed according to the natural bent of his mind, and the flow of the subject. Let me direct attention to the subsequent lines, for the same reason; they are part of the same speech:

> Let's march without the noise of threat'ning drum,
> That from the castle's tatter'd battlements
> Our fair appointments may be well perused.

> Methinks, King Richard and myself should meet
> With no less terror than the elements
> Of fire and water, when their thundering shock
> At meeting tears the cloudy cheeks of heaven.

Having proceeded thus far with the exaggeration of his own importance, York again checks him, and Bolingbroke adds, in a very different strain,

> He be the fire, I'll be the yielding water:
> The rage be his, while on the earth I rain
> My waters; on the earth, and not on him.

I have thus adverted to the three great personages in this drama, Richard, Bolingbroke, and York; and of the whole play it may be asserted, that with the exception of some of the last scenes (though they have exquisite beauty) Shakespeare seems to have risen to the summit of excellence in the delineation and preservation of character.

## Walter Pater

## Shakespeare's English Kings (1889)

A brittle glory shineth in this face;
As brittle as the glory is the face.

The English plays of Shakespeare needed but the completion of one unimportant interval to possess the unity of a popular chronicle from Richard the Second to Henry the Eighth, and possess, as they actually stand, the unity of a common motive in the handling of the various events and persons which they bring before us. Certain of his historic dramas, not English, display Shakespeare's mastery in the development of the heroic nature amid heroic circumstances; and had he chosen, from English history, to deal with Coeur-de-Lion or Edward the First, the innate quality of his subject would doubtless have called into play something of that profound and sombre power which in *Julius Caesar* and *Macbeth* has sounded the depths of mighty character. True, on the whole, to fact, it is another side of kingship which he has made prominent in his English histories. The irony of kingship—average human nature, flung with a wonderfully pathetic effect into the vortex of great events; tragedy of everyday quality heightened in degree only by the conspicuous scene which does but make those who play their parts there conspicuously unfortunate; the utterance of common humanity straight from the heart, but refined like other common things for kingly uses by Shakespeare's unfailing eloquence: such, unconsciously for the most part, though palpably enough to the careful reader, is the conception under which Shakespeare has arranged the lights and shadows of the story of the English kings, emphasizing merely the light and shadow inherent in it, and keeping very close to the original authorities, not simply in the general outline of these dramatic histories but sometimes in their very expression. Certainly the history itself, as he found it in Hall, Holinshed, and Stowe, those somewhat picturesque old chroniclers who had themselves an eye for the dramatic "effects" of human life, has much of this sentiment already about it. What he did not find there was the natural prerogative—such justification, in kingly, that is to say, in exceptional, qualities, of the exceptional position, as makes it practicable in the result. It is no *Henriade* he writes, and no history of the English people, but the sad fortunes of some English kings as conspicuous examples of the ordinary human condition. As in a children's story, all princes are in extremes. Delightful in the sunshine above the wall into which chance lifts the flower for a season, they can but plead somewhat more touchingly than others their everyday weakness in the storm. Such is the motive that gives unity to these unequal and intermittent contributions toward a slowly evolved dramatic chronicle, which it would have taken many days to rehearse; a not distant story from real life still well remembered in its general course, to which people might listen now and again, as long as they cared, finding human nature at least wherever their attention struck ground in it.

He begins with John, and allows indeed to the first of these English kings a kind of greatness, making the development of the play center in the counteraction of his natural gifts—that something of heroic force about him—by a madness which takes the shape of reckless impiety, forced especially on man's attention by the terrible circumstances of his end, in the delineation of which Shakespeare triumphs, setting, with true poetic tact, this incident of the king's death, in all the horror of a violent one, amid a scene delicately suggestive of what is perennially peaceful and genial in the outward world. Like the sensual humours of Falstaff in another play, the presence of the bastard Faulconbridge, with his physical energy and his unmistakable family likeness—"those limbs which Sir Robert never holp to make"[1]—contributes to an almost coarse assertion of the force of nature, of the somewhat ironic preponderance of nature and circumstance over men's artificial arrangements, to the recognition of a certain potent natural aristocracy, which is far from being always identical with that more formal, heraldic one. And what is a coarse fact in the case of Faulconbridge becomes a motive of pathetic appeal in the wan and babyish Arthur. The magic with which nature models tiny and delicate children to the likeness of their rough fathers is nowhere more justly expressed than in the words of King Philip.—

> Look here upon thy brother Geoffrey's face!
> These eyes, these brows were moulded out of his:
> This little abstract doth contain that large
> Which died in Geoffrey; and the hand of time
> Shall draw this brief into as huge a volume.

It was perhaps something of a boyish memory of the shocking end of his father that had distorted the piety of Henry the Third into superstitious terror. A frightened soul, himself touched with the contrary sort of religious madness, doting on all that was alien from his father's huge ferocity, on the genialities, the soft gilding, of life, on the genuine interests of art and poetry, to be credited more than any other person with the deep religious expression of Westminster Abbey, Henry the Third, picturesque though useless, but certainly touching, might have furnished Shakespeare, had he filled up this interval in his series, with precisely the kind of effect he tends towards in his English plays. But he found it completer still in the person and story of Richard the Second, a figure—"that sweet lovely rose"—which haunts Shakespeare's mind, as it seems long to have haunted the minds of the English people, as the most touching of all examples of the irony of kingship.

Henry the Fourth—to look for a moment beyond our immediate subject, in pursuit of Shakespeare's thought—is presented, of course, in general outline, as an impersonation of "surviving force": he has a certain amount of kingcraft also, a real fitness for great opportunity. But still true to his leading motive, Shakespeare, in *King Henry the Fourth*, has left the high-water mark of his poetry in the soliloquy which represents royalty longing vainly for the toiler's sleep; while the popularity, the showy heroism, of Henry the Fifth, is used to give emphatic point to the old earthy commonplace about "wild oats." The wealth of homely humor in these plays, the fun coming straight home to all the world, of Fluellen especially in his unconscious interview with the king, the boisterous earthiness of Falstaff and his companions, contribute to the same effect. The keynote of Shakespeare's treatment is indeed expressed by Henry the Fifth himself, the *greatest* of Shakespeare's kings.—"Though I speak it to you," he says *incognito*, under cover of night, to a common soldier on the field, "I think the king is but a man, as I am: the violet smells to him as it doth to me: all his senses have but human conditions; and though his affections be higher mounted than ours yet when they stoop they stoop with like wing." And, in truth, the really kingly speeches which Shakespeare assigns to him, as to other kings weak enough in all but speech, are but a kind of flowers, worn for, and effective only as personal embellishment. They combine to one result with the merely outward and ceremonial ornaments of royalty, its pageantries, flaunting so naively, so credulously, in Shakespeare, as in that old medieval time. And then, the force of Hotspur is but transient youth, the common heat of youth, in him. The character of Henry the Sixth again, *roi fainéant*, with La Pucelle[2] for his counterfoil, lay in the direct course of Shakespeare's design: he has done much to fix the sentiment of the "holy Henry." Richard the Third, touched, like John, with an effect of real heroism, is spoiled like him by something of criminal madness, and reaches his highest level of tragic expression when circumstances reduce him to terms of mere human nature.—

> A horse! A horse! My kingdom for a horse!

The Princes in the Tower recall to mind the lot of young Arthur:—

> I'll go with thee,
> And find the inheritance of this poor child,
> His little kingdom of a forced grave.

And when Shakespeare comes to Henry the Eighth, it is not the superficial though very English splendor of the king himself, but the really potent and ascendant nature of the butcher's son on the one hand, and Katharine's subdued reproduction of the sad fortunes of Richard the Second on the other, that define his central interest.³

With a prescience of the Wars of the Roses, of which his errors were the original cause, it is Richard who best exposes Shakespeare's own constant sentiment concerning war, and especially that sort of civil war which was then recent in English memories. The soul of Shakespeare, certainly, was not wanting in a sense of the magnanimity of warriors. The grandiose aspects of war, its magnificent apparelling, he records monumentally enough—the "dressing of the lists," the lion's heart, its unfaltering haste thither in all the freshness of youth and morning.—

> Not sick although I have to do with death—
> The sun doth gild our armour: Up, my Lords!—
> I saw young Harry with his beaver on,
> His cuisses on his thighs, gallantly arm'd,
> Rise from the ground like feather'd Mercury.

Only, with Shakespeare, the afterthought is immediate:—

> They come like sacrifices in their trim.
>
> —Will it never be to-day? I will trot to-morrow a mile, and my way shall be paved with English faces.

This sentiment Richard reiterates very plaintively, in association with the delicate sweetness of the English fields, still sweet and fresh, like London and her other fair towns in that England of Chaucer, for whose soil the exiled Bolingbroke is made to long so dangerously, while Richard on his return from Ireland salutes it—

> That pale, that white-fac'd shore,—
> As a long-parted mother with her child.—
> So, weeping, smiling, greet I thee, my earth!
> And do thee favour with my royal hands.—

Then (of Bolingbroke)

> Ere the crown he looks for live in peace,
> Ten thousand bloody crowns of mothers' sons
> Shall ill become the flower of England's face;

> Change the complexion of her maid-pale peace
> To scarlet indigestion, and bedew
> My pastures' grass with faithful English blood.—
>
> Why have they dared to march?—

asks York,

> So many miles upon her peaceful bosom,
> Frighting her pale-fac'd visages with war?—

waking, according to Richard,

> Our peace, which in our country's cradle,
> Draws the sweet infant breath of gentle sleep:—

bedrenching "with crimson tempest"

> The fresh green lap of fair king Richard's land:—

frighting "fair peace" from "our quiet confines," laying

> The summer's dust with showers of blood,
> Rained from the wounds of slaughter'd Englishmen:

bruising

> Her flowerets with the armed hoofs
> Of hostile paces.

Perhaps it is not too fanciful to note in this play a peculiar recoil from the mere instruments of warfare, the contact of the "rude ribs," the "flint bosom," of Barkloughly Castle or Pomfret or

> Julius Caesar's ill-erected tower:

the

> Boisterous untun'd drums
> With harsh-resounding trumpets' dreadful bray
> And grating shock of wrathful iron arms.

It is as if the lax, soft beauty of the king took effect, at least by contrast, on everything beside.

One gracious prerogative, certainly, Shakespeare's English kings possess: they are a very eloquent company, and Richard is the most sweet-tongued of them all. In no other play perhaps is there such a flush of those gay, fresh, variegated flowers of speech—color and figure, not lightly attached to, but fused into, the very phrase itself—which Shakespeare cannot help dispensing to his characters, as in this "play of the Deposing of King Richard the Second," an exquisite poet if he is nothing else, from first to last, in light and gloom alike, able to see all things poetically, to give a poetic turn to his conduct of them, and refreshing with his golden language the tritest aspects of that ironic contrast between the pretensions of a king and the actual necessities of his destiny. What a garden of words! With him, blank verse, infinitely graceful, deliberate, musical in inflection, becomes indeed a true "verse royal," that rhyming lapse, which to the Shakespearean ear, at least in youth, came as the last touch of refinement on it, being here doubly appropriate. His eloquence blends with that fatal beauty, of which he was so frankly aware, so amiable to his friends, to his wife, of the effects of which on the people his enemies were so much afraid, on which Shakespeare himself dwells so attentively as the "royal blood" comes and goes in the face with his rapid changes of temper. As happens with sensitive natures, it attunes him to a congruous suavity of manners, by which anger itself became flattering; it blends with his merely youthful hopefulness and high spirits, his sympathetic love for gay people, things, apparel —"his cote of gold and stone, valued at thirty thousand marks," the novel Italian fashions he preferred, as also with those real amiabilities that made people forget the darker touches of his character, but never tire of the pathetic rehearsal of his fall, the meekness of which would have seemed merely abject in a less graceful performer.

Yet it is only fair to say that in the painstaking "revival" of *King Richard the Second,* by the late Charles Kean, those who were very young thirty years ago were afforded much more than Shakespeare's play could ever have been before—the very person of the king based on the stately old portrait in Westminster, "the earliest extant contemporary likeness of any English sovereign," the grace, the winning pathos, the sympathetic voice of the player, the tasteful archaeology confronting vulgar modern London with a scenic reproduction, for once really agreeable, of the London of Chaucer. In the hands of Kean the play became like an exquisite performance on the violin.

The long agony of one so gaily painted by nature's self, from his "tragic abdication" till the hour in which he

> Sluiced out his innocent soul thro' streams of blood,

was for playwrights a subject ready to hand, and became early the theme of a popular drama, of which some have fancied surviving favorite fragments in the rhymed parts of Shakespeare's work:

> The king Richard of Yngland
> Was in his flowris then regnand:
> But his flowris efter sone
> Fadyt, and ware all undone:—

says the old chronicle. Strangely enough, Shakespeare supposes him an overconfident believer in that divine right of kings, of which people in Shakespeare's time were coming to hear so much; a general right, sealed to him (so Richard is made to think) as an ineradicable gift by the touch—stream rather, over head and breast and shoulders—of the "holy oil" of his consecration at Westminster; not, however, through some oversight, the genuine balm used at the coronation of his successor, given, according to legend, by the Blessed Virgin to Saint Thomas of Canterbury. Richard himself found that, it was said, among other forgotten treasures, at the crisis of his changing fortunes, and vainly sought reconsecration therewith—understood, wistfully, that it was reserved for his happier rival. And yet his coronation, by the pageantry, the amplitude, the learned care, of its order, so lengthy that the king, then only eleven years of age, and fasting, as a communicant at the ceremony, was carried away in a faint, fixed the type under which it has ever since continued. And nowhere is there so emphatic a reiteration as in *Richard the Second* of the sentiment which those singular rites were calculated to produce.

> Not all the water in the rough rude sea
> Can wash the balm from an anointed king,—

as supplementing another, almost supernatural, right.—"Edward's seven sons," of whom Richard's father was one,

> Were as seven phials of his sacred blood.

But this, too, in the hands of Shakespeare, becomes for him, like any other of those fantastic, ineffectual, easily discredited, personal graces, as capricious in its operation on men's wills as merely physical beauty, kindling himself to eloquence indeed, but only giving double pathos to insults which "barbarism itself" might have pitied—the dust in his face, as he returns, through the streets of London, a prisoner in the train of his victorious enemy.

> How soon my sorrow hath destroyed my face!

he cries, in that most poetic invention of the mirror scene, which does but reinforce again that physical charm which all confessed. The sense of "divine right" in kings is found to act not so much as a secret of power over others, as of infatuation to themselves. And of all those personal gifts the one which alone never altogether fails him is just that royal utterance, his appreciation of the poetry of his own hapless lot, an eloquent self-pity, infecting others in spite of themselves, till they too become irresistibly eloquent about him.

In the Roman Pontifical, of which the order of Coronation is really a part, there is no form for the inverse process, no rite of "degradation," such as that by which an offending priest or bishop may be deprived, if not of the essential quality of "orders," yet, one by one, of its outward dignities. It is as if Shakespeare had had in mind some such inverted rite, like those old ecclesiastical or military ones, by which human hardness, or human justice, adds the last touch of unkindness to the execution of its sentences, in the scene where Richard "deposes" himself, as in some long, agonizing ceremony, reflectively drawn out, with an extraordinary refinement of intelligence and variety of piteous appeal, but also with a felicity of poetic invention, which puts these pages into a very select class, with the finest "vermeil and ivory" work of Chatterton or Keats.

> Fetch hither Richard that in common view
> He may surrender!—

And Richard more than concurs: he throws himself into the part, realizes a type, falls gracefully as on the world's stage.— Why is he sent for?

> To do that office of thine own good will
> Which tired majesty did make thee offer.—
>
> . Now mark me! how I will undo myself.

"Hath Bolingbroke deposed thine intellect?" the Queen asks him, on his way to the Tower:—

> Hath Bolingbroke
> Deposed thine intellect? hath he been in thy heart?

And in truth, but for that adventitious poetic gold, it would be only "plume-plucked Richard."—

> I find myself a traitor with the rest,
> For I have given here my soul's consent
> To undeck the pompous body of a king.

He is duly reminded, indeed, how

> That which in mean men we entitle patience
> Is pale cold cowardice in noble breasts.

Yet at least within the poetic bounds of Shakespeare's play, through Shakespeare's bountiful gifts, his desire seems fulfilled.—

> O! that I were as great
> As is my grief.

And his grief becomes nothing less than a central expression of all that in the revolutions of Fortune's wheel goes *down* in the world.

No! Shakespeare's kings are not, nor are meant to be, great men: rather, little or quite ordinary humanity, thrust upon greatness, with those pathetic results, the natural self-pity of the weak heightened in them into irresistible appeal to others as the net result of their royal prerogative. One after another, they seem to lie composed in Shakespeare's embalming pages, with just that touch of nature about them, making the whole world akin, which has infused into their tombs at Westminster a rare poetic grace. It is that irony of kingship, the sense that it is in its happiness child's play, in its sorrows, after all, but children's grief, which gives its finer accent to all the changeful feeling of these wonderful speeches:—the great meekness of the graceful, wild creature, tamed at last.—

> Give Richard leave to live till Richard die!

his somewhat abject fear of death, turning to acquiescence at moments of extreme weariness:—

> My large kingdom for a little grave!
> A little little grave, an obscure grave!—

his religious appeal in the last reserve, with its bold reference to the judgment of Pilate, as he thinks once more of his "anointing."

And as it happens with children he attains contentment finally in the merely passive recognition of superior strength, in the naturalness of the result of the great battle as a matter of course, and experiences something of the royal prerogative of poetry to obscure, or at least to attune and soften men's griefs. As in some sweet anthem of Handel, the sufferer, who put finger to the organ under the utmost pressure of mental conflict, extracts a kind of peace at last from the mere skill with which he sets his distress to music.—

> Beshrew thee, Cousin, that didst lead me forth
> Of that sweet way I was in to despair!

"With Cain go wander through the shades of night!"—cries the new king to the gaoler Exton, dissimulating his share in the murder he is thought to have suggested; and in truth there is something of the murdered Abel about Shakespeare's Richard. The fact seems to be that he died of "waste and a broken heart": it was by way of proof that his end had been a natural one that, stifling a real fear of the face, the face of Richard, on men's minds, with the added pleading now of all dead faces, Henry exposed the corpse to general view; and Shakespeare, in bringing it on the stage, in the last scene of his play, does but follow out the motive with which he has emphasized Richard's physical beauty all through it—that "most beauteous inn," as the Queen says quaintly, meeting him on the way to death—residence, then soon to be deserted, of that wayward, frenzied, but withal so affectionate soul. Though the body did not go to Westminster immediately, his tomb,

> That small model of the barren earth
> Which serves as paste and cover to our bones,[4]

the effigy clasping the hand of his youthful consort, was already prepared there, with "rich gilding and ornaments," monument of poetic regret, for Queen Anne of Bohemia, not of course the "Queen" of Shakespeare, who however seems to have transferred to this second wife something of Richard's wildly proclaimed affection for the first. In this way, through the connecting link of that sacred spot, our thoughts once more associate Richard's two fallacious prerogatives, his personal beauty and his "anointing."

According to Johnson, *Richard the Second* is one of those plays which Shakespeare has "apparently revised"; and how doubly delightful Shakespeare is where he seems to have revised! "Would that he had blotted a thousand"—a thousand hasty phrases, we may venture once more to say with his earlier critic, now that the tiresome German superstition has passed away which challenged us to a dogmatic faith in the plenary verbal inspiration of every one of Shakespeare's clowns. Like some melodiously contending anthem of Handel's, I said, of Richard's meek "undoing" of himself in the mirror-scene; and, in fact, the play of *Richard the Second* does, like a musical composition, possess a certain concentration of all its parts, a simple continuity, an evenness in execution, which are rare in the great dramatist. With *Romeo and Juliet*, that perfect symphony (symphony of three independent poetic forms set in a grander one[5] which it is the merit of German criticism to have detected) it belongs to a small group of plays, where, by happy birth and consistent evolution, dramatic form approaches to something like the unity of a lyrical ballad, a lyric, a song, a single strain of music. Which sort of poetry we are to account the highest, is perhaps a barren question. Yet if, in art generally, unity of impression is a note of what is perfect, then lyric poetry, which in spite of complex structure often preserves the unity of a single passionate ejaculation, would rank higher than dramatic poetry, where, especially to the reader, as distinguished from the spectator assisting at a theatrical performance, there must always be a sense of the effort necessary to keep the various parts from flying asunder, a sense of imperfect continuity, such as the older criticism vainly sought to obviate by the rule of the dramatic "unities." It follows that a play attains artistic perfection just in proportion as it approaches that unity of lyrical effect, as if a song or ballad were still lying at the root of it, all the various expression of the conflict of character and circumstance falling at last into the compass of a single melody, or musical theme. As, historically, the earliest classic drama arose out of the chorus, from which this or that person, this or that episode, detached itself, so, into the unity of a choric song the perfect drama ever tends to return, its intellectual scope deepened, complicated, enlarged, but still with an unmistakable singleness, or identity, in its impression on the mind. Just there, in that vivid single impression left on the mind when all is over, not in any mechanical limitation of time and place, is the secret of the "unities"—the true imaginative unity—of the drama.

NOTES

1.  *Elinor.* Do you not read some tokens of my son (Coeur-de-Lion)
    In the large composition of this man?

2. Perhaps the one person of *genius* in these English plays.

    The spirit of deep prophecy she hath,
    Exceeding the nine Sibyls of old Rome:
    What's past and what's to come she can descry.

3. Proposing in this paper to trace the leading sentiment in Shakespeare's English Plays as a sort of *popular dramatic chronicle*, I have left untouched the question how much (or, in the case of *Henry the Sixth* and *Henry the Eighth*, how little) of them may be really his: how far inferior hands have contributed to a result, true on the

whole to the greater, that is to say, the Shakespearean elements in them.
4. Perhaps a *double entendre*:—of any ordinary grave, as comprising, in effect, the whole small earth now left to its occupant: or, of such a tomb as Richard's in particular, with its actual model, or effigy, of the clay of him. Both senses are so characteristic that it would be a pity to lose either.
5. The Sonnet : the Aubade : the Epithalamium.

# E.K. Chambers

## The Tragedy of King Richard the Second (1891)

The histories of Shakespeare have a threefold burden. They are largely epical in character, a bead-roll, as it were, of English kings, stretching from Magna Charta to the coming of the Tudors. The period from Richard II onwards is practically complete; the rest remains unfinished, but the interval left after *King John* is partly bridged over by Peele's *Edward I*, by Marlowe's *Edward II*, and by the play of *Edward III*, wherein Shakespeare himself may have had a hand. It is easy to find the motive for such a drama-cycle in the "new spring" of patriotic enthusiasm born in England of the Spanish Wars: to this spirit the youthful poet,[1] for all his deeper insight into things, fully and frankly yielded himself; the expression of it is the common prerogative of all the personages in these plays, of John and Richard no less than of Henry V himself. In the sixteenth century, History was just beginning to fill the place of mere contemporary Chronicle; Englishmen were just awaking to a wider outlook over the world, and with it to a sense that they had, as a people, a past in which they were bound to feel an interest and a pride. At such a time it was natural that Poetry too should take a retrospect, and make her harvest of all that was pity-moving or soul-stirring in the national record.

Secondly, there is the element of purely human, of tragic interest in the spectacle of so many men called one after another, not from any grace or gift of their own, but by the accident of being kings, to grapple with dangerous moral and social forces, and, most often, failing in their task. The Vergilian "sense of tears in mortal things" is nowhere more manifest than in the annals of Roman emperors or English sovereigns.[2]

Though this is much, there is "more in it." At bottom Shakespeare is always a student, and these plays are the outcome of a student's reflection on grave questions concerning the well-being of a nation. For Shakespeare, as for Thucydides, History becomes at once a judgment of the past and a forecast of the future; no longer merely a tale of "forgotten, far off things," it is an "eternal possession," and a potent factor in determining the conduct of life. Thus *Richard II* and the rest are studies in kingship, wherein, to those who can read, the poet has laid bare his mind upon the problems of government in the form which they appeared in to our ancestors. His answer to them is one which Plato might have applauded. He finds the true foundation of regal authority neither in an imaginary divine right nor in the will of a parliamentary assembly: the genuine king and leader of men is he who best understands and sympathizes with the needs and aspirations of his people, and is best fitted to guide them in the working out of their proper destiny. John forgot this, and left his country in the hands of a foreign invader; Richard II and Henry IV failed to regard it, and overwhelmed her with all the horrors of the Wars of the Roses.

In the days in which this message was delivered, it was sorely needed. The Tudors wrought a great work for England, but their task was already achieved when Shakespeare wrote. The country was at last free, united, prosperous, a pleasant and a merry land to dwell in. And now the evils inherent in the Tudor conception of monarchy began to outweigh its influence for good; the gradual extension of the royal prerogative threatened to swamp the liberties of the people. As yet the danger was hardly felt; it was reserved for the next century to preach once more the doctrines, dangerous to princes as princes themselves to those who put their trust in them, of the "divine right of kings," but Shakespeare saw more clearly than People, Parliament, or Queen: his wider vision stretched back to Runnymede and to Pontefract, and on, with vague poetic foresight, to the scaffold outside Whitehall. The English histories are his word of warning to a regardless nation, and the fatality which has always hung around revivals of *Richard II* forms a curious commentary on the text.[3]

There are thus threads of unity running through all these plays; in all we find a common dramatic treatment of history; but the smaller group, almost an English trilogy, which deals with Richard II and his two immediate successors, is woven even more closely into one web. It exhibits to us three types of king, one of them perfect, Shakespeare's ideal ruler, the other two imperfect, because lacking in the essential elements of that ideal. Henry V has all the notes of a true king. He has gone through no degrading intrigues to win his crown; neither is he weak and vain, but rather full of resource and overflowing with energy. This superabundant vitality made him wanton in his youth, but once he is on the throne it is soon converted into more fitting channels. Above all, he is neither unjust nor self-seeking; fully in harmony with the life of his people, he is ready to put himself at their head and lead them on to the accomplishment of their high fortunes. It is true that Shakespeare regards these fortunes as inextricably bound up with foreign conquest; there he is the child of his age; but, however much his spirit may resound to the "pomp and circumstance of glorious war," yet we feel that the horrors and the "pity of it" are never far from his thoughts.

The other two kings, in different ways, fall short of the ideal. Both are purely selfish in their aims, and unscrupulous of the rights of the nation in their pursuit of uncontrolled power. Moreover, Richard is unstable and frivolous; Henry has the blot of treachery and murder upon his soul. Thus both their lives are failures; it is good to be a lawful king, and it is good to be strong and self-reliant, but it is only devotion to a people's cause that can save from ruin. Yet Shakespeare does not choose to paint in crude colors; both these men have the outward aspect, the speech and bearing of a king.

*Richard II* forms part of a trilogy, and its meaning is amplified and enriched by comparison with the plays that follow it; yet, as it stands, it has a self-centered, independent unity of its own. It seems to have been written some years before *Henry IV* and *Henry V*, and perhaps slightly modified at a subsequent period in order to take its place in the series. The first essential of every work of art is a principle of unity, and the English romantic drama—having rejected the so-called classical or formal unities of place, time, and action—gradually evolved for itself an inner spiritual unity of thought. In Shakespeare this takes the form of an underlying central idea whose truth is illustrated by the development of the action. These ideas are generally human in their bearing; they deal with Character and Love and Kingship, or, in many of the later plays, with the deepest problems of the origin and destinies of man and the government of the world. The central idea of *Richard II* is a tragical one; it is a tragedy of failure, the necessary failure of a king, however rightfully he may reign, however "fair a show" he may present, if he is weak and self-seeking and lawless. The action of the play presents the working-out of this tragedy; it traces the downfall of Richard from the scenes where he appears as a powerful monarch, disposing with a word of the lives of his subjects, to that where his unkinged, murdered corpse is borne on to the stage. The instrument of his ruin is his cousin Henry, and therefore Bolingbroke's rise becomes a natural parallel to Richard's fall. The king's own image of the two buckets holds good: in the first act Richard is supreme, Henry at the lowest depth; gradually one sinks, the other ascends, until they are on a level, when they meet at Flint Castle. As is often the case, the turning-point of the action is put precisely in the middle of the play. Still the same process continues, and when the final catastrophe of the last act occurs, the original positions of the two are exactly reversed; it is now Henry's word that is potent to doom Richard. Whether the play has been revised or not, it is at least a marvel of careful workmanship; situations and phrases constantly occur in the second half of the play which are pointed inversions of others at the beginning. The moving forces of the play are thus to be found in the characters of the chief personages, in the clash of two spirits, one capable, the other incapable, of making circumstances the stepping-stones to his own end. This is carefully brought out in the first scene; the opposition between the kings, hidden as yet from others, is here clearly revealed to themselves, and the key-note of the whole play is touched. A comparison of the two natures is ample to explain the outcome of the struggle between them.

On the delineation of Richard all the resources of Shakespeare's genius have been poured: it is a work of art and of love. We have presented to us the portrait of a finely tempered man, gifted and graced in mind and body. He "looks like a king" for beauty and majesty, with his fair face in which the blood comes and goes. His marvellous wealth of eloquent imaginative speech irradiates the play. His power of personal fascination, no less than his intense selfishness and pitiful fate, remind us of Charles Stuart, the melancholy-eyed man, who lured Strafford to his doom; it enthrals the queen, it enthrals Aumerle, it enthrals even the "poor groom of his stable." He meets them with answering affection that twines itself around not men and women only, but the horse he rides upon and the earth he treads. The very root of his nature is an exquisite sensitiveness, intellectual and emotional; he reads his cousin's thoughts in his face; he is a lover of music and of pageantry, of regal hospitality and refined luxurious splendor. And withal there are lacking in him the elements which go to make up the backbone of a character. This beautiful, cultured king, for all his delicate half-tones of feeling and thought, is a being devoid of moral sense, treacherous, unscrupulous, selfish; he murders his uncle, robs his cousin, and oppresses his people; he trails the fair name of England in the dust; even in the days of his captivity he regrets his follies, but scarcely regards his crimes. It is not in moral sense only that he is deficient, but in moral and intellectual fiber; like Plato's "musical man" he has "piped away his soul with sweet and plaintive melodies";[4] he can divine Bolingbroke's wishes, but he cannot judge his character aright, nor can he forecast the results of his own lawless acts. In prosperity he yields himself to flatterers; in adversity he puts an idle confidence in a supposed God-given commission to reign. Contrary events are for him not a spur to action, but an incentive to imagination; he plays around them with lambent words; he is always "studying how to compare." The best side of him appears when he is fallen; he becomes the part of victim better than that of tyrant; the softer qualities in him move our pity, the sterner ones that he has not are less needed. True, he strikes no blow, and finds a ready comfort in despair, but he keeps his plaining and poetic laments for his friends, and meets the rebel lords with subtle scorn and all the dignity of outraged royalty. Yet even here he betrays, like another of Shakespeare's characters—Orsino in *Twelfth Night*—what we are accustomed to think of as essentially modern faults; he is a shade too self-conscious, a touch too theatrical in his attitude.

To the checkered lights and shadows of such a disposition Bolingbroke presents the most complete contrast. He leaves the impression of little grace and intense power. A man of iron will and subtle pertinacious intellect, a true "crown-grasper," he clearly envisages his end and remorselessly pursues it, playing with a masterly hand upon the hates and loves and ambitions of other men. Rarely does he betray any emotion; very rarely does he speak an uncalculated word. He can "steal courtesy from heaven" to win the hearts of the citizens or the favors of the Percies, but his genuine temper is shown in the undertone of studied sarcasm which runs through his bearing towards Richard in the first act, and makes itself heard at intervals throughout the play. His life is a web of intrigue; the disillusioned Hotspur in *Henry IV* calls him "subtle king" and "vile politician," while upon his unhappy death-bed he whispers to the watching prince "by what bypaths and indirect crooked ways he met his crown." His schemes are for the time successful, but before long they recoil upon him in the alienation of the nobles he has tricked and the wild life of his son.

As is not seldom the case in the early plays, many of the minor characters are less carefully wrought. They fall mainly into two groups, clustering respectively around Richard and Bolingbroke; but their interest is purely subordinate, as there is no secondary plot. Between the opposing parties stand the two dukes, York and Lancaster. John of Gaunt represents the heroic age of England, of "noble Edward" and the Black Prince; he unites the loyalty and piety of the olden days with a deep hatred of the king's crimes and newfangled vanities. Yet he is no rebel; he has a private grief in the banishment of his son, a public one in the inglorious peace and shameful misgovernment of the realm, but he is content to "put his quarrel to the will of heaven," and his death removes the last barrier between Richard and ruin. The Duke of York is of quite another type; he too is pious, old-fashioned and loyal, but with the loyalty not of the high-principled statesman, warrior, and idealist, but of the weak, indolent opportunist, content to maintain the established order, and serve whatever king may reign. Among Richard's supporters, Aumerle is interesting as the champion of his cousin's claims, but personally he is shadowy. Mowbray is a plain, upright soldier and servant of his king; his unjust exile comes like a thunderbolt upon him; he utters only a few words of dignified remonstrance and leaves his country, to die of a broken heart. The Bishop of Carlisle plays the part of the stern ascetic prelate; it is his function to emphasize Richard's claim to rule by divine right, and pronounce the curse of heaven on the usurper. The king's flatterers are curiously characterless; so too are the Percies and Fitzwaters who surround Bolingbroke; they typify the headstrong, boisterous nobility of the day, whom he duped and made his tools. On the other hand the women, though they have little share in the action, are important; they touch the world of politics and intrigue with the warmth of human personal emotion. The Duchess of Gloucester makes us feel Richard's villainy; the queen makes us feel his sorrow; the first scene where she speaks brings about a change in our attitude towards him.

And after all, in this play, it is the effect on the emotions that is the great thing; there is hardly another that moves us, that overwhelms us, like this. For here Shakespeare has not been content with producing a single type of unity; he has attempted to secure it not alone in the sphere of imagination but in that of feeling, the unity of music as well as of painting. He would have us leave the play with something of the impression that we get from a faultless lyric—a sense of some over-mastering emotion, that satisfies our consciousness for the moment, and stirs the "god within us." Whether such an effect is really within the scope of a drama may be doubtful; certainly none has so nearly attained it as *Richard II*. Here it is a divine pity that wells up as we watch the slowly-gathering fate of the beautiful, sad king. About the same time Shakespeare made a similar experiment with the intenser, more personal emotions of love in *Romeo and Juliet*. Afterwards he seems to have preferred to develop the drama on lines distinct from those of the lyric, and to find its proper province in the delineation of character rather than the expression of passion. Yet one is almost tempted to wish that, even at the expense of skillful workmanship and stage capabilities, he had given us some more of these soul-piercing, poignant poem-plays, so suffused with warmth and color, each of them, as has been said of those of the master-singer of our own day, like

> Some pomegranate which, if cut deep down the middle,
> Shows a heart within blood-tinctured, of a veined humanity.

The element of lyricism is strong in *Richard II*, as it is throughout the early plays, in details of style, no less than in general outline of structure; it shows itself in the character of the versification, in the proportion of rhyming lines,[5] in the alternating one-line dialogue, akin to the στ-χομνθιά of Greek tragedy, and in the couplets, quatrains, and sestets which occasionally occur. In *Love's Labour's Lost* entire sonnets are inserted in the text, while in *Romeo and Juliet* an acute criticism has traced the influence of the great forms of love-poetry, the Sonnet, Epithalamium, and Aubade: possibly the "parting-song" between Bolingbroke and Gaunt and Richard and his queen may owe something to a similar origin.[6]

Another indication of the early date of the play is to be seen in the prevalence of alliteration and also of puns and other verbal conceits. Sometimes, as at the end of act III, sc. i, these are used with splendid effect; they express the grim humor which is the nearest approach to a laugh in this tragedy; but often they are farfetched and out of place. Prose is not used; that is proper only to light scenes, and there are none here. A peculiar effect is occasionally produced by the broken irregular meter which serves to express strong and bewildering emotions. The complete absence of comedy makes the play rather unique, and it receives especial distinction from the wonderful magic of phrase, above all when the king himself speaks. It is not the terse, pregnant phrase of the later plays, but a picturesque, exuberant, imaginative one, where the language is at times almost too rich, too full for the thought.

The influence of Shakespeare's two greatest predecessors, John Lyly and Christopher Marlowe, is plainly perceptible. The mocks which the poet threw at certain forms of Euphuism in

*Love's Labour's Lost* have somewhat served to conceal the debt which he owed to the real, if affected, genius of Lyly. *Midsummer Night's Dream* is largely inspired by him, and the present play shows traces of a very careful study of his masterpiece, *Euphues*. Moreover the tendency to alliteration and verbal conceits is eminently characteristic of the earlier writer.[7] As for Marlowe, the resemblance in general outline to *Edward II* leaves little room for doubt that Shakespeare used it as a model. It could hardly be otherwise, considering the force and beauty of Marlowe's play, and the strange parallel between the fortunes of the two kings: the wonder is that the plays should be so different, not that they should be so alike. Nor is it easy to agree with Mr. Swinburne that the death of Edward is more striking than that of Richard: the self-restraint of the younger poet is incomparably in advance of the extravagance and long-drawn-out horror in which the elder one revels. The spirit of Marlowe may also be seen in the "strained passion" and occasional bombast that mark some passages of this play, notably the opening scene.

The inevitable question arises as to Shakespeare's conception of history, and his treatment of historic facts. It must be dismissed here very briefly. It seems certain that he meant to record faithfully, within the limits imposed by the scope of a drama, the spirit of the past, to give actions their true proportions, and trace the real forces that underlay the sequence of events. We, from a modern standpoint, and with the results of modern research to work upon, may perhaps see our way to a different view of Richard and his age; but, so far as an Elizabethan might, Shakespeare means to pass an honest and final judgment upon them. On the other hand, it is equally clear that he held lightly the value of details; the mere fact that they happened is not enough by itself to render them precious to him. In this play he remorselessly rehandles chronology, he alters the ages of most of his characters, he confuses Richard's two Queens and makes two Duchesses of York into one. Sometimes these inaccuracies would seem to be due purely to want of care, more often they have a meaning; while he is willing to preserve the most trivial touches if they seem to bear a significance beyond themselves. The treatment of Aumerle and of John of Gaunt will serve to illustrate the manner of his more purposeful alterations. Aumerle was really a double-dyed traitor; he deserted to Henry at an early stage, then plotted against him, and finally betrayed his confederates. Shakespeare needs someone to make the balance between the two parties even, to represent Richard's cause when he is in prison, and to link him to the claims of the House of York. Therefore he takes Aumerle and does his best to whitewash him. Quite similarly, John of Gaunt was really a selfish, ambitious man, a bad general, and an unpopular minister; Shakespeare makes him an impersonation of the patriotic, chivalrous spirit that really shone in his brother, the Black Prince, in order to provide a striking contrast to the degenerate days of Richard. . . .

NOTES

1. All Shakespeare's historical plays belong to the first half of his literary life, i.e., to the period before 1600, with the exception of *Henry VIII*. He was born in April 1564. *Henry VIII* must not be ranked with the earlier group; it is a work of the poet's closing days, probably the last he touched. He only wrote half a dozen scenes of it; the rest is by Fletcher.
2. Browning's poem of *Protus*, in *Dramatic Romances*, might almost be an epitome of *Richard II*. The whole of this side of the matter has been worked out by Mr. Pater in an essay on *Shakespeare's English Kings* (reprinted in the volume called *Appreciations*), the most graceful bit of Shakespearean criticism since Coleridge.
3. See pp. ix–x.
4. Cf. the Third Book of the *Republic*, 410 E, K.T.λ.
5. The ratio of rhyme to blank verse in *Richard II*, according to Mr. Fleay's calculation, is 1 to 4. In only three plays is it greater: *Love's Labour's Lost* (5 to 3), *Midsummer Night's Dream* (1 to 1), and *Comedy of Errors* (1 to 3). In *Hamlet* (1602), it is 1 to 30; in *The Winter's Tale* (1611) there is no rhyme.
6. See Prof. Gervinus on *Romeo and Juliet*: act I, sc. v; act II, sc. ii; act III, sc. v.
7. Several passages from *Euphues* illustrating *Richard II* have been quoted in the *Notes*, including some from which the poet has evi-borrowed. See, e.g., I.iii.275, *n*. and V.iii.6, *n*., but they do not adequately represent the general resemblance in style between the two works.

*Brents Stirling*

# Bolingbroke's "Decision" (1951)

When interpreting *Richard II* we are aware, of course, that the king's dethronement was a symbol of challenge to royal authority during Elizabeth's reign, that the deposition scene was censored in certain editions, and that because of its connotations, the play was used by the Essex conspirators to set off their abortive rising. It is not that *Richard II* contained unorthodox political doctrine; on the contrary, in the deposition scene itself Carlisle proclaims that no subject may judge a king and that, should Bolingbroke be crowned, "The blood of English shall manure the ground, / And future ages groan for this foul act."

Throughout Shakespeare's cycle of history plays this prophecy of Carlisle is recalled again at intervals to give unity and meaning to the whole. In *Henry V* the burden of the king's prayer at the play's high point of suspense before Agincourt is "Not today, Lord, / O, not today, think not upon the fault / My father made in compassing the crown!" This is but one of the commonly recognized allusions in Shakespeare which hark back to the usurpation by Bolingbroke of Richard's throne. The deed was viewed by Tudor historians as a kind of secular fall of man which tainted generations unborn until England was redeemed from consequent civil war by appearance of the Tudor Messiah, Henry Earl of Richmond. The doctrine of *Richard II* and the succeeding plays is thus wholly conventional, and the uneasiness which led to banning of the deposition scene must have been evoked, not by any avowed point of view in the play, but by the fact that its theme of usurpation was an issue too critical even to be presented with conservative commentary.

It is well understood that this attitude of concern could have been derived from the characterization which accompanies Shakespeare's presentation of history. Without authority from the established sources, Shakespeare's Richard becomes a royal sentimentalist, a defeatist who resigns the throne as though he preferred acting a role of tragedy to one of governing men. With warrant from these sources, Shakespeare's Bolingbroke becomes a victim of extortion who takes over a kingship already bankrupt from abuse and incompetency, and in the play both the extortion and the defunct kingship are dramatically magnified. Carlisle's castigation of Bolingbroke for the "foul act" of revolution is thus easy to interpret as a concession to authority, as a piece of stiff morality almost intrusive in Shakespeare's active world of mixed right and wrong where characters are not to be measured by rigid moral standards.

The only difficulty with such an interpretation is that it is too simple. Granted, it rejects a form of criticism which disregards the tangle of events in which Bolingbroke acted, and would find Shakespeare's moral in Carlisle's prophecy alone. But while rejecting one form of simplicity it substitutes another in introducing the principle that men are too complex to be judged strictly, a point of view long useful in Shakespeare study, but unfortunately misused by those who consider complexity of character to be incompatible, at least in drama, with clear moral judgment.

There will be an assumption in this essay that the political moral of *Richard II* can be described adequately only in terms of the play itself, that the structure of the idea and the structure of the play are inseparable, as they need to be in all good dramatic art. But this uncontroversial premise does not imply that Shakespeare's meaning lacks precision. If we postpone conclusions until we have traced his idea in terms of dramatic action and characterization, it is possible that it will emerge not only as more mature than Carlisle's absolutism, but as less confused than the moral tangle which results if Carlisle's judgment is minimized. It is possible, moreover, that the dramatic structure and motivation of *Richard II* will likewise be found clearer and more mature than before, and the play may thus emerge in several new ways as a landmark in Shakespeare's early development as a dramatist.

In II.i, as resistance against Richard takes form, Northumberland first tells us of the purpose entertained by Bolingbroke's faction:

> If then we shall shake off our slavish yoke,
> Imp out our drooping country's broken wing,
> Redeem from broking pawn the blemished crown,
> Wipe off the dust that hides our sceptre's gilt
> And make high majesty look like itself.

So far, nothing of deposition; Northumberland's statement is the first of many which stress a goal modestly short of the throne. Two scenes later Bolingbroke's suit is pressed again; the place is Gloucestershire where the insurgent forces encounter old York, regent in Richard's absence. To York's charge of treason "in braving arms against thy sovereign" the reply by Bolingbroke is that he "was banish'd Hereford" but returns "for Lancaster," that he remains a subject of the king, and that having been denied "attorneys" for lawful redress, he has appeared in person. Before Bolingbroke's assembled power which belies his peaceful aims, and before the claim for Henry's inheritance rights, York stands as the absolutist, the strict constructionist:

> My lords of England, let me tell you this;
> I have had feeling of my cousin's wrongs
> And labour'd all I could to do him right;
> But in this kind to come, in braving arms,
> Be his own carver and cut out his way,
> To find out right with wrong, it may not be.

Thus in a scene of unusual strength are the rebels confronted with clear disposition of their pragmatic notions of morality and justice. Ironically, however, in the lines which follow, York collapses pathetically and almost absurdly:

> But if I could, by Him that gave me life,
> I would attach you all and make you stoop
> Unto the sovereign mercy of the king;

> But since I cannot, be it known to you
> I do remain as neuter.

This luxury of neutrality is denied to York, however, in Bolingbroke's request that he accompany the rebels to Bristol in order to "weed and pluck away" Bushy and Bagot, the "caterpillars of the commonwealth." York, the erstwhile absolutist, cannot even decide this incidental issue: "It may be I will go with you; but yet I'll pause; / For I am loath to break our country's laws." And in any event, "Things past redress are now with me past care."

In the first two scenes of Act III Shakespeare now presents Bolingbroke and Richard in characterization which emphasizes the utter difference in temperament between them; then, having shown each individually in parallel scenes, he brings them together for an episode in which the issue of deposition is determined, an issue which arises naturally and dramatically as a direct result of character clash. Dramatic structure, characterization, and presentation of idea (the deposition theme) are thus fused to the extent that none of these qualities can properly be discussed without reference to the others.

Scene i presents Bolingbroke, and in keeping with the character it is short and concentrated. It opens in the midst of events with Henry's terse "Bring forth these men"; Bushy and Green are then presented for his brief but unhurried recitation of the counts against them: they have misled and "disfigur'd clean" the king; they have "made a divorce betwixt his queen and him"; they have forced Bolingbroke to taste "the bitter bread of banishment" and disinheritance. These deeds condemn them to death. "My Lord Northumberland, see them dispatch'd." Next, the queen must be remembered; to York: "Fairly let her be entreated." And lastly Owen Glendower and his forces must be met; unhurried orders are so given. In a little over forty lines Bolingbroke has passed a death sentence, attended to the amenities of courtesy, and has set a campaign in motion.

Scene ii presents Richard and his retinue in a parallel situation and the contrast of this episode with Bolingbroke's scene lies in its portrayal of the king, initially by soliloquies of self-regard, then by wordy defiance which collapses as Richard learns of the Welsh defection, and finally by near hysteria as Aumerle cautions, "Comfort my liege; remember who you are." As Scroop enters with worse news, Richard proceeds from the false stoicism of anticipated defeat into insults directed at his absent favorites, and back again into sentimental despair:

> Let's choose executors and talk of wills;
> And yet not so; for what can we bequeath
> Save our deposed bodies to the ground?
> Our lands, our lives, and all are Bolingbroke's.

The word "deposed" is repeated three times as a kind of refrain in the next few lines as Richard offers to "sit upon the ground / And tell sad stories of the death of kings." A short speech of defiance as Carlisle warns against this sitting and wailing of woes, and a final descent into sentimental resignation as Scroop reports the joining of York with Bolingbroke, these acts complete Richard's performance in the scene. Lest our account of it end by being merely descriptive, two factors of Shakespeare's inventiveness should be set forth; to Holinshed's version of Richard's misfortune he adds the king's embracing of deposition far in advance of demand or suggestion,[1] and this external behavior he shows to be derived from motives of playing the martyr's role. The scene to come is thus inevitable; Richard in effect will depose himself in an agony of play-acting before the unsentimental Bolingbroke. But Shakespeare reserves a surprise; not the realist but the sentimentalist will call the turn.

The dramatic situation created for this event in the episode before Flint Castle is thus one of encounter between a self-contained realist who has come but "for his own" and an emotional defeatist who has determined to give him everything. And at the end of the Flint scene Shakespeare will answer with clear irony our question: *when* did Bolingbroke, after all his protests to the contrary, decide to seize the crown? For one point of the play, it will appear, is that this question has no point.

In a literal reading, Bolingbroke makes no decision prior to Act IV, and there he is scarcely more than at hand to take the throne. Now this set of facts is subject to several interpretations. First, we may assume that prior to the deposition scene there is no stage of the play at which the deviousness of Bolingbroke becomes clear, that there are obvious *lacunae* between his disclaimers of ambition in the first three acts and his sudden coronation in Act IV. In that event *Richard II* is just a bad play, and the fact that Henry's coronation is also sudden in the chronicles does not make it better. Or, secondly, we may assume that the historical reputation of Bolingbroke would have led an Elizabethan audience to recognize that his denials of royal ambition were insincere, and that he intended from the beginning to be king.[2] This could be the case, but the play, at least to us, would still be the worse for it. Nor is it Shakespeare's custom to allow major characterization to rest upon undramatized historical background, this in spite of occasional statements to the contrary. Finally, a third explanation of our "indecisive" Bolingbroke is that opportunism, of which he becomes the living symbol, is essentially a tacit vice: that although the opportunist is aware in a sense of the ends to which means commit him, he relies upon events, not upon declarations, to clarify his purposes. On the basis of the scene before Flint Castle (III.iii) and of two prominent episodes which follow it, I believe that the interpretation just expressed is one which fits the dramatic facts.

By the time the Flint scene opens we are aware of Richard's impulses toward virtual abdication, but Bolingbroke has never exceeded his demands for simple restitution of rank and estate. Nor have his followers done so. True, we have heard York tell him that his very appearance in arms is treason, but Bolingbroke's rejoinder to this was both disarming and apparently genuine. At Flint, however, dramatic suggestion begins to take shape. As Henry's followers parley before the castle, Northumberland lets slip the name "Richard" unaccompanied by its title of king. York reprieves him with a remark that such brevity once would have seen Northumberland shortened by a head's length. Bolingbroke intercedes: "Mistake not, uncle, further than you should." To which York: "Take not, cousin, further than you should." This suggestive colloquy is followed by Bolingbroke's characteristic statement of honest intention: "Go to . . . the castle . . . and this deliver: Henry Bolingbroke / On both his knees does kiss King Richard's hand / And sends allegiance and true faith of heart / To his most royal person." He will lay down his arms provided only that his lands are restored and his banishment repealed. If not, war is the alternative. With dramatic significance, however, Northumberland, who bears this message from a Bolingbroke "on both his knees," fails himself to kneel before Richard and thus becomes again the medium of "unconscious" disclosure. Richard, in a rage, sends word back to Henry that "ere the crown he looks for live in peace, / Ten thousand bloody crowns of mothers' sons" shall be the price in slaughter. Northumberland's rejoinder is a yet more pious assertion of Bolingbroke's limited aims: "The King of heaven forbid our lord the King / Should so with civil and uncivil arms / Be rush'd upon! Thy thrice noble cousin / Harry Bolingbroke . . . swears . . . his coming hath no further scope / Than for his lineal royalties."

Richard's response is to grant the demands, to render a wish in soliloquy that he be buried where his subjects "may hourly trample on their sovereign's head," and, when summoned to the "base court," to cry out symbolically that down, down he comes "like glist'ring Phaeton, / Wanting the manage of unruly jades." He enters the base court, and the scene concludes with a priceless mummery of sovereignty, each participant speaking as a subject to his king.

> *Boling.* Stand all apart,
> And show fair duty to His Majesty. [*He kneels down.*]
> My gracious lord—
> *K. Rich.* Fair Cousin, you debase your princely knee
> To make the base earth proud with kissing it.
> Me rather had my heart might feel your love
> Than my unpleased eye see your courtesy.
> Up, Cousin, up. Your heart is up, I know,
> Thus high at least, although your knee be low.
> *Boling.* My gracious lord, I come but for mine own.
> *K. Rich.* Your own is yours, and I am yours, and all.
> *Boling.* So far be mine, my most redoubted lord,
> As my true service shall deserve your love.
> *K. Rich.* Well you deserve. They well deserve to have
> That know the strong'st and surest way to get. . . .
> Cousin, I am too young to be your father,
> Though you are old enough to be my heir.
> What you will have, I'll give, and willing too,

> For do we must what force will have us do.
> Set on towards London, Cousin, is it so?
> *Boling.* Yea, my good lord.
> *K. Rich.* Then I must not say no.

There is no question of what "London" means. It is dethronement for Richard and coronation for Bolingbroke, an implication which is plain enough here but which Shakespeare underscores in the very next scene where the Gardener, asked by the Queen (line 77), "Why dost thou say King Richard is deposed?" concludes his explanation with "Post you to London, and you will find it so." Bolingbroke's answer to Richard, "Yea, my good lord," is the aptly timed climax of the Flint episode, and of the play. With this oblique admission, coming with great effect immediately after his statement of loyalty and subjection, Henry's purposes become clear, and the significant fact is that not he but Richard has phrased his intent. The king's single line, "Set on towards London, cousin, is it so?" is the ironic instrument for exposing a long line of equivocation which the rebels seem to have concealed even from themselves.[3] And in dramatic fact, Bolingbroke is still trying to conceal it; his short answer is the minimum articulation of his conduct, an opportunist's falling back upon "what must be" in order to evade a statement of purpose.

The quality of this turn in the play rests upon a skillful fusion of plot unfoldment, disclosure of political "moral," and characterization, all of which present parallel irony. In plotting, first among these ingredients, the end of the Flint scene is the point at which conflicting forces reach their determination in a climactic disclosure of Henry's true purpose. But this climax is also a studied anticlimax, for the rebels advance upon Flint Castle only, as it were, to find it abandoned with the words, "Come to London," written upon the walls. They, and the audience, had expected not quiet exposure of their aims (the actual climax) but dramatic opportunity for "constitutional" manifestoes.

As for disclosure of political meaning, the second element here, it is during the encounter at Flint that the rebels achieve their most eloquent statement of legality in seeking only a subject's claim to justice from his king. But the luxury of that statement collapses at the end of the scene, again with the word "London." It becomes suddenly apparent that York's previous judgment was sound, that Bolingbroke's use of force to gain just concessions from his sovereign has committed him to the destruction of sovereignty.

The third component at the end of the Flint scene is characterization, a quality which is the basis for all the drama and irony in the direction the play has taken. Shakespeare's prior establishment of Bolingbroke's realism, self-containment, and resourcefulness, along with Richard's romantic defeatism, near-hysteria, and pathetic reliance upon others, has furnished a decided pattern for the meeting of the two at Flint. Bolingbroke and Northumberland thus fulfill their previously set traits of stability and restraint; Richard repeats the performance he had enacted before his own followers in the preceding scene, a performance which richly justifies the description of him by one critic as an inveterate spectator at his own tragedy. Full characterization of Bolingbroke and Richard, both before and during the Flint Castle episode, thus provides all of the expansiveness which is so deliberately deflated in the last lines. There, with Richard's knowing reference to London and Bolingbroke's one-line reply, the ironic shift in characterization materializes. The unstable Richard, who had fled from facts through every form of emotional exaggeration, now drops his sentimental role and states the truth of his position with quiet wit and candor; the plain-dealing Bolingbroke who had offered his demands with such consistency and seeming honesty now admits his sham of rebellion which was to stop short of rebellion.

The end of Act III, scene iii, is thus a pivotal stage of *Richard II*. Here, upon a question asked by the king and an answer given by Henry, the trend of the play becomes dramatically apparent in plot, in political meaning, and in ultimate characterization. We have also observed that perhaps the main achievement at this point of multiple effect has been a disclosure of ambiguity in Henry Bolingbroke. In concluding this essay I hope to show that, by the time Shakespeare's portrait of Bolingbroke is completed, this ambiguity is presented twice again by means of the same dramatic method.

The first of these repetitions occurs in IV.i (the deposition) which runs directly parallel to the Flint Castle scene. Here again we have Richard confronted by the rebels, and here also he is in turn both defiant and submissive; his sentimental display is likewise in dramatic contrast with Henry's simplicity, forbearance, and directness. But again in the closing lines the paradox comes.

> K. *Rich.* I'll beg one boon,
> And then be gone and trouble you no more.
> Shall I obtain it?
> *Boling.* Name it, fair Cousin.
> K. *Rich.* "Fair Cousin"? I am greater than a king.
> For when I was a king, my flatterers
> Were then but subjects. Being now a subject,
> I have a King here to my flatterer.
> Being so great, I have no need to beg.
> *Boling.* Yet ask.
> K. *Rich.* And shall I have?
> *Boling.* You shall.
> K. *Rich.* Then give me leave to go.
> *Boling.* Whither?
> K. *Rich.* Whither you will, so I were from your sights.
> *Boling.* Go, some of you convey him to the Tower.

Just as at the end of III.iii, "London" meant deposition, so here the Tower means imprisonment and ultimate death. This colloquy between the king and his adversary is exactly parallel in technique to the one which concluded the scene at Flint. In it Richard, who has again run his course of theatrical emotion, now becomes pointedly realistic; in it Bolingbroke, who has again exhibited every sign of gracious honesty, reveals duplicity in a concluding line.

There remains a third and final step in the portrayal of Henry which is analogous in all essentials to the two scenes we have examined. The fact that Shakespeare here drew upon the chronicles might imply that he found in them a suggestion of Bolingbroke's taciturnity marked by sudden revelations of shifting purpose. Piers of Exton, in the short fourth scene of Act V, ponders something he has heard. "Have I no friend will rid me of this living fear?" Was not that what the new king said? And did he not repeat it? Exton satisfies himself that Bolingbroke did so and convinces himself that in the saying of it Henry "wistly look'd on me." It is enough, for Exton promptly murders Richard and returns with the body. Henry's lines which conclude the play are well known; he admits desiring Richard's death but disowns Exton's act and pledges expiation in a voyage to the Holy Land.

Three times—at the end of the Flint Castle scene, at the end of the deposition scene, and in the Exton scenes at the end of the play—Henry has taken, if it may be so called, a decisive step. Each time the move he has made has been embodied in a terse statement, and each time another has either evoked it from him or stated its implications for him. Never, in an age of drama marked by discursive self-revelation, has a character disclosed his traits with such economy and understatement. The Elizabethan character with a moral contradiction usually explains his flaw before, during, and after the event. And at length. Until the short choral "confession" at the very end of the play, Bolingbroke, however, exhibits his deviousness in one-line admissions spaced at intervals which are aptly arranged in parallel series for cumulative effect. And while each of these admissions marks a step in characterization, it indicates at the same time a critical stage of plot development. The conflict of forces is resolved with the line on London concluding the Flint Castle scene, for there Richard and Henry reach mutual understanding on the dethronement issue which the king alone has previously entertained. The falling action becomes defined with the line near the end of the deposition scene which sends Richard to the Tower. The catastrophe is precipitated by the line to Exton which sends him to death.

Finally, at each of these three points of characterization and plot unfoldment the doctrine implicit in the play evolves to a new clarity. At Henry's line on London at Flint Castle it becomes apparent that a "constitutional" show of force against sovereignty leads inevitably to the deposition of sovereignty; at Henry's line in the dethronement scene it appears that deposition of sovereignty requires imprisonment and degradation of the sovereign; and at Henry's line to Exton it becomes plain that murder of sovereignty must be the final outcome. The chronicle accounts of Richard's latter days disclose neither a suggestion of these cumulative steps nor a basis for Bolingbroke's over-insistence on lawful aims which dramatically precedes them; we learn only that Henry returned vowing allegiance and shortly became king (Boswell-Stone, pp. 109ff.). As usual, a play-source comparison emphasizes Shakespeare's artistry both in structure and motivation.[4]

In passages such as Ulysses' lines on degree in *Troilus and Cressida* Shakespeare excels in a poet's expression of Tudor political dogma. In *Richard II*, however, and early in his career, he shows control of a much more difficult art, that of revealing doctrine integrally with progressive growth of plot and of characterization. With our debt to the English and American revolutions we cannot admire the doctrine as such, but we can recognize in *Richard II* a stage of Shakespeare's development at which, so far as fundamentals are concerned, political morality and artistry become inseparable.

### NOTES

1. See Boswell-Stone, *Shakespere's Holinshed* (London, 1896). It is true that the chronicles show Richard in an early state of despair, but with no preconception of dethronement (p. 106), and in a mood, much later, of willingness to abdicate after arrival in London (p. 113). Shakespeare, however, presents a king determined to abdicate as early as the landing in Wales (III.ii), before Richard has even encountered Bolingbroke, and continues to portray him in this mood from there onward.
2. Samuel Daniel indicates that in Shakespeare's time Bolingbroke's motives were commonly viewed as suspect. He develops the subject at some length (*Civil Wars*, Book I, Stanzas 87-89) and concludes that, in charity, judgment should be suspended on the issue of whether Henry intended originally to seize the throne.
3. Self-delusion on Bolingbroke's part is a trait clearly suggested by Daniel in his enigmatic stanzas on Henry's motives (*Civil Wars*, Book I, Stanzas 90-91). I mention this only to show that such an interpretation was made overtly at the time *Richard II* was written.
4. Daniel (*Civil Wars*, Books I and II, London, 1595) likewise fails to present Bolingbroke's opportunistic conduct in the telling manner

of Shakespeare. He does amply suggest the possibility of "unconscious" drift toward usurpation but in no way dramatizes this action in successive steps of cumulative disclosure. Daniel is not to be regarded with certainty as a source of Shakespeare; it is possible that similarities between the *Civil Wars* and *Richard II* are to be accounted for by Daniel's having seen the play. But, in any event, a comparison of Shakespeare and Daniel is revealing.

# PART IV
*RICHARD II*
Poetry and Rhetoric

*Alessandro Manzoni*

# Letter to Mr. Chauvet concerning the unities of time and place in Tragedy (1820)

This, then, is what art and philosophy gain by accepting arbitrary rules: forcing great men to concoct subterfuges in order to avoid improprieties and to come up with subtle arguments to evade the thing by adopting the word!

But if, in choosing as the subject of dramatic action those illustrious events worthy of tragedy, that Corneille mentions, we wish to avoid the error of heaping them up in an implausible manner, we fall perforce into another blunder; we must then abandon a part of those events, sometimes the most interesting one; we must give up all thought of providing the rest with a natural development: in other words, tragedy has to be made less poetic than history.

The shortest way to convince you that this is indeed the case is to examine one of the tragedies conceived on the historical plan, a tragedy whose action is unified, lofty and interesting; and to see if its most dramatic qualities can be preserved by squeezing it into the framework of the unities. As our example, let us consider Shakespeare's *Richard II*, which is by no means the finest of the plays he drew from English history.

The action of this tragedy is the deposition of Richard from the English throne and the elevation of Bolingbroke in his stead. The play begins at the moment when schemes of these two characters are found to be openly opposed, when the king, truly disquieted by his cousin's ambitious projects, rashly attempts to thwart them by measures which eventually lead Bolingbroke to carry out his plans. Richard banishes Bolingbroke; once the latter's father, the Duke of Lancaster, is dead, the king confiscates his property and leaves for Ireland. Bolingbroke violates the order of his expulsion and returns to England, on pretext of claiming the inheritance which has been seized from him by an illegal act. His followers flock to him in droves: as their number increases, he changes his tune, shifts gradually from claims to threats; and soon the subject who came to demand justice is a powerful rebel laying down the law. The King's uncle and lieutenant, the Duke of York, who goes to meet Bolingbroke intending to fight him, ends up coming to terms with him. The personality of this character unfolds along with the action he is involved in: the Duke speaks in a series of stages, first to the rebellious subject, then to the leader of a sizeable faction, finally to the new king; and this progression is so natural, so exactly parallel to events that the spectator is not surprised to find, by the play's end, a loyal servant of Henry IV in the same character who had learned of Bolingbroke's landing with the greatest indignation. Once Bolingbroke's early successes are known, our interest and curiosity naturally turn to Richard. We are eager to see the effect of so great a *coup* on the soul of this petulant and haughty king. Thus, Richard is called on stage both by the spectator's expectations and by the course of the action.

He has been informed of Bolingbroke's disobedience and his venture; he hurriedly quits Ireland and lands in England just when his adversary is occupying Gloucestershire: but of course the king should not march directly on the audacious aggressor until he has been properly equipped to resist him. Here plausibility, as deliberately as history itself, repudiated unity of place, and Shakespeare has not followed either of them to any extent. He shows us Richard in Wales: he could have easily arranged his action so as to display the two rivals on the same territory in succession; but think of the things he would have had to sacrifice for that! And what would his tragedy have gained by it? Unity of action? Certainly not. For where could one find a tragedy with a more unified action than this one?

Richard deliberates with his remaining friends on what he is to do, and here it is that the king's character begins to assume so natural and so unforeseen a development. The spectator has already met this remarkable person, and flattered himself that he had scanned him through and through; but he has in him something secret and profound which made no appearance during his prosperity and that misfortune alone can cause to burst forth. The basis of his character remains the same: it is still pride, it is still the loftiest notion of his dignity; but this same pride, when it went hand-in-hand with power, was manifested as frivolity, impatience with any obstacle, a recklessness that prevented him from even suspecting that all human might has its judges and its limitations; this pride, once stripped of force, has become grave and earnest, solemn and moderate. What upholds Richard is an unalterable awareness of his greatness, the assurance that no human event has been able to destroy him, since nothing could undo his birth and his kingship. He has lost the gratifications of power; but the notion of his calling to the highest rank remains: in what he is, he persists in honoring what he was; and this stubborn respect for a title that no one continues to acknowledge removes from the sense of his misfortune anything that might humiliate or discourage him. The ideas and emotions through which this revolution in Richard's character occurs in Shakespeare's tragedy are of great originality, the most exalted poetry, and are even quite touching.

But this historical depiction of Richard's soul and the events that modify it necessarily encompasses more than twenty hours, as is the case with the progress of the other deeds, passions and characters that develop over the course of the action. The clash of the two factions, the ardor and growing activity of the king's enemies, the tergiversations of those who await a victory so as to find out precisely which cause decent people ought to espouse; the courageous loyalty of one lone man, a loyalty the poet has described just as history has sanctioned, with all the ideas, true and false, that decided this man to pay homage to adversity in despite of force; all this is admirably portrayed in this tragedy. A few improprieties which might be deleted without altering the arrangement should not delude us about the greatness and beauty of the whole.

I am almost ashamed to provide so barebones a sketch of so majestic a painting; but I flatter myself that I've said enough to show at least that the most characteristic features of the subject demand more latitude than the rule of two unities grants it.

Let's suppose now that Shakespeare, having written his *Richard II*, had submitted it to a critic who was convinced of the necessity of that rule. He probably would have said: "There are some lovely situations in your play, and some admirable sentiments in particular; but plausibility is deplorably shocked by it. You transport your audience from London to Coventry, from Gloucestershire to Wales, from Parliament to Flint Castle; the spectator cannot possibly manage the suspension of disbelief needed to follow you. There is a contradiction between the various situations you wish to put him in, and the actual situation in which he exists. He is too sure that he has not moved to be able to imagine he has done all the travelling you demand of him."

I don't know for sure, but I think Shakespeare would have been rather surprised by such objections. "For Heaven's sake!" he might have replied, "what's all this talk of moving about and travelling! There's none of that here; I never dreamt of such a thing, nor did my audience. I laid before their eyes an action that unfolds by degrees and is composed of events, each of which is begotten by the previous one and takes place somewhere else; it is the audience member's mind that follows them, he doesn't have to travel or pretend he's travelling. Do you imagine he came to the theatre to see actual events? And did I ever have it in mind to produce such an illusion on him? to make him believe that what he knows to have already occurred some centuries ago is happening again today? that these actors are men actually involved in the passions and concerns they are talking about, and talking about in verse?"

But, sir, I have lost sight of the fact that you do not base your support of the rules on an objection derived from plausibility, but in fact on the impossibility of preserving unity of action and soundness of characters without them. Then let us see if this objection can be applied to the tragedy of *Richard II*. So! How—I ask this out of genuine curiosity—how would one go about proving that its action is not unified, that the characters are not consistent, and that this results from the poet staying within the places and times supplied by history, instead of enclosing himself in the space and duration that the critics have meted out of their authority as proper for all tragedies?

What would Shakespeare have replied to a critic who came and countered him with this law of twenty-four hours? "Twenty-four hours!" he would have said, "What for? Reading Holinshed's chronicles furnished my mind with the notion of a great and simple action, unified and varied, full of interest and homilies; and I was supposed to disfigure and truncate this action on a mere whim! I was not to seek to render the impression a chronicler made on me, in my own manner, for spectators who ask nothing better! I would have been less a poet than my source is! I see an event whose every incident relates to every other and serves to motivate them; I see stable characters develop over a period of time and in specific places; and to present an idea of that event and portray those characters, I would have absolutely had to mutilate one and the other just so that a twenty-four hour span and the precincts of a palace would suffice for their development?"

I confess, sir, you do have in your system one other reply to make to Shakespeare: you might tell him that the attention he paid to reproducing deeds in their natural order and with the best-documented principal circumstances likens him rather to an historian than to a poet. You might add that the rule of two unities would have made him a poet by forcing him to create an action, a tangled skein, sudden reversals; for "thus it is," you say, "that the limits of art give wings to an artist's imagination, and compel him to become creative." That, indeed, I agree, is the true consequence of that rule; and the slightest acquaintance with plays that have followed it proves moreover that it has not failed of its effect. In your opinion, it is a great advantage: I dare to be of a different mind, and, on the contrary, I regard the effect in question to be the most serious drawback to the rules that cause it. Yes, this need for creating, arbitrarily imposed on art, makes it stray from truth, and impairs it both in its results and in its techniques.

I don't know if what I'm about to say runs counter to commonly approved notions; but I believe I'm merely speaking a very plain truth when I declare that the essence of poetry does not consist in inventing deeds: such invention is the easiest, commonest thing in the workings of the mind, and takes the least thought and even the least imagination. Then too, there is nothing more profuse than creations of this kind; whereas all the great monuments of poetry are based on events provided by history or, what comes to the same thing, by what was once taken to be history.

As for dramatic poets in particular, the greatest ones of every nation have avoided, in proportion to their genius, the insertion into drama of deeds of their creation; and on every occasion when they were told they had substituted invention for history at essential points, far from accepting this judgment as praise, they dismissed it as blame. Did I not know the temerity that lurks in over-generalized historical assertions, I should venture to state that in what has come down to us of Greek drama and even Greek poetry, there is not a single example of this kind of creativity, which consists in substituting wantonly invented causes for known principal causes. The Greek poets took their plots, with all their major circumstances, from national traditions. They did not make up events: they accepted them just as their contemporaries transmitted them: they included, they respected history for what individuals, peoples and eras had made it.

## Algernon Charles Swinburne

## "King Richard II" (1909)

It is a truth more curious than difficult to verify that there was a time when the greatest genius ever known among the sons of men was uncertain of the future and unsure of the task before it; when the one unequalled and unapproachable master of the one supreme art which implies and includes the mastery of the one supreme science perceptible and accessible by man stood hesitating between the impulsive instinct for dramatic poetry, the crown and consummation of all philosophies, the living incarnation of creative and intelligent godhead, and the facile seduction of elegiac and idyllic verse, of meditative and uncreative song: between the music of Orpheus and the music of Tibullus. The legendary choice of Hercules was of less moment than the actual choice of Shakespeare between the influence of Robert Greene and the influence of Christopher Marlowe.

The point of most interest in the tragedy or history of *King Richard II* is the obvious evidence which it gives of the struggle between the worse and the better genius of its author. "'Tis now full tide 'tween night and day." The author of *Selimus* and *Andronicus* is visibly contending with the author of *Faustus* and *Edward II* for the mastery of Shakespeare's poetic and dramatic adolescence. Already the bitter hatred which was soon to vent itself in the raging rancor of his dying utterance must have been kindled in the unhappy heart of Greene by comparison of his original work with the few lines, or possibly the scene or two, in his unlovely though not unsuccessful tragedy of *Titus Andronicus*, which had been retouched or supplied by Shakespeare; whose marvellous power of transfiguration in the act of imitation was never overmatched in any early work of a Raffaelle while yet the disciple of a Perugino. There are six lines in that discomfortable play which can only have been written, if any trust may be put in the evidence of intelligent comparison, by Shakespeare; and yet they are undoubtedly in the style of Greene, who could only have written them if the spirit of Shakespeare had passed into him for five minutes or so:

> King, be thy thoughts imperious, like thy name.
> Is the sun dimmed that gnats do fly in it?
> The eagle suffers little birds to sing,
>   And is not careful what they mean thereby,
> Knowing that with the shadow of his wing
>   He can at pleasure stint their melody.

There is nothing so fine as that in the elegiac or rhyming scenes or passages of *King Richard II*. And yet it is not glaringly out of place among the *sottes monstruosités*—if I may borrow a phrase applied by Michelet to a more recent literary creation—of the crazy and chaotic tragedy in which a writer of gentle and idyllic genius attempted to play the part which his friend Marlowe and their supplanter Shakespeare were born to originate and to sustain. To use yet another and a more admirable French phrase, the author of *Titus Andronicus* is evidently a *mouton enragé*. The mad sheep who has broken the bounds of his pastoral sheepfold has only, in his own opinion, to assume the skin of a wolf, and the tragic stage must acknowledge him as a lion. Greene, in his best works of prose fiction and in his lyric and elegiac idyls, is as surely the purest and gentlest of writers as he was the most reckless and disreputable of men. And when ambition or hunger lured or lashed him into the alien field of tragic poetry, his first and last notion of the work in hand was simply to revel and wallow in horrors after the fashion, by no means of a wild boar, but merely of a wether gone distracted.

Nevertheless, the influence of this unlucky trespasser on tragedy is too obvious in too much of the text of *King Richard II* to be either questioned or overlooked. Coleridge, whose ignorance of Shakespeare's predecessors was apparently as absolute as it is assuredly astonishing in the friend of Lamb, has attempted by super-subtle advocacy to explain and excuse, if not to justify and glorify, the crudities and incongruities of dramatic conception and poetic execution which signalize this play as unmistakably the author's first attempt at historic drama: it would perhaps be more exactly accurate to say, at dramatic history. But they are almost as evident as the equally wonderful and youthful genius of the poet. The grasp of character is uncertain; the exposition of event is inadequate. The reader or spectator unversed in the byways of history has to guess at what has already happened—how, why, when, where, and by whom the prince whose murder is the matter in debate at the opening of the play has been murdered. He gets so little help or light from the poet that he can only guess at random, with blind assumption or purblind hesitation, what may be the right or wrong of the case which is not even set before him. The scolding-match between Bolingbroke and Mowbray, fine in their primitive way as are the last two speeches of the latter disclaimer, is liker the work of a pre-Marlowite than the work of Marlowe's disciple. The whole scene is merely literary, if not purely academic; and the seemingly casual interchange of rhyme and blank verse is more wayward and fitful than even in *Romeo and Juliet*. That the finest passage is in rhyme, and is given to a character about to vanish from the action of the play, is another sign of poetical and intellectual immaturity. The second scene has in it a breath of true passion and a touch of true pathos: but even if the subject had been more duly and definitely explained, it would still have been comparatively wanting in depth of natural passion and pungency of natural pathos. The third scene, full of beautifully fluent and plentifully inefficient writing, reveals the protagonist of the play as so pitifully mean and cruel a weakling that no future action or suffering can lift him above the level which divides and purifies pity from contempt. And this, if mortal manhood may venture to pass judgment on immortal godhead, I must say that Shakespeare does not seem to me to have seen. The theatrical trickery which masks and reveals the callous cruelty and the heartless hypocrisy of the histrionic young tyrant is enough to remove him once for all beyond reach of manly sympathy or compassion unqualified by scorn. If we can ever be sorry for anything that befalls so vile a sample of royalty, our sorrow must be so diluted and adulterated by recollection of his wickedness and baseness that its tribute could hardly be acceptable to any but the most pitiable example or exception of mankind. But this is not enough for the relentless persistence in spiritual vivisection that seems to guide and animate the poet's manipulation and evolution of a character which at once excites a contempt and hatred only to be superseded by the loathing and abhorrence aroused at thought of the dastardly ruffian by the deathbed of his father's noble and venerable brother. The magnificent poetry which glorifies the opening scene of the second act, however dramatically appropriate and effective in its way, is yet so exuberant in lyric and elegiac eloquence that readers or spectators may conceivably have thought the young Shakespeare less richly endowed by nature as a dramatist than as a poet. It is not of the speaker or the hearer that we think as we read the most passionate panegyric on his country ever set to hymnal harmonies by the greatest of patriotic poets but Aeschylus alone: it is simply of England and of Shakespeare.

The bitter prolongation of the play upon words which answers the half-hearted if not heartless inquiry, "How is't with aged Gaunt?" is a more dramatic touch of homelier and nearer nature to which Coleridge has done no more than exact justice in his admirable comment: "A passion there is that carries off its own excess by plays on words as naturally, and therefore as appropriately to drama, as by gesticulations, looks, or tones." And the one thoroughly noble and nobly coherent figure in the poem disappears as with a thunderclap or the sound of a trumpet calling to judgment a soul too dull in its baseness, too decrepit in its degradation, to hear or understand the summons.

> Live in thy shame, but die not shame with thee!
> These words hereafter thy tormentors be!

But the poor mean spirit of the hearer is too narrow and too shallow to feel the torment which a nobler soul in its adversity would have recognized by the revelation of remorse.

With the passing of John of Gaunt the moral grandeur of the poem passes finally away. Whatever of interest we may feel in any of the surviving figures is transitory, intermittent, and always qualified by a sense of ethical inconsistency and intellectual inferiority. There is not a man among them: unless it be the Bishop of Carlisle: and he does but flash across the action for an ineffectual instant. There is often something attractive in Aumerle: indeed, his dauntless and devoted affection for the king makes us sometimes feel as though there must be something not unpitiable or unlovable in the kinsman who could inspire and retain such constancy of regard in a spirit so much manlier than his own. But the figure is too roughly and too thinly sketched to be thoroughly memorable as a man's: and his father's is an incomparable, an incredible, an unintelligible and a monstrous nullity. Coleridge's attempt to justify the ways of York to man—to any man of common sense and common sentiment—is as amusing in Coleridge as it would be amazing in any other and therefore in any lesser commentator.

In the scene at Windsor Castle between the Queen and her husband's minions the idyllic or elegiac style again supplants and supersedes the comparatively terse and dramatic manner of dialogue between the noblemen whom we have just seen lashed into disgust and goaded into revolt by the villainy and brutality of the rascal king. The dialogue is beautiful and fanciful: it makes a very pretty eclogue: none other among the countless writers of Elizabethan eclogues could have equalled it. But if we look for anything more or for anything higher than this, we must look elsewhere: and we shall not look in vain if we turn to the author of *Edward the Second*. When the wretched York creeps in, we have undoubtedly such a living and drivelling picture of hysterical impotence on the downward grade to dotage and distraction as none but Shakespeare could have painted. When Bolingbroke reappears and Harry Percy appears on the stage of the poet who has bestowed on him a generous portion from the inexhaustible treasure of his own immortal life, we find ourselves again among men, and are comforted and refreshed by the change. The miserable old regent's histrionic attempt to play the king and rebuke the rebel is so admirably pitiful that his last unnatural and monstrous appearance in the action of the play might possibly be explained or excused on the score of dotage—an active and feverish fit of impassioned and demented dotage.

The inspired effeminacy and the fanciful puerility which

dunces attribute to the typical character of a representative poet never found such graceful utterance as the greatest of poets has given to the unmanliest of his creatures when Richard lands in Wales. Coleridge credits the poor wretch with "an intense love of his country," intended to "redeem him in the hearts of the audience" in spite of the fact that "even in this love there is something feminine and personal." There is nothing else in it: as anybody but Coleridge would have seen. It is exquisitely pretty and utterly unimaginable as the utterance of a man. The two men who support him on either side, the loyal priest and the gallant kinsman, offer him words of manly counsel and manful cheer. He answers them with an outbreak of such magnificent poetry as might almost have been uttered by the divine and unknown and unimaginable poet who gave to eternity the Book of Job: but in this case also the futility of intelligence is as perfect as the sublimity of speech. And his utter collapse on the arrival of bad tidings provokes a counter-change of poetry as splendid in utterance of abjection and despair as the preceding rhapsody in expression of confidence and pride. The scene is still rather amoebaean than dramatic: it is above the reach of Euripides, but more like the imaginable work of a dramatic and tragic Theocritus than the possible work of a Sophocles when content to give us nothing more nearly perfect and more comparatively sublime than the *Trachiniae*. And it is even more amusing than curious that the courtly censors who cancelled and suppressed the scene of Richard's deposition should not have cut away the glorious passage in which the vanity of kingship is confronted, by the grovelling repentance of a king, with the grinning humiliation of death. The dramatic passion of this second great speech is as unmistakable as the lyric emotion of the other. And the utter collapse of heart and spirit which follows on the final stroke of bad tidings at once completes the picture of the man, and concludes in equal harmony the finest passage of the poem and the most memorable scene in the play.

The effect of the impression made by it is so elaborately sustained in the following scene as almost to make a young student wonder at the interest taken by the young Shakespeare in the development or evolution of such a womanish or semi-virile character. The style is not exactly verbose, as we can hardly deny that it is in the less passionate parts of the second and third acts of *King John*: but it is exuberant and effusive, elegiac and Ovidian, in a degree which might well have made his admirers doubt, and gravely doubt, whether the future author of *Othello* would ever be competent to take and hold his place beside the actual author of *Faustus*. Marlowe did not spend a tithe of the words or a tithe of the pains on the presentation of a character neither more worthy of contempt nor less worthy of compassion. And his Edward is at least as living and convincing, as tragic and pathetic a figure as Shakespeare's Richard.

The garden scene which closes this memorable third act is a very pretty eclogue, not untouched with tragic rather than idyllic emotion. The fourth act opens upon a morally chaotic introduction of incongruous causes, inexplicable plaintiffs, and incomprehensible defendants. Whether Aumerle or Fitzwater or Surrey or Bagot is right or wrong, honorable or villainous, no reader or spectator is given a chance of guessing: it is a mere cockpit squabble. And the scene of deposition which follows, full as it is of graceful and beautiful writing, need only be set against the scene of deposition in *Edward the Second* to show the difference between rhetorical and dramatic poetry, emotion and passion, eloquence and tragedy, literature and life. The young Shakespeare's scene is full to superfluity of fine verses and fine passages: his young compeer's or master's is from end to end one magnificent model of tragedy, "simple, sensuous, and passionate" as Milton himself could have desired: Milton, the second as Shakespeare was the first of the great English poets who were pupils and debtors of Christopher Marlowe. It is pure poetry and perfect drama: the fancy is finer and the action more lifelike than here. Only once or twice do we come upon such a line as this in the pathetic but exuberant garrulity of Richard: "While that my wretchedness doth bait myself." That is worthy of Marlowe. And what follows is certainly pathetic: though certainly there is a good deal of it.

The last act might rather severely than unfairly be described as a series of six tragic or tragicomic eclogues. The first scene is so lovely that no reader worthy to enjoy it will care to ask whether it is or is not so lifelike as to convey no less of conviction than all readers must feel of fascination in the continuous and faultless melody of utterance and tenderness of fancy which make it in its way an incomparable idyl. From the dramatic point of view it might certainly be objected that we know nothing of the wife, and that what we know of the husband does not by any means tend to explain the sudden pathos and sentimental sympathy of their parting speeches. The first part of the next scene is as beautiful and blameless an example of dramatic narrative as even a Greek poet could have given at such length: but in the latter part of it we cannot but see and acknowledge again the dramatic immaturity of the poet who in a very few years was to reveal himself as beyond all question, except from the most abject and impudent of dunces, the greatest imaginable dramatist or creator ever born into immortality. Style and metre are rough, loose, and weak: the dotage of York becomes lunacy. *Sa folie en furie est tournée.* The scene in which he clamors for the blood of his son is not in any proper sense tragic or dramatic: it is a very ugly eclogue, artificial in manner and unnatural in substance. No feebler or unlovelier example exists of those "jigging veins of rhyming mother-wits" which Marlowe's imperial rebuke should already have withered into silence on the lips of the veriest Marsyas among all the amoebaean rhymesters of his voluble and effervescent generation.

The better nature of the young Shakespeare revives in the closing scenes: though Exton is a rather insufficient ruffian for the part of so important an assassin. We might at least have seen or heard of him before he suddenly chips the shell as a full-fledged murderer. The last soliloquy of the king is wonderful in its way, and beautiful from any point of view: it shows once more the influence of Marlowe's example in the curious trick of selection and transcription of texts for sceptic meditation and analytic dissection. But we see rather more of the poet and less of his creature the man than Marlowe might have given us. The interlude of the groom, on the other hand, gives promise of something different in power and pathos from the poetry of Marlowe: but the scene of slaughter which follows is not quite satisfactory: it is almost boyish in its impetuosity of buffeting and bloodshed. The last scene, with its final reversion to rhyme, may be described in Richard's own previous words as good, "and yet not greatly good."

Of the three lines on which the greatest genius that ever made earth more splendid, and the name of man more glorious, than without the passage of its presence they could have been, chose alternately or successively to work, the line of tragedy was that on which its promise or assurance of future supremacy was first made manifest. The earliest comedies of Shakespeare, overflowing with fancies and exuberant in beauties as they are, gave no sign of inimitable power: their joyous humor and their sunbright poetry were charming rather than promising qualities. The imperfections of his first historic play, on which I trust I have not touched with any semblance of even the most unwilling or unconscious irreverence, are surely more serious, more obvious, more obtrusive, than the doubtless undeniable and indisputable imperfections of *Romeo and Juliet*. If the style of lovemaking in that loveliest of all youthful poems is fantastically unlike the actual courtship of modern lovers, it is not unliker than is the style of lovemaking in favor with Dante and his fellow-poets of juvenile and fanciful passion. Setting aside this objection, the first of Shakespeare's tragedies is not more beautiful than blameless. There is no incoherence of character, no inconsistency of action. Aumerle is hardly so living a figure as Tybalt: Capulet is an indisputably probable as York is obviously impossible in the part of a headstrong tyrant. There is little feminine interest in the earliest comedies: there is less in the first history. In the first tragedy there is nothing else, or nothing but what is so subservient and subordinate as simply to bring it out and throw it into relief. In the work of a young poet this difference would or should be enough to establish and explain the fact that though he might be greater than all other men in history and comedy, he was still greater in tragedy.

*Richard D. Altick*

# Symphonic Imagery in *Richard II* (1947)

Critics on occasion have remarked the peculiar unity of tone which distinguishes *Richard II* from most of Shakespeare's other plays. Walter Pater wrote that, like a musical composition, it possesses "a certain concentration of all its parts, a simple continuity, an evenness in execution, which are rare in the great dramatist. . . . It belongs to a small group of plays, where, by happy birth and consistent evolution, dramatic form approaches to something like the unity of a lyrical ballad, a lyric, a song, a single strain of music."[1] And J. Dover Wilson, in his edition of the play, has observed that "*Richard II* possesses a unit of tone and feeling greater than that attained in many of his greater plays, a unity found, I think, to the same degree elsewhere only in *Twelfth Night*, *Antony and Cleopatra*, and *The Tempest*."[2]

How can we account for that impression of harmony, of oneness, which we receive when we read the play or listen to its lines spoken upon the stage? The secret, it seems to me, lies in an aspect of Shakespeare's genius which has oftener been condemned than praised. Critics and casual readers alike have groaned over the fine-drawn ingenuity of the Shakespearean quibble, which, as Dr. Johnson maintained, was "the fatal Cleopatra for which he lost the world, and was content to lose it." But it is essentially the same habit of the creative imagination— a highly sensitized associational gift—that produces iterative symbolism and imagery. Simple word-play results from the poet's awareness of the diverse meanings of words, of which, however, he makes no better use than to demonstrate his own cleverness and to tickle for a moment the wit of the audience. These exhibitions of verbal agility are simply decorations scattered upon the surface of the poetic fabric; they can be ripped out without loss. But suppose that to the poet's associational sensitivity is added a further awareness of the multitudinous emotional overtones of words. When he puts this faculty to use he is no longer merely playing a game; instead, words have become the shells in which ideas and symbols are enclosed. Suppose furthermore that instead of being the occupation of a few fleeting lines of the text, certain words of multifold meanings are played upon throughout the five acts, recurring time after time like leit-motivs in music. And suppose finally that this process of repetition is applied especially to words of sensuous significance, words that evoke vivid responses in the imagination. When these things happen to certain words—when they cease to be mere vehicles for a brief indulgence of verbal fancy and, taking on a burden of serious meaning, become thematic material—the poet has crossed the borderline that separates word-play from iterative imagery. Language has become the willing servant of structure, and what was on other occasions only a source of exuberant but undisciplined wit now is converted to the higher purpose of poetic unity.

That, briefly, is what happens in *Richard II*. The familiar word-plays of the earlier Shakespearean dramas persist: John of Gaunt puns endlessly upon his own name. But in this drama a word is not commonly taken up, rapidly revolved, so that all its various facets of meaning flash out, and then discarded. Instead, certain words are played upon throughout the drama. Far from being decorations, "gay, fresh, variegated flowers of speech," as Pater called them,[3] they are woven deeply into the thought-web of the play. Each word-theme symbolizes one or another of the fundamental ideas of the story, and every time it reappears it perceptibly deepens and enriches those meanings and at the same time charges the atmosphere with emotional significance.

The most remarkable thing about these leit-motivs is the way in which they are constantly mingling and coalescing, two or three of them joining to form a single new figure, very much in the manner in which "hooked images," as Professor Lowes called them, were formed in the subconscious mind of Coleridge. This repeated criss-crossing of familiar images[4] makes of the whole text one vast arabesque of language, just as a dozen lines of *Love's Labour's Lost* form a miniature arabesque when the poet's quibbling mood is upon him. And since each image motif represents one of the dominant ideas of the play (heredity, patriotism, sycophancy, etc.) the coalescing of these images again and again emphasizes the complex relationship between the ideas themselves, so that the reader is kept ever aware that all that happens in *Richard II* results inevitably from the interaction of many elements.

It is pointless to try to explain by further generalizations this subtle and exceedingly intricate weaving together of metaphor and symbol—this glorified word-play, if you will—which is the key to the total poetic effect of *Richard II*. All I can do is to draw from the fabric, one by one, the strands that compose it, and to suggest in some manner the magical way in which they interact and by association and actual fusion reciprocally deepen their meaning.

Miss Spurgeon has pointed out how in *Antony and Cleopatra* the cosmic grandeur of the theme is constantly emphasized by the repetition of the word *world*.[5] In a similar manner the symbolism of *Richard II* is dominated by the related words *earth, land,* and *ground*. In no other play of Shakespeare is the complex of ideas represented by these words so tirelessly dwelt upon.[6] The words are but three in number, and superficially they seem roughly synonymous; but they have many intellectual ramifications, which become more and more meaningful as the play progresses and the words are used first for one thing and then for another. As our experience of the words increases, their connotation steadily deepens. In addition to their obvious meaning in a particular context they come to stand for something larger and more undefinable—a mingling of everything they have represented earlier.

Above all, *earth* is the symbol of the English nation. It is used by Shakespeare to connote those same values which we find in the equivalent synecdoche of *soil,* as in "native soil." It sums up all the feeling inherent in the sense of pride in nation—of jealousy when the country is threatened by foreign incursion, of bitter anger when its health has been destroyed by mismanagement or greed. "This earth of majesty," John of Gaunt calls England in his famous speech, ". . . This blessed plot, this earth, this realm, this England" (II.i.41, 50).[7] And a few lines further on: "This land of such dear souls, this dear dear land . . ." (II.i.57). Having once appeared, so early in the play, in such lustrous context, the words *earth* and *land* forever after have richer significance. Whenever they recur, they are more meaningful, more powerful. Thus Richard's elaborate speech upon his arrival in Wales—

> As a long-parted mother with her child
> Plays fondly with her tears and smiles in meeting.
> So, weeping, smiling, greet I thee, my earth,
> And do thee favours with my royal hands.
> . . . . . . . . . . . . . . . . . . . . . . . . . . . .
> Mock not my senseless conjuration, lords.
> This earth shall have a feeling, and these stones
> Prove armed soldiers, ere her native king
> Shall falter under foul rebellion's arms
>
> (III.ii.8-11, 23-26)

—undoubtedly gains in emotional splendor (as well as dramatic irony) by its reminiscences of John of Gaunt's earlier language. The two men between them make the English earth the chief verbal theme of the play.

Richard, we have just seen, speaks pridefully of "*my* earth." To him, ownership of the land is the most tangible and positive symbol of his rightful kingship. He bids Northumberland tell Bolingbroke that "every stride he makes upon my land / Is dangerous treason" (III.iii.92-93), and as he lies dying from the stroke of Exton's sword his last thought is for his land: "Exton, thy fierce hand / Hath with the king's blood stained the king's own land" (V.v.110-11). It is only natural, then, that *land* should be the key word in the discussions of England's sorry condition. Symbol of Englishmen's nationalistic pride and of the wealth of kings, it becomes symbol also of Englishmen's shame and kings' disgrace:

> Why, cousin, wert thou regent of the world,
> It were a shame to let this land by lease;
> But for thy world enjoying but this land,
> Is it not more than shame to shame it so?
> Landlord of England art thou now, not king.
>
> (II.i.109-113)

Northumberland's sad allusion to "this declining land" (II.i.240), York's to "this woeful land" (II.ii.99), and Richard's to "this revolting land" (III.iii.163) carry on this motif.

But *earth*, while it emblematizes the foundation of kingly pride and power, is also a familiar symbol of the vanity of human life and of what, in the middle ages, was a fascinating illustration of that vanity—the fall of kings. "Men," Mowbray sighs, "are but gilded loam or painted clay" (I.i.79); and Richard, luxuriating in self-pity, often remembers it; to earth he will return:

> Ah, Richard [says Salisbury], with the eyes of heavy mind
> I see thy glory like a shooting star
> Fall to the base earth from the firmament.
> 
> (II.iv.18-20)

The earth, Richard knows, is accustomed to receive the knees of courtiers: "Fair cousin," he tells Bolingbroke after he has given away his kingdom for the sheer joy of listening to himself do so, "you debase your princely knee / To make the base earth proud with kissing it" (III.iii.190-91). And the idea of the ground as the resting place for suppliant knees, and therefore the antithesis of kingly elevation, is repeated thrice in the two scenes dealing with Aumerle's conspiracy.[8]

The irony of this association of *earth* with both kingly glory and abasement is deepened by another role the word has in this earth-preoccupied play. For after death, earth receives its own; and in *Richard II* the common notion of the grave has new meaning, because the ubiquitous symbol of *earth* embraces it too. By the beginning of the third act, *earth* has lost its earlier joyful connotation to Richard, and this king, whose feverish imagination no amount of woe can cool, eagerly picks up a hint from Scroop:

> *Scroop:*    Those whom you curse
> Have felt the worst of death's destroying wound
> and lie full low, grav'd in the hollow ground.
> . . . . . . . . . . . . . . . . . . . . . . . . . . . . . . . .
> *Richard:* Let's talk of graves, of worms, and epitaphs;
> Make dust our paper and with rainy eyes
> Write sorrow on the bosom of the earth.

> Let's choose executors and talk of wills;
> And yet not so; for what can be bequeath
> Save our deposed bodies to the ground?
> Our lands, our lives, and all are Bolingbroke's,
> And nothing can we call our own but death,
> And that small model of the barren earth
> Which serves as paste and cover to our bones.
> For God's sake, let us sit upon the ground
> And tell sad stories of the death of kings
> 
> (III.ii.138-40, 145-56)

And later, in another ecstasy of self-pity, he conjures an elaborate image of making some pretty match with shedding tears:

> As thus, to drop them still upon one place,
> Till they have fretted us a pair of graves
> Within the earth.
> 
> (III.iii.166-68)

The same association occurs in the speeches of the other characters. Surrey, casting his gage at Fitzwater's feet, envisions his father's skull lying quietly in earth (IV.i.66-69); a moment or two later the Bishop of Carlisle brings news that the banished Mowbray, having fought for Jesu Christ in glorious Christian field, "at Venice gave / His body to that pleasant country's earth" (IV.i.97-98); and in the same scene Richard, having handed over his crown to the usurper, exclaims,

> Long mayst thou live in Richard's seat to sit,
> And soon lie Richard in an earthy pit!
> 
> (IV.i.218-19)

A final theme in the symphonic pattern dominated by the symbol of earth is that of the untended garden. Miss Spurgeon has adequately emphasized the importance of this iterated image in the history plays, and, as she points out, it reaches its climax in *Richard II*, particularly in the allegorical scene of the Queen's garden.[9] In Shakespeare's imagination the misdeeds of Richard and his followers constituted an overwhelming indignity to the precious English earth—to a nation which, in happier days, had been a sea-wall'd garden. And thus the play is filled with references to ripeness and the seasons, to planting and cropping and plucking and reaping, to furrows and plowing, and caterpillars and withered bay trees and thorns and flowers.[10]

Among the host of garden images in the play, one especially is unforgettable because of the insistence with which Shakespeare thrice echoes it. It is the terrible metaphor of the English garden being drenched by showers of blood.

> I'll use the advantage of my power
> And lay the summer's dust with showers of blood
> Rain'd from the wounds of slaughtered Englishmen;
> (III.iii.42-44)

threatens Bolingbroke as he approaches Flint castle; and when the King himself appears upon the walls, he casts the figure back in Bolingbroke's face:

> But ere the crown he looks for live in peace,
> Ten thousand bloody crowns of mothers' sons
> Shall ill become the flower of England's face,
> Change the complexion of her maid-pale peace
> To scarlet indignation, and bedew
> Her pastures' grass with faithful English blood.
> (III.iii.95-100)

The Bishop of Carlisle takes up the theme:

> And if you crown him, let me prophesy,
> The blood of English shall manure the ground,
> And future ages groan for this foul act.
> (IV.i.136-38)

And the new King—amply justifying Professor Van Doren's remark that not only are most of the characters in this play poets, but they copy one another on occasion[11]—echoes it:

> Lords, I protest, my soul is full of woe
> That blood should sprinkle me to make me grow.
> (V.vi.45-46)

This extraordinary series of four images is one of the many examples of the manner in which the principal symbols of *Richard II* so often chime together, bringing the ideas they represent into momentary conjunction and thus compounding those single emotional strains into new and revealing harmonies. In this case the "showers of blood" metaphor provides a recurrent nexus between the pervasive symbol of earth and another, equally pervasive, symbol: that of blood.

Both Professor Bradley[12] and Miss Spurgeon[13] have pointed out the splendid horror which Shakespeare achieves in *Macbeth* by his repeated allusions to blood. Curiously enough, the word *blood*, together with such related words as *bloody* and *bleed*, occurs much less frequently in *Macbeth* than it does in most of the history plays. What gives the word the tremendous force it undoubtedly possesses in *Macbeth* is not the frequency with which it is spoken, but rather the intrinsic magnificence of the passages in which it appears and the fact that in this play it has but one significance—the literal one. In the history plays, however, the word *blood* plays two major roles. Often it has the same meaning it has in *Macbeth*, for these too are plays in which men's minds often turn toward the sword:

> . . . our kingdom's earth should not be soil'd
> With that dear blood which it hath fostered
>
> (I.iii.125-26)

says Richard in one more instinctive (and punning!) association of blood and earth. But *blood* in the history plays also stands figuratively for inheritance, descent, familial pride; and this is the chief motivating theme of the play—the right of a monarch of unquestionably legitimate blood to his throne. The two significances constantly interplay, giving the single word a new multiple connotation wherever it appears. The finest instance of this merging of ideas is in the Duchess of Gloucester's outburst to John of Gaunt. Here we have an elaborate contrapuntal metaphor, the basis of which is a figure derived from the familiar medieval genealogical symbol of the Tree of Jesse, and which is completed by a second figure of seven vials of blood. The imposition of the figure involving the word *blood* (in its literal and therefore most vivid use) upon another figure which for centuries embodied the concept of family descent thus welds together with extraordinary tightness the word and its symbolic significance. The occurrence of *blood* in other senses on the borders of the metaphor (in the first and next-to-last lines of the passage) helps to focus attention upon the process occurring in the metaphor itself.

> Hath love in thy old blood no living fire?
> Edward's seven sons, whereof thyself art one,
> Were as seven vials of his sacred blood,
> Or seven fair branches springing from one root.
> Some of those seven are dried by nature's course,
> Some of those branches by the Destinies cut;
> But Thomas, my dear lord, my life, my Gloucester,
> One vial full of Edward's sacred blood,
> One flourishing branch of his most royal root,
> Is crack'd, and all the precious liquor spilt,
> Is hack'd down, and his summer leaves all faded,
> By Envy's hand and Murder's bloody axe.
> Ah, Gaunt, his blood was thine!
>
> (I.ii.10–22)

Because it has this multiple function, the word *blood* in this play loses much of the concentrated vividness and application it has in *Macbeth* where it means but one unmistakable thing; but its ambiguity here gives it a new sort of power. If it is less effective as imagery, it does serve to underscore the basic idea of the play, that violation of the laws of blood descent leads but to the spilling of precious English blood. That is the meaning of the word as it pulses from beginning to end, marking the emotional rhythm of the play.

In *Richard II*, furthermore, the word has an additional, unique use, one which involves an especially striking symbol. It has often been remarked how Shakespeare, seizing upon a hint in his sources, plays upon Richard's abnormal tendency to blanch and blush. In the imagery thus called forth, *blood* has a prominent part. How, demands the haughty king of John of Gaunt, dare thou

> with thy frozen admonition
> Make pale our cheek, chasing the royal blood
> With fury from his native residence.
>
> (II.i.117–19)

And when the King hears the news of the Welshmen's defection, Aumerle steadies his quaking body:

> Comfort, my liege; why looks your Grace so pale?
> *Richard:* But now the blood of twenty thousand men
> Did triumph in my face, and they are fled;
> And, till so much blood thither come again,
> Have I not reason to look pale and dead?
>
> (III.ii.75-79)

This idiosyncrasy of the King is made the more vivid because the imagery of the play constantly refers to pallor, even in contexts far removed from him. The Welsh captain reports that "the pale-fac'd moon looks bloody on the earth" (II.iv.10). In another speech, the words *pale* and *blood*, though not associated in a single image, occur so close to each other that it is tempting to suspect an habitual association in Shakespeare's mind:

> Pale trembling coward, there I throw my gage,
> Disclaiming here the kindred of the King,
> And lay aside my high blood's royalty.
>
> (I.i.69-71)

And as we have already seen, the King prophesied that "ten thousand bloody crowns of mothers' sons / Shall . . . change the complexion of [England's] maid-pale peace" (III.iii.96-98). Elsewhere Bolingbroke speaks of "pale beggar-fear" (I.i.189); the Duchess of Gloucester accuses John of Gaunt of "pale cold cowardice" (I.ii.34); and York describes how the returned exile and his army fright England's "pale-fac'd villages" with war (II.iii.94).

The idea of pallor and blushing is linked in turn with what is perhaps the most famous image-motif of the play, that of Richard (or the fact of his kingship) emblematized by the sun. More attention probably has been paid to the sun-king theme than it is worth, for although it occurs in two very familiar passages, it contributes far less to the harmonic unity of the play than do a number of other symbol strains. In any event, the conjunction of the sun image with that of blushing provides one more evidence of the closeness with which the poetic themes of the play are knit together. In the first of the sun-king speeches, Richard compares himself, at the length to which he is addicted, with "the searching eye of heaven" (III.ii.37). Finally, after some ten lines of analogy:

## Poetry and Rhetoric

> So when this thief, this traitor, Bolingbroke,
> Who all this while hath revell'd in the night
> Whilst we were wand'ring with the antipodes,
> Shall see us rising in our throne, the east,
> His treasons will sit blushing in his face. . . .
>
> (III.ii.47-51)

And Bolingbroke in a later scene does him the sincere flattery of imitation:

> See, see, King Richard doth himself appear,
> As doth the blushing discontented sun
> From out the fiery portal of the east.
>
> (III.iii.62-64)

Another occurrence of the sun image provides a link with the pervasive motif of tears. Salisbury, having envisioned Richard's glory falling to the base earth from the firmament, continues:

> Thy sun sets weeping in the lowly west,
> Witnessing storms to come, woe, and unrest.
>
> (II.iv.21-22)

In no other history play is the idea of tears and weeping so insistently presented.[14] It is this element which enforces most strongly our impression of Richard as a weakling, a monarch essentially feminine in nature, who has no conception of stoic endurance or resignation but a strong predilection for grief. This is why the play seems so strangely devoid of the heroic; the King and Queen are too much devoted to luxuriating in their misery, and the other characters find a morbid delight in at least alluding to unmanly tears. Characteristically, Richard's first question to Aumerle when the latter returns from bidding farewell to Bolingbroke is, "What store of parting tears were shed?" (I.iv.5). Bushy, discussing with the Queen her premonitions of disaster, speaks at length of "sorrow's eye, glazed with blinding tears" (II.ii.16). Richard greets the fair soil of England with mingled smiles and tears; and from that point on, his talk is full of "rainy eyes" (III.ii.146) and of making "foul weather with despised tears" (III.iii.161). He counsels York,

> Uncle, give me your hands: nay, dry your eyes:
> Tears show their love, but want their remedies.
> (III.iii.202-203)

In the garden scene the Queen, rejecting her lady's offer to sing, sadly tells her:

> 'Tis well that thou hast cause;
> But thou shouldst please me better wouldst thou weep.
> *Lady*: I could weep, madam, would it do you good.
> *Queen*: And I could sing, would weeping do me good,
> And never borrow any tear of thee.
> (III.iv.19-23)

And echoing that dialogue, the gardener, at the close of the scene, looks after her and says:

> Here did she fall a tear; here in this place
> I'll set a bank of rue, sour herb of grace.
> Rue, even for ruth, here shortly shall be seen,
> In the remembrance of a weeping queen.
> (III.iv.104-107)

The theme reaches a climax in the deposition scene, in which the agonized King, handing his crown to Bolingbroke, sees himself as the lower of the two buckets in Fortune's well:

> . . . full of tears am I,
> Drinking my griefs, whilst you mount up on high.
> (IV.i.188-89)

And a few lines later he merges the almost ubiquitous motif of tears with another constant theme of the play: "With mine own tears I wash away my balm" (IV.i.207). Of the frequent association of the anointing of kings, blood, and the act of washing, I shall speak a little later.

Professor Van Doren, in his sensitive essay on *Richard II*, eloquently stresses the importance of the word *tongue* in the play.[15] *Tongue*, he says, is the key word of the piece. I should prefer to give that distinction to *earth*; but there is no denying the effectiveness of Shakespeare's tireless repetition of the idea of speech, not only by the single word *tongue* but also by such allied words as *mouth*, *speech*, and *word*. A few minutes' study of

Bartlett's *Concordance* will show that *Richard II* is unique in this insistence upon the concept of speech; that the word *tongue* occurs here oftener than in any other play is but one indication.

This group of associated words heavily underscores two leading ideas in the play. In the first place, it draws constant attention to the propensity for verbalizing (as Shakespeare would not have called it!) which is Richard's fatal weakness. He cannot bring himself to live in a world of hard actuality; the universe to him is real only as it is presented in packages of fine words. Aumerle tries almost roughly to recall him from his weaving of sweet, melancholy sounds to a realization of the crucial situation confronting him, but he rouses himself only momentarily and then relapses into a complacent enjoyment of the sound of his own tongue. It is of this trait that we are constantly reminded as all the characters regularly use periphrases when they must speak of what they or others have said. By making the physical act of speech, the sheer fact of language so conspicuous, they call attention to its illusory nature—to the vast difference between what the semanticists call the intensional and extensional universes. That words are mere conventional sounds molded by the tongue, and reality is something else again, is constantly on the minds of all the characters. The initial dispute between Mowbray and Bolingbroke is "the bitter clamour of two eager tongues" (I.i.49); Mowbray threatens to cram his antagonist's lie "through the false passage of thy throat" (I.i.125); and later, in a fine cadenza, he conceives of his eternal banishment in terms of the engaoling of his tongue, whose "use is to me no more / Than an unstrung viol or a harp," and concludes:

> What is thy sentence [then] but speechless death,
> Which robs my tongue from breathing native breath?
> (I.iii.161-62, 172-73)

Bolingbroke, for his part, marvels over the power of a single word to change the lives of men:

> How long a time lies in one little word!
> Four lagging winters and four wanton springs
> End in a word: such is the breath of kings.
> (I.iii.213-15)

Gaunt too is preoccupied with tongues and speech; and when Aumerle returns from his farewell with Bolingbroke, from tears the image theme swiftly turns to tongues:

> *Richard*: What said our cousin when you parted with him?
> *Aumerle*: "Farewell!"
>    And, for my heart disdained that my tongue
>    Should so profane the word, that taught me craft
>    To counterfeit oppression of such grief
>    That words seem'd buried in my sorrow's grave.
>    Marry, would the word "farewell" have length'ned hours
>    And added years to his short banishment,
>    He should have had a volume of farewells.
>                                                       (I.iv.10-18)

And we have but reached the end of Act I; the remainder of the play is equally preoccupied with the unsubstantiality of human language.[16]

But the unremitting stress laid upon tongues and words in this play serves another important end: it reminds us that Richard's fall is due not only to his preference for his own words rather than for deeds, but also to his blind predilection for comfortable flattery rather than sound advice. Words not only hypnotize, suspend the sense of reality: they can sting and corrupt. And so the tongues of *Richard II* symbolize also the honeyed but poisonous speech of the sycophants who surround him. "No," replies York to Gaunt's suggestion that his dying words might yet undeaf Richard's ear,

>        it is stopp'd with other flattering sounds,
>    As praises, of whose taste the wise are found,
>    Lascivious metres, to whose venom sound
>    The open ear of youth doth always listen.
>                                                       (II.i.17-20)

The venom to which York refers and the snake which produces it form another theme of the imagery of this play. The snake-venom motif closely links the idea of the garden on the one hand (for what grossly untended garden would be without its snakes?) and the idea of the tongue on the other. All three meet in the latter part of Richard's speech in III.ii:

> But let thy spiders, that suck up thy venom,
> And heavy-gaited toads lie in their way,
> Doing annoyance to the treacherous feet
> Which with usurping steps do trample thee
> Yield stinging nettles to mine enemies;
> And when they from thy bosom pluck a flower,
> Guard it, I pray thee, with a lurking adder
> Whose double tongue may with a mortal touch
> Throw death upon thy sovereign's enemies.
>
> (III.ii.14-22)

And the double association occurs again in the garden scene, when the Queen demands of the gardener,

> Thou, old Adam's likeness, set to dress this garden,
> How dares thy harsh rude tongue sound this unpleasing news?
> What Eve, what serpent, hath suggested thee
> To make a second fall of cursed man?
>
> (III.iv.73-76)

Mowbray elsewhere speaks of "slander's venom'd spear" (I.i.171), and to Richard, the flatterers who have deserted him are, naturally enough, "villains, vipers, damn'd without redemption! / . . . Snakes, in my heart-blood warm'd, that sting my heart!" (III.ii.129-31).

Although England's sorry state is most often figured in the references to the untended garden and the snakes that infest it, the situation is emphasized time and again by at least four other recurrent themes, some of which refer as well to the personal guilt of Richard. One such theme—anticipating a similar motif in *Hamlet*—involves repeated references to physical illness and injury. Richard in seeking to smooth over the quarrel between Mowbray and Bolingbroke says:

> Let's purge this choler without letting blood.
> This we prescribe, though no physician;
> Deep malice makes too deep incision.
>
> (I.i.153-55)

There are repeated allusions to the swelling caused by infection. Richard in the same scene speaks of "the swelling difference of your settled hate" (I.i.201), and much later, after he has been deposed, he predicts to Northumberland that

> The time shall not be many hours of age
> More than it is, ere foul sin gathering head
> Shall break into corruption
>
> (V.i.57-59)

Thus too there are vivid mentions of the remedy for such festering:

> Fell Sorrow's tooth doth never rankle more
> Than when he bites, but lanceth not the sore.
>
> (I.iii.302-303)

> This fest'red joint cut off, the rest rest sound.
>
> (V.iii.85)

*Plague, pestilence,* and *infection* are words frequently in the mouths of the characters of this play. Aumerle, during the furious gage-casting of IV.i, cries, "May my hands rot off" if he does not seize Percy's gage (IV.i.49); and elsewhere York, speaking to the unhappy Queen, says of the King,

> Now comes the sick hour that his surfeit made;
> Now shall he try his friends that flatter'd him.
>
> (II.ii.84-85)

Indeed, the imagery which deals with bodily injury directly associates the wretchedness of the monarch and his country with the tongues of the sycophants. A verbal juxtaposition of *tongue* and *wound* occurs early in the plays: "Ere my tongue / Shall wound my honour with such feeble wrong" (I.i.190-91). Gaunt carries the association one step further when he explicitly connects Richard's and England's illness with the presence of gross flatterers in the King's retinue:

> Thy death-bed is no lesser than thy land
> Wherein thou liest in reputation sick;
> And thou, too careless patient as thou art,
> Commit'st thy anointed body to the cure
> Of those physicians that first wounded thee.

> A thousand flatterers sit within thy crown,
> Whose compass is no bigger than thy head.
> 
> (II.i.95-101)

And Richard himself completes the circuit between the tongue-wound association and his personal grief: "He does me double wrong / That wounds me with the flatteries of his tongue" (III.ii.215-16).

Again, the evil that besets England is frequently symbolized as a dark blot upon fair parchment—an image which occurs oftener in this play than in any other. The suggestion for the image undoubtedly came from contemplation of the deeds and leases by which the king had farmed out the royal demesnes; as John of Gaunt said, England "is now bound in with shame, / With inky blots and rotten parchment bonds" (II.i.63-64). The image recurs several times. "No, Bolingbroke," says Mowbray in I.iii, "if ever I were traitor, / My name be blotted from the book of life" (I.iii.201-202). Richard sighs through blanched lips, "Time hath set a blot upon my pride" (III.ii.81) and later speaks of the record of Northumberland's offenses as including

> one heinous article,
> Containing the deposing of a king
> And cracking the strong warrant of an oath,
> Mark'd with a blot, damn'd in the book of heaven.
> 
> (IV.i.233-36)

Carlisle and Aumerle in a duet harmonize the image with the two other motifs of gardening and generation:

> *Carlisle*: The woe's to come; the children yet unborn
>   Shall feel this day as sharp to them as thorn.
> *Aumerle*: You holy clergymen, is there no plot
>   To rid the realm of this pernicious blot?
> 
> (IV.i.322-25)

Aumerle's conspiracy which stems from this conversation is itself spoken of by Bolingbroke in Aumerle's own terms: "Thy abundant goodness shall excuse / This deadly blot in thy digressing son" (V.iii.65-66). The vividness of the image is increased by the presence elsewhere of allusions to books and writing: "He should have had a volume of farewells" (I.iv.18); "The purple testament of bleeding war" (III.iii.94);

> Let's talk of graves, of worms, and epitaphs;
> Make dust our paper and with rainy eyes
> Write sorrow on the bosom of the earth
>
> (III.ii.145-47)

(an interesting example of double association of imagery—tears, earth-grave, and writing); and in the deposition scene, when Richard calls for a mirror:

> I'll read enough,
> When I do see the very book indeed
> Where all my sins are writ, and that's myself.
>
> (IV.i.273-75)

The blot image has a very direct relationship with another class of figures by which Shakespeare symbolizes guilt or evil: that of a stain which must be washed away. This image is most commonly associated with *Macbeth*, because of the extraordinary vividness with which it is used there. But the theme is much more insistent in *Richard II*. Twice it is associated, as in *Macbeth*, with blood:

> Yet, to wash your blood
> From off my hands, here in the view of men
> I will unfold some causes of your deaths
>
> (III.i.5-7)

> I'll make a voyage to the Holy Land
> To wash this blood off from my guilty hand.
>
> (V.vi.49-50)

Elsewhere the association is with the story of the crucifixion, in a repetition of which Richard fancies he is the sufferer:

> Nay, all of you that stand and look upon me
> Whilst that my wretchedness doth bait myself,
> Though some of you with Pilate wash your hands
> Showing an outward pity; yet you Pilates
> Have here deliver'd me to my sour cross,
> And water cannot wash away your sin.
>
> (IV.i.237-42)

But in this play the absolution of guilt requires not merely the symbolic cleansing of bloody hands; it entails the washing-off of the sacred ointment of royalty—the ultimate expiation of kingly sin. The full measure of Richard's fall is epitomized in two further occurrences of the metaphor, the first spoken when he is in the full flush of arrogant confidence, the second when nemesis has overtaken him:

> Not all the water in the rough rude sea
> Can wash the balm off from an anointed king.
> (III.ii.54-55)

> With mine own tears I wash away my balm,
> With mine own hands I give away my crown.
> (IV.i.207-208)

Whatever the exact context of the image of washing, one suggestion certainly is present whenever it appears: a suggestion of momentous change—the deposition of a monarch, the cleansing of a guilt-laden soul.

But the most unusual of all the symbols of unpleasantness which occur in *Richard II* is the use of the adjective *sour*, together with the repeated contrast of sweetness and sourness. A reader of the play understandably passes over the frequent use of *sweet* as a conventional epithet used both of persons and of things. But the word, however commonplace the specific phrases in which it occurs, has a role in the poetic design which decidedly is not commonplace, for it acts as a foil for the very unaccustomed use of its antonym. There is nothing less remarkable in Shakespeare than such phrases as "sweet Richard," "your sweet majesty," "sweet York, sweet husband," even such passages as this:

> And yet your fair discourse hath been as sugar,
> Making the hard way sweet and delectable.
> (II.iii.6-7)

But what is remarkable is the manner in which, in this play alone, mention of *sweet* so often invites mention of *sour*: "Things sweet to taste prove in digestion sour" (I.iii.236); "Speak sweetly, man, although thy looks be sour" (III.ii.193); "how sour sweet music is!" (V.v.42);

> Sweet love, I see, changing his property,
> Turns to the sourest and most deadly hate.
> (III.ii.135-36)

In addition to this repeated collocation of *sweet* and *sour*, the text of *Richard II* is notable for a persistent use, unmatched in any other play, of *sour* alone, as an adjective or verb:

> Not Gloucester's death, nor Hereford's banishment
> Not Gaunt's rebukes, nor England's private wrongs,
> . . . . . . . . . . . . . . . . . . . . . . . . . . . . . . . . . . .
> Have ever made me sour my patient cheek.
> (II.i.165-66, 169)

"I'll set a bank of rue, sour herb of grace" (III.iv.105: this in significant collocation with the motif of tears, as the next is joined with the motif of washing—"yet you Pilates / Have here deliver'd me to my sour cross" (IV.i.240-41);

> The grand conspirator, Abbot of Westminster,
> With clog of conscience and sour melancholy
> Hath yielded up his body to the grave.
> (V.vi.19-21)

The occurrence of *sour* thus lends unmistakable irony to every occurrence of *sweet*, however unimportant the latter may be in itself. Even at a distance of a few lines, mention of one quality seems to invite mention of the other, as if Shakespeare could never forget that the sour is as frequent in life as the sweet:

> *Duchess*: The word is short, but not so short as sweet;
>   No word like "pardon" for kings' mouths so meet.
> *York*: Speak it in French, King; say *"Pardonne moi."*
> *Duchess*: Dost thou teach pardon pardon to destroy?
>   Ah, my sour husband, my hard-hearted lord,
>   That set'st the word itself against the word!
> (V.iii.117-22)

This contrapuntal use of *sweet* and *sour* is one of the most revealing instances of the artistry by which the poetry of *Richard II* is unified.[17]

Two more image themes, one of major importance, the other less conspicuous, remain to be mentioned. For one of them, we must return to the Tree of Jesse passage (I.ii.10-22) quoted above. This passage is the fountainhead of one of the chief themes of the play—the idea of legitimate succession, of hereditary kingship. We have already noticed how, largely as a result of this early elaborate metaphor, the close identification of the word *blood* with the idea of family descent deepens the symbolic significance of the word as it recurs through the play. In addition, as Miss Spurgeon has pointed out, in *Richard II* there are many other cognate images derived from the ideas of birth and generation, and of inheritance from father to son.[18] The Tree of Jesse metaphor (whose importance Miss Spurgeon failed to note) is followed in the next scene by one involving the symbol of earth and thus suggesting the vital relationship between generation and patriotism:

> Then, England's ground, farewell; sweet soil, adieu;
> My mother, and my nurse, that bears me yet!
> (I.iii.306–307)

In John of Gaunt's dying speech, earth and generation again appear, significantly, in conjunction:

> This blessed plot, this earth, this realm, this England,
> This nurse, this teeming womb of royal kings.
> (II.i.50–51)

In her scene with Bagot and Bushy, the Queen dwells constantly on the idea of birth:

> Some unborn sorrow, ripe in fortune's womb,
> Is coming towards me.
> . . . . . . . . . . . . . . . . . . . . . . . .
>     Conceit is still deriv'd
> From some forefather grief; mine is not so,
> For nothing hath begot my something grief,
> . . . . . . . . . . . . . . . . . . . . . . . .
> So, Green, thou art the midwife to my woe,
> And Bolingbroke my sorrow's dismal heir.
> Now hath my soul brought forth her prodigy,
> And I, a gasping new-deliver'd mother,
> Have woe to woe, sorrow to sorrow join'd.
> (II.ii.10–11, 34–36, 62–66)

Richard's last soliloquy begins with the same sort of elaborated conceit:

> My brain I'll prove the female to my soul,
> My soul the father; and these two beget
> A generation of still-breeding thoughts,
> And these same thoughts people this little world,
> In humours like the people of this world.
> For no thought is contented.
>
> (V.v.6-11)

And throughout the play, as Miss Spurgeon notes, "the idea of inheritance from father to son . . . increases the feeling of the inevitable and the foreordained, as also of the unlimited consequences of action."

The word *crown* as the symbol of kingship is of course common throughout the history plays. In *Richard II*, however, the vividness of the image and the relevance of its symbolism to the grand theme of the play are heightened by several instances in which its metaphorical function goes beyond that of a simple, conventional metonymy:

> A thousand flatterers sit within thy crown,
> Whose compass is no bigger than thy head;
>
> (II.i.100-101)

> for within the hollow crown
> That rounds the mortal temples of a king
> Keeps Death his court,
>
> (III.ii.160-62)

> But ere the crown he looks for live in peace,
> Ten thousand bloody crowns of mothers' sons
> Shall ill become the flower of England's face,
>
> (III.iii.95-97)

> Now is this golden crown like a deep well
> That owes two buckets, filling one another,
> The emptier ever dancing in the air,
> The other down, unseen, and full of water.
>
> (IV.i.184-87)

In addition, the actual image of the crown is made more splendid by the occurrence, in the play's poetic fabric, of several images referring to jewels:

## Poetry and Rhetoric

> A jewel in a ten-times-barr'd-up chest
> Is a bold spirit in a loyal breast.
> *Gaunt*: The sullen passage of thy weary steps
> Esteem as foil wherein thou art to set
> The precious jewel of thy home return.
> *Bolingbroke*: Nay, rather, every tedious stride I make
> Will but remember me what a deal of world
> I wander from the jewels that I love.
> (I.iii.265-70)

And again: "I'll give my jewels for a set of beads" (III.iii.147), "This precious stone set in the silver sea" (II.i.46), and "Love to Richard / Is a strange brooch in this all-hating world" (V.v.65-66).

Keeping in mind the leading metaphors and verbal motifs which I have reviewed—*earth-ground-land*, *blood*, pallor, garden, sun, tears, *tongue-speech-word*, *snake-venom*, physical injury and illness, *blot*, washing, *sweet-sour*, generation, and jewel-crown—it is profitable to re-read the whole play, noting especially how widely the various themes are distributed, and how frequently their strands cross to form new images. There is no extended passage of the text which is not tied in with the rest of the play by the occurrence of one or more of the familiar symbols. However, the images are not scattered with uniform evenness. As in *The Merchant of Venice*, metaphorical language tends to be concentrated at the emotional climaxes of *Richard II*. At certain crucial points in the action, a large number of the unifying image-threads appear almost simultaneously, so that our minds are virtually flooded with many diverse yet closely related ideas. The first part of II.i (the prophecy of Gaunt) offers a good instance of this rapid cumulation of symbols and the resultant heightening of emotional effect. The whole passage should be read as Shakespeare wrote it; here I list simply the phrases that reveal the various image themes, omitting a number which glance obliquely at the themes but are not directly connected with them:

| line | | |
|---|---|---|
| | 5 | the tongues of dying men |
| | 7 | words |
| | 8 | words |
| | 12 | the setting sun |

| | |
|---|---|
| 13 | As the last taste of sweets, is sweetest last |
| 14 | Writ in remembrance |
| 17 | flattering sounds |
| 19 | Lascivious metres, to whose venom sound |
| 23 | limps |
| 41 | The earth of majesty |
| 44 | infection |
| 45 | breed |
| 46 | This precious stone |
| 49 | less happier lands |
| 50 | This earth |
| 51 | This nurse, this teeming womb of royal kings |
| 52 | breed . . . birth |
| 57 | land . . . land |
| 64 | With inky blots and rotten parchment bonds |
| 83 | hollow womb |
| 95 | land |
| 96 | sick [followed by extended metaphor] |
| 100 | thy crown |
| 103 | thy land |
| 104-105 | thy grandsire . . . his son's son . . . his sons |
| 110-13 | this land . . . this land . . . landlord |
| 116 | ague |
| 118 | pale . . . blood |
| 122 | This tongue |
| 126 | blood |
| 131 | blood |
| 134 | To crop at once a too long withered flower |
| 136 | words |
| 141 | words |
| 149 | His tongue |
| 153 | The ripest fruit first falls |
| 157 | Which live like venom where no venom else |

Thus in the first 157 lines of the scene we meet no less than twelve of the motifs of the play.

In another sort of harmonization, Shakespeare strikes a long chord containing a number of the image strains and then in the following minutes of the play echoes them separately. The

"Dear earth, I do salute thee with my hand" speech at the beginning of III.ii interweaves at least six themes which shortly are unravelled into individual strands. The idea of the garden which is the framework for the whole speech (6-26) recurs in the line "To ear the land that hath some hope to grow" (212). The repeated references to weeping in the initial speech ("I weep for joy" . . . "with her tears" . . . "weeping") are echoed in "as if the world were all dissolv'd to tears" (108) and "rainy eyes" (146). Richard's "Nor with thy sweets comfort his ravenous sense" (13) is recalled in Scroop's "Sweet love . . . changing his property, / Turns to the sourest and most deadly hate" (135-36) and in Richard's "speak sweetly, man, although thy looks be sour" (193) and "that sweet way I was in to despair" (205). The lurking adder and the venom which the spiders suck up (20, 14) find their sequel in Richard's later "vipers . . . snakes . . . that sting my heart" (129-31). The double tongue (21) is succeeded by "discomfort guides my tongue" (65), "my care-tun'd tongue" (92), the tongue that "hath but a heavier tale to say" (197), and the one whose flatteries wound the King at the end of the scene (216). The initial reference to wounding ("though rebels wound thee with their horses' hoofs," 7) is succeeded by "death's destroying wound" (139); and the same general motif of bodily hurt is carried out by "this ague fit of fear is over-blown" (190), which links the disease-theme to that of the garden. Finally, the frequent use of *earth* in Richard's first speech (6, 10, 12, 24) prepares the ear for the five-times-repeated occurrence of the idea (earth . . . ground . . . lands . . . earth . . . ground) in the "Let's talk of graves, of worms, and epitaphs" speech. This progressive analysis of the components of the original chord of images is accompanied by a succession of other images not included in the chord: an extended sun metaphor (36-50), a reference to washing (54-55), the most famous instance of the pallor-blood motif (76-81), two references to the crown (59, 115), and two allusions to writing (81, 146-47). And thus the mind is crowded with a richly overlapping series of images.

Another example of the close arraying of image patterns (without the initial chord) occurs in III.iii.85-100:

| | |
|---|---|
| Yet know, my master, God omnipotent, | |
| Is mustering in his clouds on our behalf | |
| Armies of pestilence; and they shall strike | (illness) |
| Your children yet unborn and unbegot, | (generation) |
| That lift your vassal hands against my head | |
| And threat the glory of my precious crown. | (crown) |
| Tell Bolingbroke—for yon methinks he stands— | |
| That every stride he makes upon my land | (earth) |
| Is dangerous treason. He is come to open | |
| The purple testament of bleeding war; | (books, blood) |
| But ere the crown he looks for live in peace, | (crown) |
| Ten thousand bloody crowns of mothers' sons | (blood, crown, generation) |
| Shall ill become the flower of England's face, | (garden) |
| Change the complexion of her maid-pale peace | (pallor) |
| To scarlet indignation, and bedew Her pastures' grass with faithful English blood. | (blood) |

Curiously, the deposition scene, though it is rich enough in individual appearances of the familiar themes, does not mesh them so closely as one might expect.

A final aspect of the use of iterative imagery in *Richard II* is the manner in which a particularly important passage is prepared for by the interweaving into the poetry, long in advance, of inconspicuous but repeated hints of the imagery which is to dominate that passage. The method is exactly analogous to that by which in a symphony a melody appears, at first tentatively, indeed almost unnoticed, first in one choir of the orchestra, then another, until ultimately it comes to its reward as the theme of a climactic section. In such a manner is the audience prepared, although unconsciously, for Richard's last grandiose speech. One takes little note of the first timid appearance of a reference to beggary or bankruptcy in Bolingbroke's "Or with pale beggar-fear impeach my height" (I.i.189). But in the second act the motif recurs:

> Be York the next that must be bankrupt so!
> Though death be poor, it ends a mortal woe,
> (II.i.151-52)

and a hundred lines later the idea is repeated: "The king's grown bankrupt, like a broken man" (II.i.257). The haunting dread of destitution, then, however obliquely alluded to, is a recurrent theme, and adds its small but perceptible share to the whole atmosphere of impending disaster. It forms the burden of two plaints by Richard midway in the play:

> Let's choose executors and talk of wills;
> And yet not so; for what can we bequeath
> Save our deposed bodies to the ground?
> Our lands, our lives and all are Bolingbroke's.
> (III.ii.148-51)

> I'll give my jewels for a set of beads,
> My gorgeous palace for a hermitage,
> My gay apparel for an almsman's gown,
> My figur'd goblets for a dish of wood,
> My sceptre for a palmer's walking-staff,
> My subjects for a pair of carved saints,
> And my large kingdom for a little grave.
> (III.iii.147-53)

But the time is not ripe for the climactic utterance of this motif. It disappears, to return for a moment in a verbal hint in the deposition scene:

> Let it command a mirror hither straight,
> That it may show me what a face I have
> Since it is bankrupt of his majesty.
> (IV.i.265-67)

> Being so great, I have no need to beg.
>
> (IV.i.309)

The Duchess of York momentarily takes up the motif: "A beggar begs that never begg'd before" (V.iii.78), and Bolingbroke replies:

> Our scene is alt'red from a serious thing,
> And now chang'd to "The Beggar and the King."
>
> (V.iii.79-80)

And now finally comes the climax toward which these fleeting references have been pointing: a climax which illuminates the purpose and direction of the earlier talk about beggary and bankruptcy:

> Thoughts tending to content flatter themselves
> That they are not the first of fortune's slaves,
> Nor shall not be the last; like silly beggars
> Who, sitting in the stocks, refuge their shame,
> That many have and others must sit there;
> And in this thought they find a kind of ease,
> Bearing their own misfortunes on the back
> Of such as have before endur'd the like.
> Thus play I in one person many people,
> And none contented. Sometimes am I king;
> Then treasons make me wish myself a beggar;
> And so I am. Then crushing penury
> Persuades me I was better when a king.
>
> (V.v.23-35)

A similar process can be traced in the repetition of the word *face*, which, besides being obviously connected with the idea of Richard's personal comeliness, underscores the hovering sense the play contains of the illusory quality of life, of the deceptions that men accept as if they were reality. The word occurs casually, unremarkably, often without metaphorical intent; but its frequent appearance not only reinforces, however subtly, a dominant idea of the play, but also points toward a notable climax. "Mowbray's face" (I.i.195) . . . "Now never look upon each other's face" (I.iii.185) . . . "the northeast wind / Which then blew bitterly against our faces" (I.iv.6-7) . . . "His face thou hast, for even so look'd he" (II.i.176) . . . "Frighting her pale-fac'd villages with war" (II.iii.94) . . . "The pale-fac'd moon looks bloody on the earth" (II.iv.10) . . . "His treasons will sit blushing in his face" (III.ii.51) . . . "But now the blood of twenty thousand men / Did triumph in my face" (III.ii.76-77) . . .

> Ten thousand bloody crowns of mothers' sons
> Shall ill become the flower of England's face.
> (III.iii.96-97)

Meanwhile Bushy has introduced the corollary idea of shadow:

> Each substance of a grief hath twenty shadows,
> Which shows like grief itself, but is not so
> (II.ii.14-15)

> Which, look'd on as it is, is nought but shadows
> Of what it is not.
> (II.ii.23-24)

The related themes merge as, in retrospect, it is plain they were destined to do, in the deposition scene:

> Was this face the face
> That every day under his household roof
> Did keep ten thousand men? Was this the face
> That, like the sun, did make beholders wink?
> Is this the face which fac'd so many follies,
> That was at last out-fac'd by Bolingbroke?
> A brittle glory shineth in this face;
> As brittle as the glory is the face,
> For there it is, crack'd in an hundred shivers.
> Mark, silent king, the moral of this sport,
> How soon my sorrow hath destroy'd my face.
> *Bolingbroke*: The shadow of your sorrow hath destroy'd
> The shadow of your face.
> *Richard*:       Say that again.
> The shadow of my sorrow! Ha! let's see.
> (IV.i.281-94)

And thus from beginning to end *Richard II* is, in a double sense of which Shakespeare would have approved, a play on words. As countless writers have affirmed, it is entirely fitting that this should be so. King Richard, a poet *manqué*, loved words more dearly than he did his kingdom, and his tragedy is made the more moving by the style, half rhetorical, half lyrical, in which it is told. Splendid words, colorful metaphors, pregnant poetic symbols in this drama possess their own peculiar irony.

But the language of *Richard II*, regarded from the viewpoint I have adopted in this paper, has another significance, entirely apart from its appropriateness to theme. It suggests the existence of a vital relationship between two leading characteristics of Shakespeare's poetic style: the uncontrolled indulgence of verbal wit in the earlier plays and the use of great image-themes in the plays of his maturity. As I suggested in the beginning, word-play and iterative imagery are but two different manifestations of a single faculty in the creative imagination—an exceedingly well developed sense of association. In *Richard II* we see the crucial intermediate stage in the development, or perhaps more accurately the utilization, of Shakespeare's singular associative gift. In such passages as John of Gaunt's speech upon his name, we are reminded of the plays which preceded this from Shakespeare's pen. But, except on certain occasions when they contribute to the characterization of the poet-king, the brief coruscations of verbal wit which marked the earlier plays are less evident than formerly. On the other hand, when we stand back and view the play as a whole, its separate movements bound so closely together by image themes, we are enabled to anticipate the future development of Shakespeare's art. The technique that is emerging in *Richard II* is the technique that eventually will have its part in producing the poetry of *Lear* and *Macbeth* and *Othello*. Here we have the method: the tricks of repetition, of cumulative emotional effect, of interweaving and reciprocal coloration. What is yet to come is the full mastery of the artistic possibilities of such a technique. True, thanks to its tightly interwoven imagery *Richard II* has a poetic unity that is unsurpassed in any of the great tragedies; so far as structure is concerned, Shakespeare has levied from iterative language about all the aid that it will give. The great improvement will come in another region. Taken individually, in *Richard II* Shakespeare's images lack the qualities which they will possess in the later plays. They are, many of them, too conventional for our tastes; they are marred by diffuseness; they bear too many lingering traces of Shakespeare's affection for words for words' sake. The ultimate condensation, the compression of a universe of meaning into a single bold metaphor, remains to be achieved. But in the best imagery of *Richard II*, especially in those passages which combine several themes into a richly complex pattern of meaning, we receive abundant assurance that Shakespeare will be equal to his task. The process of welding language and thought into a single entity is well begun.

NOTES

1. "Shakespeare's English Kings," *Appreciations*, library ed. (London, 1910), pp. 202-203.
2. *Richard II*, ed. J. Dover Wilson (Cambridge, 1939), pp. xiv-xv.
3. *Appreciations*, p. 194.
4. Throughout this paper I use the words *image* and *imagery* in their most inclusive sense of metaphorical as well as "picture-making" but non-figurative language.
5. Caroline F.E. Spurgeon, *Shakespeare's Imagery* (Cambridge, 1936), pp. 352-53. I should add a word concerning a relatively little-known book which anticipated Miss Spurgeon's general method of image-study as well as two or three of my own observations concerning *Richard II*. This is *Shakespeare's Way: A Psychological Study*, by the Rt. Rev. Msgr. F.C. Kolbe (London, 1930).
6. In *Richard II* the three words occur a total of 71 times; in *King John*, the nearest rival, 46.—I should note at this point that my identification of all the word- and image-themes to be discussed in this essay is based upon statistical study. A given word or group of related words is called a "theme" (a) if Bartlett's *Concordance* shows a definite numerical preponderance for *Richard II* or (b) if the word or group of words is so closely related to one of the fundamental ideas of the play that it is of greater importance than the comparative numerical frequency would imply. I have not included any arithmetic in this paper because all such tabulations obviously must be subjective to some degree. No two persons, doing the same counting for the same purpose, would arrive at precisely the same numerical results. But I am confident that independent tabulation would enable anyone to arrive at my general conclusions. Statistics here, as in all such critical exercises, are merely grounds upon which to base a judgment that must eventually be a subjective one.
7. I am using the text of William A. Neilson and Charles J. Hill (Boston, 1942).

8. The much admired little passage about the roan Barbary takes on added poignancy when the other overtones of *ground* are remembered:

> *King Richard*: Rode he on Barbary? Tell me, gentle friend,
> How went he under him?
> *Groom*: So proudly as if he disdain'd the ground.
>
> (V.v.81-83)

9. *Shakespeare's Imagery*, pp. 216-24.
10. We must not, of course, take *garden* too literally. Shakespeare obviously intended the term in its wider metaphorical sense of fields and orchards.
11. Mark Van Doren, *Shakespeare* (New York, 1939), p. 88.
12. A.C. Bradley, *Shakespearean Tragedy*, 2d ed. (London, 1905), pp. 335-56.
13. *Shakespeare's Imagery*, p. 334.
14. There are many more references to tears and weeping in *Titus Andronicus*, but the obvious inferiority of the poetry and the crudity of characterization make their presence far less remarkable.
15. *Shakespeare*, pp. 85-87.
16. Another way in which Shakespeare adds to the constant tragic sense of unsubstantiality in this play—the confusion of appearance and reality—is the repeated use of the adjective *hollow*, especially in connection with death: "our hollow parting" (I.iv.9), the "hollow womb" of the grave (II.i.83), "the hollow eyes of death" (II.i.270), a grave set in "the hollow ground" (III.ii.140), "the hollow crown" in which Death keeps his court (III.ii.160).
17. The *sweet-sour* contrast occurs five times in *Richard II*; no more than twice in any other play.—Compare a similar juxtaposition in three of the sonnets:

> Such civil war is in my love and hate
> That I an accessary needs must be
> To that sweet thief which sourly robs from me.   (No. 35)

> O absence, what a torment wouldst thou prove
> Were it not thy sour leisure gave sweet leave
> To entertain the time with thoughts of love.   (No. 39)

> For sweetest things turn sourest by their deeds.   (No. 94)

It is interesting to note that in the same two groups of sonnets in which the *sweet-sour* collocation occurs can be found another word whose use is noteworthy in *Richard II*:

## Poetry and Rhetoric

> And dost him grace when clouds do blot the heaven (No. 28)
>
> So shall those blots that do with me remain,
> Without thy help by me be borne alone. (No. 36)
>
> But what's so blessed-fair that fears no blot? (No. 92)
>
> Where beauty's veil doth cover every blot (No. 95)

If we accept the hypothesis that at a given period in his life Shakespeare habitually thought of certain abstract ideas in terms of particular metaphors, there is a good case for dating these sonnets at the time of *Richard II*. Conventional though the sweet-sour and blot ideas may be, it is plain that Shakespeare had them constantly in mind when writing *Richard II*; they are a hallmark of the style of the play. Their occurrence in these sonnets is possibly significant.

18. *Shakespeare's Imagery*, pp. 238–41.

DAVID GLENN HUNT
MEMORIAL LIBRARY
GALVESTON COLLEGE

**DAVID GLENN HUNT
MEMORIAL LIBRARY
GALVESTON COLLEGE**